ASSESSMENT

OF

DEVELOPMENTAL

LEARNING

DISORDERS

ASSESSMENT

OF

DEVELOPMENTAL

LEARNING

DISORDERS

A Neuropsychological Approach

RITA G. RUDEL

WITH

Jane M. Holmes and Joan Rudel Pardes

Basic Books, Inc., Publishers

NEW YORK

Library of Congress Cataloging-in-Publication Data

Rudel, Rita G. (Rita Gillis), 1921–1984.
  Assessment of developmental learning disorders.

  Bibliography: p. 235
  Includes index.
  1. Learning disabilities—diagnosis. 2. Developmentally disabled children. 3. Pediatric neuropsychology. I. Holmes, Jane M. II. Pardes, Joan Rudel. III. Title. [DNLM: 1. Child Development Disorders—diagnosis. 2. Learning Disorders—diagnosis. WS 110 R915a]
RJ506.L4R83 1988   618.92′8588   87–47836
ISBN 0-465-00509-8

This book was completed in memory of
Dr. Rita Gillis Rudel

Contents

PART THREE

EDUCATIONAL IMPLICATIONS

Foreword

T HERE has never been anyone quite like Rita Rudel, and there probably never will be. Like another unique person in modern neuropsychology, Edith Kaplan, Rita Rudel came along when nineteenth-century giants were still among us and twentieth-century methods were being elaborated. From the days when—as she loved to tell it—she had been Kurt Goldstein's "pregnant fellow" to the days after I left New York and she became a diagnostic clinician supervising others, Rita was a psychologist who spanned subspecialties, who was always *integrating* neurological, clinical, educational, and developmental psychology. When I was first introduced to Rita, she was entirely engaged in neuropsychological research with Hans-Lukas Teuber and Tom Twitchell, a productive period she dubbed her "Eastern Shuttle research program," since she was firmly based in New York while her colleagues were in Boston. From H.-L. Teuber, Rita brought to any research design the concept that language should be, insofar as it is possible with human subjects, a minimal factor in administration, task mediation, and response requirements; when she teamed up with me, that nonverbal tradition complemented my Geschwindian aphasia-based frame of reference. By the time our all-too-brief (and, for me, idyllic) research partnership was disrupted by my departure from the New York area, Rita had become more sophisticated about language development than I had ever been, and I had become (and remain) fascinated by nonverbal perception, learning, and memory.

Rita learned from Kurt Goldstein, from Hans-Lukas Teuber, from Tom Twitchell, and even from me; but she transformed what she learned into approaches and constructs distinctively her own. She was a brilliant research designer of the deliberately "low-tech" school, so that ample replication of virtually all her work has been produced. Rita was capable of splendid bursts of intuitive insight and sustained periods of critical analytic reasoning. Alternately artistic and legalistic, she was always a stimulation to colleagues. She was innovative without ever being impulsive; she was compulsive without ever being bogged down in details.

When she became (at first willy-nilly, then with increasing enthusiasm) a clinician, Rita insisted that neuropsychological evaluation was defined not by what tests you gave but by how you conceived of their dimensions, by what you observed while giving the tests, and by how you put the puzzle together from the results. As chapters 1–4 in this volume illustrate, Rita believed in her own witticism, "Don't assault me with your battery." She and I would become suspicious of our own expertise if, year by year, we did *not* change some of our test procedures or the tests themselves. Domains of functioning (as Jane Holmes explains so well) rather than particular tests that operationalize domains were what Rita was seeking from the evaluation. She was also a superb developmentalist, keenly aware of the changing demands of tasks (for example, the Wechsler subtest Block Design, as it goes from the four- to the nine-block matrix; "reading," as it goes from "barking at print" to comprehending text) called by the same names but changing across crucial developmental inflection points. Rita understood that the developing brain and the increasingly demanding school or home environment had to be evaluated within a load-matching paradigm, that is, what can sustain each level.

Rita was the first to point out so many phenomena that by now I have lost count; two examples that come to mind are her insistence that I add foot movements, repetitive and alternating, to my timed neuromotor battery, citing the importance in early childhood of cephalocaudad (from head toward feet) skill development; and noting sex differences in order effects during a variety of discrimination and matching experiments.

Rita was a prodigious worker and not one to look kindly on excuses for lack of productivity. It amazes me now to look back at how much I accomplished in so few years of working with her. She never minced words about quality control and never tolerated sloppy or loose interpretations of data. Yet she knew how to have fun, and lunches with Rita, punctuating our hard-working days, were filled with laughter.

This book was in progress when Rita became ill; she kept working at it until very shortly before her untimely death. The first four chapters are essentially Rita's words, with some editorial work and provision of references by Joan Rudel Pardes, Rita's firstborn of three children, who also contributed chapter 8, on principles of remediation. I know how proud Rita would have been of Joan's contribution; clear thinking and no-nonsense observation shine through Joan's pages. Like mother, like daughter.

The midsection of the book was undertaken by Jane Holmes with my urging as well as blessing. In a nonbiological and indirect sense, Jane is a daughter in neuropsychology of Rita Rudel. Selected by me to become the developmental neuropsychologist for the Learning Disabilities Clinic at Boston Children's Hospital Medical Center when I became the clinic's director in 1976, Jane is now herself director of neuropsychology at that hospital. Trained by Edith Kaplan and (via myself) by Rita Rudel, Jane Holmes brings to this volume not only her rich educational background but also her own superb skills as observer and thinker. Given the need to continue where Rita Rudel's chapters perforce stopped, nobody but Jane Holmes could have carried on the tradition, in her own voice, itself as strong as Rita's. Jane has the same kind of dynamic grasp of developmental neuropsychological diagnosis that characterized Rita's work.

I am happy to introduce this book. Within its covers the reader will meet three extraordinarily gifted experts and learn state-of-the-art neuropsychologically oriented principles applied to learning disabilities. My only regret remains that each and every reader cannot have the privilege of knowing Rita Rudel herself.

MARTHA BRIDGE DENCKLA, M.D.
Professor of Neurology and Pediatrics,
Johns Hopkins University School of Medicine, and
Director, Developmental Neurobehavior Clinic,
The Kennedy Institute for Handicapped Children

Preface and Acknowledgments

W HEN my mother, Rita Gillis Rudel, died in 1984, she left an extraordinary personal and professional legacy. A small part of that legacy is represented in this book. However, in order to fully appreciate the professional contribution found here, it is necessary to understand, at least in part, the very personal aspect of this work and how it came to be published.

My mother's long battle with cancer and the many months that followed her death forced me to feel my familial loss most keenly. I hoped to gain comfort from the fact that my mother left us a part of her unceasing love of life and learning. Still, it seemed unfathomable that I would never again be able to seek her advice or simply hear her voice. I looked for some way to ease my pain, and I suppose to some degree I found it in the completion of this book. I began by reading all of my mother's published works, where I discovered not only a wealth of professional knowledge but also the sound of her voice.

In addition to the special understanding of life and love my mother bequeathed her family, she made many significant contributions to the field of neuropsychology. I wanted at least some of those contributions to be memorialized in the book she had begun and that her illness had prevented her from completing. I knew that many of my mother's colleagues would miss the originality and clarity of her research projects, the direct and often biting wit of her lectures, and the insightful brilliance of her writing. I knew these things about my mother's professional life in part because our fields of work sometimes touched. As a college professor, I have worked with teachers and students as they learned about the cognitive bases of reading and writing, curriculum development, and the psychology of education. In this capacity, I sometimes helped my mother answer specific questions about types of curriculum materials best suited to the learning needs of a particular patient. And I would frequently ask her technical questions about the advisability of using certain diagnostic tools for a child who came to school with a puzzling set of learning difficulties.

After reading and studying all my mother's writings, I devised a plan to edit and expand the existing manuscript. I decided that adding chapters on the rationale, process, and procedures of testing, with a final chapter on educational implications, would result in a forceful and significant book. This book would summarize a part of my mother's professional legacy. I then contacted Dr. Jane M. Holmes, a noted neuropsychologist at Harvard Medical School and Children's Hospital in Boston, who agreed to contribute three chapters on testing (chapters 5, 6, and 7). Dr. Holmes is a leader in her field, and has for many years studied and tested children with learning difficulties. She had always been a colleague whose work and wit my mother valued and respected. Dr. Holmes has made an important contribution to this book, one that the reader will find original, thorough, and practical. Her unremitting energy and patience made the task of completing this book possible. It should be noted that there are some aspects of assessment that are covered by both Dr. Rudel and Dr. Holmes. However, we hope that readers will view any such redundancies as the application of similar concepts by compatible practitioners with a different focus.

In editing this volume, one of my tasks was to construct a bibliography for the first four chapters from the hundreds of empty parentheses my mother had left in the manuscript. This was a time-consuming and often frustrating task that was made much easier by Marge Cronin, who, having worked in my mother's laboratory, was familiar with many of the research references. For many months she and I turned detective and were able to find all but two references. (These two are noted in the text. Perhaps some enterprising researcher will recognize his or her work and let us know.)

I wrote the chapter that goes beyond the diagnostic applications and into the area of education (chapter 8) in the full understanding that my mother always concluded her detailed clinical evaluations with specific recommendations for the patient's educational and vocational planning. It is in the spirit of focusing the energy of assessment on a child's learning strengths as well as weaknesses that this volume is written.

I would like to thank Dr. Martha Denckla for her advice and support. I also extend my appreciation to Dr. Rita Haggarty for helping search out and collect missing pieces. Thanks also to our editor at Basic Books, Jo Ann Miller, who was willing to listen to and endorse a rather unorthodox approach to assembling a book. I would like to thank my husband for introducing me to the word processor and for having a job that kept him traveling and too busy to notice that dinner was often takeout or leftover. And to my three wonderful children, Rachel, Jennifer, and Daniel: I hope the assembling of this book has taught you how much time and energy a worthwhile project must take!

JOAN RUDEL PARDES
August 1987

PART ONE

DEFINING THE PROBLEM

Chapter 1

Concepts and Issues

RITA G. RUDEL

Introduction

The tendency to "name" or "label" conditions and to believe that one has thereby explained or understood them is an all-too-human weakness. We see this practice in many areas—political, economic, social, medical, and educational. For some time now, children with an infinite variety of learning problems have been labeled "perceptually" or "neurologically" impaired, as if these terms explain the condition or, better still, lead to some appropriate remediation. Further, these labels frequently are based on examinations that fail to isolate perception or to determine whether it refers to vision, audition, or touch, and they rarely test the intactness of the nervous system. Evidence for perceptual or neurological impairment is often inferred from performance on a single, poorly validated test.

The antilabeling movement—indeed, the antitesting movement—has a history of being equally uninformed and vociferous. I once lectured before a graduate neuroscience seminar on various types of learning disabilities. A young man in the back of the room kept shaking his head from left to right. Unable to continue, I stopped the lecture and asked what was troubling him. He said that he objected to "this current trend of stigmatizing innocent children with labels." I said that I, too, was against labeling but thought that what I had to present was at least a step beyond the practice, fashionable years ago, of dismissing children who couldn't learn the three R's as "dummies." While the need to label, to identify, is human, labels are worthless and misleading unless they describe and explain the condition and direct remediation.

As diagnosis becomes increasingly refined, one should be able to identify a disorder with a single diagnostic term, just as one uses the word *measles* to indicate a rash, fever, sensitivity to light, contagion, and a mode of treatment. Even some of our key words in the field of learning disorders are only vaguely understood, poorly defined in terms of symptoms, and even more inadequately suggestive of therapy. Consider the many connotations of the word *dyslexia*. I have been at various times asked to diagnose whether children unable to cope with nursery school or adults unable to climb the ladder of professional success were possibly "dyslexic."

SYMPTOMS

A survey of the research literature provides evidence that dyslexia has at least the following correlated symptoms:

1. Letter reversals during reading (or writing), in or out of the context of a "perceptual" disorder
2. Eye movement abnormalities
3. Poor phonetic analysis
4. Poor visual memory
5. Difficulties with serial ordering
6. Inadequate syllable segmentation
7. Excessively long visual fixations
8. Short-term memory deficits
9. Inadequate learning strategies
10. Word-retrieval difficulties
11. Paraphasic word errors
12. Global language disorder
13. Problems with verbal abstraction

The list seems endless: Doehring has reported sixty-eight tests on which dyslexic children performed significantly more poorly than controls (Doehring 1968). There are undoubtedly children with reading problems or with general learning problems who can be demonstrated to have one or more of these deficits at any given time; however, it is inconceivable that all of these symptoms are necessary to the condition, and it is unknown whether any *one* symptom is sufficient.

Most of the investigations that have produced this mass of evidence have failed to determine whether the specific problem area is age-related; that is, whether the symptom is common early in the school experience of the reading-disabled child but is transient, or whether it occurs relatively late in (possibly as a result of) the history of the reading disability. There are few longitudinal, prospective studies that are much more than anecdotal. Further, few cross-sectional investigations of the correlates of reading disability have carefully defined and selected the groups being studied; therefore, one cannot be certain whether the results relate to a specific reading disorder or to learning disorders generally. It seems apparent that the reading disorder of a child who fails to learn because of a failure to pay attention in the classroom would be characterized by very different symptoms than the reading disorder of one who cannot learn despite paying careful attention. The fact that the reading-disabled child may eventually develop an attentional problem in response to boredom and frustration further complicates the issue for diagnosis as well as for research.

These correlated symptoms of dyslexia do not begin to exhaust the list. Since the 1930s it has been known that some children with unspecified learning disabilities have excess slow wave activity on EEG recordings. Within the last ten years, sophisticated computer analysis of these readings implicates the connections between the two hemispheres as insufficiently integrated; that is, one side of the brain apparently is not keeping the other side adequately informed. Further, evoked response research has demonstrated differences between approximately 40 percent of reading-disabled and normal readers. Whatever merit these findings may have in directly relating differences in electrophysiological events of the brain to reading disability, their usefulness is limited. Finding that a reading-disabled child has an electrophysiological abnormality helps only to more securely label him or her; it does not diagnose how this child is functionally different from children of equal (or even lesser) intelligence who learn to read. Only with such functional comparisons can one make a diagnosis (in contrast to affixing labels) and devise individual courses of remediation.

AGE FACTORS

The earlier the diagnosis is made and remediation begun, the better the prognosis. Strag, for example, reported that "when the diagnosis of dyslexia was made in the first two grades of school, nearly 82 percent of the students could be brought up to their normal classroom work, while only 46 percent of the dyslexic problems identified in the third grade were remediated and only 10 to 15 percent of those observed in grades 5–7 could be helped. . . ." (Strag 1972, 52). In a five-year follow-up study, Muehl and Forell (1974) found that only early identification and remediation resulted in better reading ability. In a longitudinal study at grades two and five of children originally tested in kindergarten, Satz and Fletcher (1978) found that many of the children with only mild reading disorders in second grade were severely impaired by fifth grade, raising the proportion of children in that category from 12 percent to 20 percent. The problem doesn't go away without remediation and may, in fact, get worse. Children who had been found to have mild or severe reading disorders in earlier grades were rated, in fifth grade, as being deficient in handwriting skills, and the severely reading impaired were, by then, two to five years behind in arithmetic. The need for early detection, and, clearly, the earlier the better, is critical, but the effectiveness of any diagnosis depends upon an understanding of the nature of the disorder.

Although there are many problems with the cumulative data provided by research into learning disorders, there is a necessary reciprocal relationship between research and clinical diagnosis. Clinically recognized disorders constitute the starting point for much of the research that is done; in turn, clinical diagnosis is both guided and informed by research findings. For example, only when a child performs deficiently in areas that have been defined as deficit areas in dyslexia can one diagnose these reading problems as dyslexia instead of as an environmentally or motivationally engendered difficulty. Ideally, only research findings with demonstrated validity and reliability should be utilized in making such assessments. Even when these findings form the basis of an assessment, however, there is a problem in the transfer of group findings to the evaluation of a single child. The significance of research data is established in terms of statistical probability; therefore, they are not really applicable in every individual instance. One must determine what constitutes "sufficient" evidence: on how many tests must the child fall significantly below average to achieve a deficit profile? It is at this point—in the weighing of a great many probabilities to determine the adequacy of their "fit" for the individual case under scrutiny—that diagnosis becomes an art.

Given the difficulties of diagnosis and the inherent danger of affixing a potentially prejudicial label on a child, why do it at all? After all, when a child cannot read, spell, do arithmetic, or write legibly, a "diagnosis" of sorts has already been achieved. Asserting that a child unable to read at grade level is "dyslexic" provides only a translation (from English into Greek) and neither helps the child in any substantive way nor aids an understanding of the processes involved. Extra teaching, especially in a one-to-one setting, may overcome the child's specific problem without benefit of prior diagnosis. However, when remediation fails to help, or when solution of one academic problem only yields another, a diagnosis is called for to determine (1) the underlying cause of the difficulty, (2) how the child is or is not functioning, and (3) the recommended direction for remediation.

Major Sources of Clinical Referrals

Most children brought for clinical diagnosis are referred by some frustrated individual or group: the tutor who has been providing "extra help" with no concomitant improvement, the special educator who has exhausted the resources of the "resource room," the school administrator who wants to transfer the child somewhere else, the parent who resists such action, the parent who wants to know what a diagnostic designation like "perceptually impaired" means, the neurologist who is unable to find a "cause" within the nervous system for the child's inability to learn, or the psychiatrist (or other therapist) who is unable to find or cure the child's "emotional block" to learning.

Parental referrals are undoubtedly the most problematic and the most extreme, as many parents overreact to the slightest difficulties or refuse to see what is apparent to everyone else. Some parents see danger signals everywhere: one mother wanted to know whether her son was "brain damaged" when he was taken out of the "intellectually gifted" class. Some parents arrive for a diagnostic interview weighted down with previous assessments dating back to the child's infancy. They seem impelled to get a reading of the child's intellectual temperature every six months. They see every previous diagnosis as somehow inadequate and challenge the examiner to come up with a "real" diagnosis. In sharp contrast, there are parents who see their child's continuing problems as reflections of the school's inadequacy: the teacher who "turned him off," the current, inadequate teachers, scapegoating by other children, or the child's superior individuality (nonconformity) and particular brand of misunderstood brilliance. Often, such parents will bring the child for diagnosis only after the school has threatened the repeating of a grade or expulsion. Many children are referred for diagnosis by a preschool teacher or caregiver, who may suggest a clinical evaluation when the child's language and/or general development seems out-of-step with that of his or her peers. However, except for the child with an overanxious parent or a parent with inflated expectations, the school is usually the original source of referral for learning disorders. After all, it is because the child is unable to cope with the demands of schooling that he or she has a problem to be diagnosed. In that sense, learning disorders constitute a "social disease," and it is in this context that they have raised a great many controversial social issues.

SOCIAL ISSUES

There are arguments about the basic skills needed by children for whom English is not the home or primary language: can one fairly describe as learning disabled children who have had little or no access to the oral component of the language that they are required to read? Further, early exposure to testing situations can make a difference: the simple experience of paying attention to a question before answering it can alter performance. Merely administering an alternate form of a test after an initial experience can result in higher scores, when young children are tested for intelligence. Preschool exposure to the tools of education (pencils, papers, books, pictures, et cetera) and learning to listen to and answer questions can improve early school performance even if the benefits have not been shown to be long-lasting. There is no question that many social conditions, including unstable or alcoholic parents, adversely affect scholastic performance, and they provide the background against which the causes or correlates of learning disorders must be considered.

Broader social issues also affect the education of learning-disabled children. As the national economy moves from a manufacturing base to a service base, from doing things to analyzing what is being done, the need for literacy increases. Robots may be able to build cars, but the system still needs people capable of feeding mathematical or verbal symbols, often in precise serial order, into calculators or computers. It requires literate human beings to explain computer findings by turning them into comprehensible language arranged in a logical order. I have seen for diagnosis several young adults, with childhood histories of reading problems, whose business careers foundered when they were promoted from the task of feeding information into computers to the task of communicating the computer findings to others.

The social goal of universal literacy often translates into mandatory college attendance, particularly in the middle class, even for children who have been unable to cope adequately with lower levels of schooling. One of the great concerns of parents who bring in their children (some as young as six) for assessment is, "Will he [or she] be able to get into a decent college?" The fact that there are colleges available for young people who were never able to adequately acquire or develop their basic skills raises questions about the nature of higher education. For better or worse, there has been an evolution away from some of the older standards of a college education. Some graduates have not achieved formerly expected levels of literacy, and their shortcomings often become painfully apparent outside the college environment. There is also the question of the price many of these young people pay in loss of self-esteem when they are forced to cope with inadequate basic skills in still another school setting. Many of them are seen for diagnosis through psychiatric referral.

There was a time when illiteracy was not life threatening, when large segments of the population earned their livelihood carving church doors, weaving fabrics, sewing tapestries, building and ornamenting cathedrals, or making shoes. It was not expected (nor considered necessary) that skilled artisans could read or write, and if we are to believe the many genetic studies of dyslexia, the present-day reading-disabled population may be counted among their descendents. There are, however, decreasing numbers of jobs available for them to fill.

Undoubtedly, a great many social issues—personal, familial, economic, and historical—are associated with learning disabilities. Although these issues will be noted from time to time, this book deals primarily with the delineation of whatever brain-behavior relationships characterize a variety of learning disorders, that is, the neuropsychological approach to diagnosis. This approach demands some definition of how the clinical neuropsychologist views the brain and of those behaviors that are essential to the functions being evaluated.

The Neuropsychological Approach to Diagnosis

A great deal of what is known about specific brain areas essential to the performance of particular functions was gleaned through the study of the effects of brain damage on adults. By extrapolating from the deficits of people who have suffered localized trauma to the brain, scientists have correlated certain areas of the brain with certain functions. For example, a lesion that disconnects the visual from the verbal areas of the left hemisphere (in right-handed people as well as in most left-handed people), and that also interrupts the flow of information from the visual association area of the right hemisphere to the homologous area on the left will result in a loss of the capacity to read, which is called *alexia*. While this type of "localization" may provide a useful map for the neuropsychologist, it is inadequate for extrapolation to the childhood condition. Developing the capacity to read may depend upon the intactness of only some small part of that circumscribed but extended pathway, or it may depend upon much more, for example, the frontal attentional system. Adult brain trauma studies shed light on what is essential for the *performance* of a function but not for its *development*. Conceivably, a disturbance anywhere in the visual-verbal connections or within the visual or verbal areas will impede the process of learning to read, and, perhaps, the extent of that disturbance will define the severity of the deficit. Considering the plasticity of the developing brain, the necessary level of disturbance may be much greater and may comprise both the language and the attentional centers.

In providing the adult example of alexia, I mentioned a "lesion," but in the childhood examples, I spoke only vaguely of a "disturbance" or lack of "intactness." A child with reading problems, or one whose language development does not meet with age expectations, is not necessarily brain damaged. One cannot predict a lesion from such behavioral information for the following reasons:

1. Statistical probability: by definition, there are children who fall two standard deviations or more below average on every normative curve.
2. Brain dysfunction (as opposed to damage) could follow some event or condition (temporary deafness or inadequate exposure to language) during the critical years of language acquisition. There may be electrophysiological or neuro-chemical transmission abnormalities that impede or slow down learning without any identifiable "lesion."
3. Brain differences, deviations, or alterations from expected brain organization can be the result of variations in genetic encoding or early nonspecific, nonlocalizable brain trauma. Following such trauma, the plasticity of the developing brain may result in neuronal shifts providing, for the child, alternate (although possibly less efficient) routes for the performance of certain functions and, for the neuropsychologist, unchartable differences in brain organization.

The child who cannot perform at the level expected for his or her age (and intelligence), then, may be suffering from brain damage, brain dysfunction, or brain difference. If you preface these possibilities with the word "minimal," you have three alternatives for what has been bandied about as "minimal brain damage."

The isolation of some impairment of brain mechanisms in development does not imply the presence of an observable structural lesion, nor is there a test (a measurement of behavior) that can localize a problem in a specific hemisphere, lobe, or gyrus of the cerebral cortex. Since an established pathway may or may not be essential for the *development* of a function (in contrast to its performance), and since the plasticity of the developing brain makes some shift of locus possible, neuropsychologists cannot localize functions with children quite as they can with adults. Further, since diagnosis in children is not likely to be followed by any sort of verification of localization, neurosurgical intervention, CAT scan, or angiogram, one can never be wrong nor, for that matter, right. The aim of developmental diagnosis is to identify the functional (behavioral) system that is impaired and to establish the way and the degree to which it is impaired.

Unfortunately, the brain is not neatly arranged according to academic requirements, with one area devoted to reading and another to mathematics, social studies, or even to paying attention. It takes a great many brain areas, even in the adult with well-established abilities, just to make the decoding of print possible. Neither reading nor arithmetic are one-dimensional activities; they both demand the confluence of a great many abilities and, therefore, the activation of more than one functional system in the brain. Diagnosis lies in determining the strength and weakness of functional systems, individually and collectively, and not in determining the localization of "damage." The latter approach not only is questionable and unverifiable but, in the present state of our knowledge, cannot lead to remediation. Determining which functional system works poorly and which works well, however, can lead to tutorial therapy, compensatory techniques, or alternative forms of education.

Just as one cannot localize the acquisition of skills involved in reading, writing, or arithmetic, there are no tests that depend on the intactness of a single locus in the brain. During a neuropsychological meeting, a slide "localizing" the *Peabody Picture Vocabulary Test* in the left angular gyrus was greeted with universal embarrassment. This test involves (at a minimum) attention, visual discrimination, choice behavior, comprehension of words, and retrieval from memory! The behaviors that the clinician evaluates in establishing intact or impaired brain-behavior relationships are manifold; deficits detected on one test must be broken down and retested in another way to determine *which* of the functions is impaired. For example, one study showed, as it has been shown before, that dyslexic children do more poorly than matched controls (children who read at grade level) on the *Bender Visual-Motor Gestalt Test* (Owen et al. 1971). This finding had been interpreted as evidence that the underlying reading disability was a perceptual deficit. However, this very large research study ($N = 304$) involved a second step after the initial copying of nine rather complicated designs. The tester presented copies of varying degrees of exactness of each of the nine designs, along with the originals, to all the children (dyslexic and control), who were then asked to judge which of the copies was closest to the original. This step eliminated the copying, or the motor, aspect of the visual-motor test, thus also eliminating the difference in performance between the two groups and the "perceptual deficit" hypothesis of reading disability as well. Again, statistical probability does not rule out the possibility that there may have been *some* dyslexic children in the group with perceptual problems, but there was not a statistically significant number. On the other hand, a statistically significant number did have motor problems or, at least, problems transforming their adequate *perceptions* of the forms into adequate copies, a deficit somewhere between the visual and motor functions or in the motor act itself.

In a sense, a child's performance on a test, or on a group of tests, leads the tester to form a hypothesis as to the nature of the child's problem. The tester then selects another test or group of tests to adequately challenge that hypothesis. For example, if a child's naming of pictured objects is below par for his or her age, the deficit has to be evaluated in the context of (1) other vocabulary measures, (2) the nature of the errors (does the child misperceive what the objects are or just misname the pictures), (3) naming objects in response to auditory stimulation, and (4) visual discrimination when naming is not involved.

Since a final diagnosis is determined only after continuous hypothesis testing, making an assessment with a fixed battery of tests is difficult and may even run counter to the requirements of individualized diagnostic testing. Of course, one can use a "battery" so comprehensive that nothing is missed and every hypothesis can be tested afterward, but this could take several days to administer and certainly would strain the goodwill of the child.

Finally, in hypothesis testing, as in arriving at an evaluation, one must invoke the law of parsimony: the simplest, most basic diagnosis must take precedence. A retarded child can be learning disabled only relative to the level of his or her retardation; a deaf child may only secondarily have a language comprehension deficit; and so on. The tester must show the basic functions to be intact before higher-order deficits can be implicated in diagnosis.

THE EXCLUSIONARY FACTORS

Before one can clearly define specific learning disabilities, it is essential to delineate what a learning disability is not. A certain degree of consensus has developed on this issue, so that one does not include, among the learning disabled, children with (1) an inadequate capacity to learn (too young or unintelligent for the task at hand); (2) reduced sensory acuity (uncorrected, poor vision or hearing); (3) a psychiatric disorder (emotional disturbance that would interfere with learning or with the development of appropriate motivation to learn); (4) a neurological disturbance (evidence of brain damage sufficient to account for reduced learning capacity); and (5) inadequate educational opportunity or environment for learning. The *Diagnostic and Statistical Manual,* 3d ed., of the American Psychiatric Association (*DSM III*), runs counter to these exclusions, and has recognized that a learning disability may exist along with neurological or emotional disorders when either is present but independent of the learning disability. Such independence, however, is often difficult to establish.

Neuropsychological Examination. Brain damage usually is determined in a neurological examination of sensory and motor systems—two systems that may have little or no effect on those systems essential for learning or acquiring basic skills. However, is not the brain-damaged child (that is, the child with motor and/or sensory symptoms of brain damage who cannot read adequately) also dyslexic? Children with epilepsy, for example, are more likely to have learning disorders than are normal controls, and it is reasonable to assume (although usually unverifiable) that the brain damage causing the seizure activity is to some degree also responsible for or at least related to the learning problem.

The incidence of reading disability is very high (about one-third) among children who have suffered a depressed skull fracture. A study of eighty-eight children referred because of head injury found that 55 percent had reading levels one or more years behind their chronological ages and 33 percent were two or more years behind (Shaffer et al. 1980). It would be difficult to assume the "independence" of these symptoms, just as it is impossible to ignore that some children without histories of head injury and without classic signs of neurological impairment often have more subtle, "soft" signs of dysfunction along with their learning disability. Ruling out neurological damage in the definition of learning-disabled children would exclude those with hemiplegia (paralysis of one side of the body), yet Denckla (1979b) has described signs of a right hemi-syndrome (not as severe as a hemiplegia) in some learning-disabled dyslexic children, which implies some inadequacy of left-hemisphere development. Similarly, although the diagnosis of learning disability would exclude children with aphasia (those who have not acquired language), many learning-disabled children have mild forms of receptive, expressive, or repetition disorders of language. Although they may not have demonstrable visual field defects (areas of blindness), studies have demonstrated slowing of visual processing in general (Stanley and Hall 1973; Blank, Berezweig, and Bridges 1975; Broman and Rudel 1982) and problems with letter recognition (Gross et al. 1978; Marcel, Katz, and Smith 1974). Thus, although free of hard neurological evidence of damage to the visual system, these children may have soft signs in the form of less direct or less rapid access of visual information to the language areas.

Excluding children with neurological damage from the definition or diagnosis of learning disorders raises two separate substantive issues. While children with identifiable brain damage may or may not also be learning disabled, the chances that they will be learning disabled are greater than among children without brain damage. Therefore, identifying the correlates of learning disabilities among those with brain damage may be useful (1) in determining the nature and site of brain damage that will not produce deficits in academic achievement and (2) for formulating plans to remediate learning deficits in children where information about the probable site of the damage can be useful. Just as neuropsychology developed out of the analysis of residual behavior following specific and local brain damage, so a true neuropsychology of learning disabilities may develop out of the assessment of academic achievement in the light of known brain abnormalities. Of course, learning-disabled children must be clearly characterized as with or without brain damage in research or diagnosis.

Even when, in accord with consensus, one excludes children with neurological damage from definitions of learning disabilities, the exclusion is not absolute but one of degree. In fact, it is the presence of these and other soft, or developmental, signs—the hemi-syndrome (rather than hemiplegia), the language problems (rather than the absence of language or aphasia), and the slow visual processing (rather than visual field defects)—that confirm the presence of a learning disability rather than some motivational, emotional, or social problem as the cause of inadequate functioning in school.

An emotional disturbance determined by psychiatric evaluation is not always or necessarily the cause of a child's learning disability and, in fact, may be a reaction to rather than the cause of the problem. Epidemiological studies have shown that delinquent children with emotional problems and reading disabilities have the same kinds of reading disturbances as dyslexic children without such psychiatric problems, whereas those with only antisocial behavior were very dissimilar (Rutter 1970; Varlaam 1974). Should the diagnosis of learning disability, and possible remediation of that condition, be withheld from children with both learning and emotional problems? For example, children from disadvantaged environments, who constitute possibly the largest group of learning disabled, are not defined as such because their environmental opportunities for acquiring the basic skills have been less than optimal.

Definition and Diagnosis. Defining learning disability by excluding certain possibly causative factors aims at "pure" groups of children with cognitive disabilities of constitutional origin (Critchley 1964). As long as these exclusionary factors are specified, such consensus is essential for defining subjects used in research. In diagnosis, however, clinicians need to weigh the various factors and evaluate them for their relevance to the chief complaint of learning disability in the specific case.

Attentional disorders, which may or may not include hyperactivity, constitute another, even more complex issue and, paradoxically, have received less consideration than the other possibly predisposing factors. Although recognized as a possible source of learning disability, attentional disorders are not usually excluded from the definition of reading disability or other learning disorders, nor are children ruled out of research studies (or from a diagnosis of learning disability) on that basis. Yet, a child unable to learn because he or she is unable to sustain attention in the learning situation is constitutionally very different from one with adequate attention but with impairment of a cognitive system essential to the acquisition of a basic skill. There are also reactive attentional disorders (just as there are reactive emotional disorders) secondary to the frustration of being unable to cope with classroom requirements or to keep up with peers. This type of secondary effect is very different from a primary attentional deficit, which in itself may be the *cause* of a learning disability.

While attentional disorders are not excluded by consensus from the definition of learning disability, they constitute a source of confusion and mistaken identity in research and diagnosis. Many of the correlates of learning disability that have been demonstrated in research may be correlates of attentional disorders, neither identified nor ruled out in the groups being studied. Denckla and Rudel (1978) demonstrated the effect of this confusion in a study comparing two groups of children with reading disorders on tests of motor coordination. Whereas dyslexic children without attentional disorders were not significantly different from age-matched controls, a similarly constituted group, unscreened for attentional problems, were slower than controls and had more qualitative signs of motor immaturity. The difference between the two groups had to be in the presence or absence of attentional problems and not in the nature of their reading disability. It seems likely that at least some of the many identified correlates of reading disability may be reflections of immature or impaired attentional systems.

Conversely, deficits said to characterize hyperactive children may be correlates of learning disorders. One study comparing hyperactive children with and without reading disability demonstrated that only the former were deficient on the *Matching Familiar Figures* test, which is said to be sensitive to the impulsive-response tendencies of hyperactive children (Halperin et al. 1984). In fact, the test may have been sensitive to the demonstrated tendency of *learning-disabled* children to fail to search a visual field selectively (Dykman, Ackerman, and Oglesby 1979) rather than to the failures of impulse control in hyperactive children. Further studies have attempted to differentiate hyperactive groups with and without reading disorders or learning-disabled groups with and without attentional disorders.

All future research into the correlates or causes of learning disorders should indicate whether or not the subject groups were screened for attentional problems along with other impairments (psychiatric, neurological, sensory, environmental, and intellectual) that are usually excluded. Ultimately, such screening (and exclusion-inclusion) information will aid in delineating more specifically the brain-behavior relationships essential to the acquisition of basic skills as distinct from the attentional mechanisms. Many learning-disabled children have deficits of *both* attention and the cognitive systems essential to the acquisition of basic skills; in these cases, one must determine whether the attentional disorder is another primary disorder or a behavioral reaction to the learning disability. In chapter 2, the attentional deficit disorder will be considered as a distinct and separate learning disability, a disorder of the capacity to learn to deploy and sustain attention or to respond in the learning situation as other children do.

The Concept and Use of Discrepancy Scores

How much educational or sensory deprivation, or how much psychiatric or neurological impairment, would have to be demonstrated before these factors could be seen as responsible for a learning disorder? Just how much incapacity to learn constitutes grounds for diagnosing (or defining) a learning disability remains unclear, though the question has been and still is being raised. Perhaps this is because age and intelligence, which provide measures of capacity to learn, are given numerically, whereas sensory, psychiatric, and neurological data are provided in terms of the unquantified presence or absence of disabling symptoms or antecedents.

The fact that a child has regularly attended a school in which his or her peers have learned is considered sufficient evidence for adequate environmental opportunity, while an unusually poor attendance record will provide measurable evidence for inadequate educational opportunity. Cause-and-effect may be confounded here as well: children are as likely to become truants because they can't learn as they fail to learn because of their truancy. Often excessive school absences are the result of a child's negative reaction to his or her inability to learn with the ease and success demonstrated by classmates.

It has become incumbent upon anyone defining or diagnosing a learning disability to prove that the degree of discrepancy between the child's capacity to learn (as estimated from his or her age and intelligence) and what he or she has learned (as estimated from achievement scores) is sufficient to warrant a positive diagnosis. How one makes that determination, as well as what constitutes a sufficient discrepancy, have been matters of considerable controversy in the research literature and would not concern us here except that the issues, some of which are social, are very similar for diagnosis and research.

The "average" child performing at grade level is the nondiscrepant norm to which others are compared. One is rarely concerned about the child performing *above* grade level, except, perhaps, when he or she becomes inattentive through boredom. The child referred for diagnosis generally is the child with at least average capacity who performs below grade level. *Grade level*, however, has very different connotations in different places. The norm for a particular school can be below or above what is considered average almost everywhere else. The dilemma is not an uncommon one, particularly among upper-middle-class children attending a school where the average level of performance is considerably higher than it is elsewhere. One then may be put in the position of diagnosing as learning disabled a child whose achievement is appropriate for his or her age but not for the school he or she is attending. If the child's capacity is only average, then the problem becomes a social one, perhaps of finding a different, less demanding school. The situation becomes more complex if the child has above-average capacity, as measured on intelligence tests, but is performing at average levels. The degree of discrepancy between ability and performance may appear sufficient for a diagnosis of learning disability, but is there any justification for it? One can answer this question only in the psychological context of the effect the capacity-achievement discrepancy has on the child and in the course of diagnosis, which may or may not reveal cognitive impairments to explain failure of the child to acquire basic skills at levels consistent with his or her intellectual potential. Without such evidence, the child's motivation, attention, and environment must be brought under scrutiny to explain the discrepancy.

One must also consider the dilemma posed at the opposite end of the continuum—when a child of average or above-average ability attends a school where normal achievement is below his or her potential. Is such a child learning disabled if he or she performs at "grade level" at this school? Unfortunately, such children are rarely referred for evaluation, so the question remains whether many of them eventually rise above their environments and the limited demands made on them.

The discrepancy concept is based on the difference between a set of expectations and actual achievement. There are social, scholastic, and parental expectations that may change from time to time and can be rather nebulous and subjective. The intelligence test provides a different kind of expectancy, serving as an objective measure to predict academic success or failure. Most of the time, its predictive validity is quite good (Rutter and Yule 1975; Jastak and Jastak 1978), but it is precisely in those instances where the results of intelligence tests predict academic success and there is, instead, failure, that one is provided with a basis for considering a diagnosis of a learning disability.

CAPACITY-ACHIEVEMENT DISCREPANCY

A capacity-achievement discrepancy is rarely known when a child is referred for diagnosis. There is only the chief complaint that something is not going right with the child's school performance. Behaviorally and/or academically, the child is unable to cope, and the neuropsychologist as diagnostician is required to determine whether some demonstrable disorder of brain function provides an explanation, that is, whether an impairment of a specific functional system (or systems) impedes acceptable school performance despite overall quantitatively adequate capacity. It is, then, only after neurological, psychiatric, and intellectual impairment and sensory and educational deficiencies have been ruled out, and a discrepancy between capacity to learn and achievement has been demonstrated, that one can begin to attribute the child's problem to a learning disability, to an attentional disorder, or to both.

The critical difference between capacity and achievement depends upon the child's age. To arbitrarily designate a one- or two-year lag as the necessary or sufficient discrepancy makes no sense in a seven- or eight-year-old who has been exposed to teaching for only a year or two. A two-year lag constitutes a much smaller proportion of learning delay, and a much less severe problem, in a fourteen-year-old as compared to a nine-year-old. Further, there is no evidence that increments in the acquisition of basic skills perfectly parallel increments in mental age or capacity, as measured in intelligence tests. Therefore, even the same proportion of delay (say 15 or 20 percent below expectation) may have very different meanings and consequences at different ages.

There are psychometric obstacles to using grade levels or school years as measures of discrepancy between aptitude or achievement or in assessing the degree of deficiency in a given child or groups of children. Reynolds (1981) makes two very important points: (1) grade-equivalent scores ignore the amount of dispersion about the mean (how much variability there is within a given grade), and (2) the relationship between grade and test score is not equivalent across grades or school subjects. Because of changes in percentile rankings in the distribution of grade-equivalent scores with increasing age, there can be considerable distortion in the interpretation of discrepancies. In the upper grades, for example, there is a flattening of the relative growth curves between age and basic skill scores when these tools of learning should have been acquired. A twelfth-grader who reads at the tenth-grade level actually may be quite average, in the fiftieth percentile. On the other hand, a fourth-grader who is reading at the second-grade level will fall far below the fiftieth percentile.

Ideally, only standard scores that are constant across age and that take into account the degree of dispersion about the mean (as in the *Wechsler Intelligence Scale for Children*) should be used in determining the degree of capacity-achievement discrepancies. Unlike grade-level equivalents, such scores have the same relationship at every age between distance from the mean and percentile ranking. For example, at every age, a score that falls two-thirds of a standard deviation below the mean has a percentile rank of 25; in contrast, a test score falling two-thirds of a grade level below the mean for that grade has a different percentile rank at every age. Standard scores, however, are not available for many tests of achievement. Future research will have to establish better norms by which one can assess the performance of children in relation to their potential. These norms would have to take into account dispersion around the mean, regression toward the mean (Cone and Wilson 1981), and the number of years the child has spent in school.

On a practical, day-to-day basis, children are judged in relation to their grade-level peers, and it is on this basis that they are referred for diagnosis or selected for research studies. It is possible, after all, that discrepant capacity-achievement ratios are typical of the school they attend. A proposed formula compares the individual child with the intelligence-achievement ratios found in the specific school and grade he or she is attending (Yule et al. 1974). This is rarely feasible in practice, since school data are based on group-administered tests, which, aside from requiring reading, are not comparable to the individually administered tests usually utilized in research and *always* utilized in diagnosis. However, even if the school data are unavailable, the diagnostician must never lose sight of the fact that the relative levels of aptitude and performance at the school the child attends are critical for evaluating whatever capacity-achievement discrepancy is found. For better or worse, the child's performance is also being compared to that of peers and not only to his or her own potential.

Not all tests of capacity (IQ tests) measure the same thing. A common practice in research studies is to use (or report) only one part of the *Wechsler Intelligence Scale for Children—Revised* (WISC-R), the Verbal or Performance score, whichever represents the child's capacity optimally. However, this practice exaggerates potential by ignoring its clearly expressed limitations. Whatever biases are ruled out (or in) by such a procedure, discrepancy scores will differ depending upon which measure of capacity is employed. Similarly, discrepancy scores (and, therefore, who is or is not diagnosed as learning disabled) will vary according to which tests of ability are used. In two unpublished studies by the author, as well as a study by Helensworth and White (1981),* groups of dyslexic children were shown to perform significantly better on tests of single-word reading (*Wide-Range Achievement Test, WRAT,* or *Woodcock Reading Mastery Tests*) than on tests of oral prose reading (*Gray Oral Reading Test* or *Gilmore Oral Reading Test*). Normal control groups do not show this difference in scores between the two types of reading; therefore, one would have to conclude that something more substantive than different standardization groups for oral prose reading and single-word reading is responsible for the difference between the two levels of reading ability in the dyslexic groups.

Selected research samples of dyslexic children, or the diagnosis of dyslexia, will differ, however, depending upon whether tests of single-word or oral prose reading are employed, and whether accuracy or comprehension is used as the essential measure of reading ability. The problem of designation is further compounded when comprehension is measured by silent reading (Vogel 1974, 1977), for then there is no way of knowing whether poor performance is a function of the inability to accurately decode the text, to comprehend what has been decoded, or to hold attention to the text long enough to process and comprehend it; nor can one then evaluate whether any correlated deficits are a function of poor decoding skill or inadequate comprehension.

Similar problems exist in assessing skill in arithmetic. Should one use verbal problems, oral or written, or submit already set-up arithmetic calculation examples to be solved? Should reading or arithmetic tests be timed or untimed, and should speed of response be a factor at all in measuring ability? Even when they are measured separately, should reading discrepancy scores be calculated on the basis of accuracy or should comprehension be included as well?

In selecting children for research, experimenters often leave such

---

* Reference unknown. See page *xiii*.

questions unanswered. As a result, test choices vary from one study to another, so that they have to be carefully evaluated for comparability. In diagnosing a learning disability, one can employ any and all measures and determine discrepancies at each level of skill, but it is essential to realize that no single measure can provide a complete picture of the learning function.

There are, then, no absolutes for determining the degree of discrepancy essential to the diagnosis of learning disability. Competence is measured relative not only to capacity but also to social expectation. While the capacity-achievement discrepancy suggests the presence of a learning disability, it is often the school and social situation that dictate how much discrepancy can be tolerated.

Chapter 2

Learning Difficulties: Disorders of Symbolic Representation

RITA G. RUDEL

Dyslexia

Once the diagnostician has excluded all other factors and determined a capacity-achievement discrepancy, a diagnosis of *dyslexia*, which means simply unexpected difficulty in learning to read, indicates some brain dysfunction as a probable cause. The most common complaint brought to a diagnostician is the failure to learn to read, to decode, to turn writing into oral language or symbols into meaning. Parents are much more likely to be concerned over a lack of progress in learning to read than over similar difficulties in other areas (Johnson, Blalock, and Nesbitt 1978); in fact, parents often overlook other academic problems while concentrating on reading remediation. It is when the child's *only* school problem is the failure to learn to read that one can speak of a specific reading disorder or a specific dyslexia. However, this condition is not likely to be encountered in clinical practice. The child who fails to learn to read rarely learns to spell or to write (as distinct from just producing letters or words) and often has difficulty with arithmetic as well. In addition, as the child progresses through the educational system, he or she must cope with academic subjects that all require reading! If the child has been unable to learn to read effectively, then the learning problems are exacerbated, resulting in school failure, which may lead to a clinical referral.

LANGUAGE IMPLICATIONS

Most of the research on learning disorders has focused on reading and has established a clear link between delayed or nonacquisition of reading skills and a developmental lag in, or impairment of, language development. Similarly, clinical research in adult neurology has found that adults who have lost the capacity to read ("alexia") also have language disorders of varying degrees of severity (Benson and Geschwind 1969). Further, studies of cerebral blood flow show that reading silently or aloud activates receptive and expressive language areas (Lassen, Ingnar, and Skinhj 1978).

Reading disorders appear to involve spoken language skills insufficient to allow for flexible adaptation to the more complex level of performance demanded in reading or writing. Thus, while the child may make all the right sounds when speaking, he or she cannot "see" those sounds when reading. Not surprisingly, the dyslexic child may make impossible sound combinations, just as he or she makes impossible semantic or syntactic word combinations when reading. Some of these sounds are not words. For example, the sentence "Mary and Dick assist him by gathering wood" was read by a ten-and-a-half-year-old boy with a WISC-R verbal IQ score of 118 as "Mary and Dick *ask* him by *graduling* wood." *Ask* in this context makes no semantic sense, and of course, there is no such word as *graduling*.

Another boy, thirteen-and-a-half years old, with a high-average verbal IQ score (117), read "excursions" as *exkerienses* and "expedition" as *expienshun*. There is little doubt that at some time in his oral language experience, this child has come in contact with these words. He must realize, at least on some intellectual level, the nonsense quality of the words he reads. A child, of almost twelve years old, with a high-average verbal IQ score (119) read "keenly" as *kneedy*. When faced with the sentence "School is scheduled to open," this child read, "School is *se-cluded* to open." A ten-year-old, with a verbal IQ score of 111, read the sentence "Bob is eleven years old" as "Bob is *very* years old." An eleven-and-a-half-year-old with a normal verbal IQ score read the phrase "The entire family insist" as *"They enter family enstants."* A twelve-year-old boy with a high-average verbal IQ score (119) read the same phrase as *"They extra family insteads."* These examples indicate the child's inability to connect the logic of spoken language with the rules and patterns of written language. None of these children speak this way, nor do they fail to note the absurdities if the sentences are read to them with these errors. Note that in these errors of misreading, the initial sounds are almost always produced correctly. This is characteristic of children who have trouble learning to read just as it is characteristic of adults with acquired alexia.

Dyslexic children often misread "small" words—articles (see *they* for "the," above); prepositions; pronouns; adverbs connoting how, where, and when; and auxiliary verbs—much as aphasic adults tend to leave out these parts of speech altogether. They also pay little or no attention to grammatical coherence, number, tense, or subject-verb correspondence. Thus, "On holidays" is read as *"One* holidays"; "there are," as *"they* are"; "her name," as *"here* name"; "during these visits," as "during *this* visits"; et cetera. One boy, age twelve, with a verbal IQ score of 122, left out small words like *by, in,* and *the;* read *are* for "her"; and often paraphrased the text, using synonyms to achieve similar meaning ("goat" read as *kid,* "lamp" read as *light*). This type of inaccurate reading is very rare in dyslexic children and resembles what has been described as "deep dyslexia" in adults (Coltheart 1979).

OBJECT NAMING

Most of the dyslexic children tested clinically fail to make sense of the text while they are reading, and the content does not provide them with cues. In view of the distortions and the misreading or omission of non-content words (prepositions, articles, adverbs), it is not surprising that their prose reading is worse than their reading of single words in isolation.

Context and syntax do not help their recognition of words but appear to hinder it. One can see the language deficiency of dyslexia even more strikingly when these children are required, not to read or to write, but simply to complete orally presented sentences with the name of an object. For example, when asked to complete the following sentence, "You hang laundry out to dry on a _____," a twelve-year-old dyslexic boy responded *clotheshanger* instead of "clothesline." When asked to complete, "When a man has a lot of hair on top of his upper lip, we say he has a _____," he substituted *beard* for "mustache." In these situations, when no translation from visual input to verbal output is required, dyslexics perform more poorly (and more slowly) than children who read but have other learning disabilities, and naming errors are more likely to be paraphasic, or linguistic.

Like many adults who have lost the ability to read (*alexia*), dyslexic children are somewhat *anomic*, having great difficulty when called upon to name objects implied in sentences or in definitions read to them or from pictures. Performance on repetitive-naming tasks differentiates dyslexic children not only from normal controls but also from children with learning disabilities other than reading (Denckla and Rudel 1976). These children tend to circumlocate—give the function of the object instead of its name—missequence word parts and syllables (*shoehorn* for "horseshoe"), or name another object in the same class (*sink* for "faucet") (Rudel et al. 1980).

These reading errors, which are often found in clinical practice, suggest that for these children, reading is a guessing game in which grammar and content play a very minor role. When dyslexics see a word that they do not recognize instantly or that they cannot sound out, they create a word that contains some of the correct letters (plus others) and looks something like the original, for example, reading "enter" as "*extra*" or *entire*, "eleven" as *very*, or "insists" as *insteads* or *instants*, even when these substitutions make neither semantic nor syntactic sense. The first letter sound of a word is usually read correctly, particularly if it is a consonant. As in the substitution of *very* for "eleven," however, dyslexic children have more difficulty reading vowels, even when they are the initial sound, perhaps because vowels rarely have their letter name sounds (*a* is pronounced "ay" only in certain contexts). Further evidence of this lack of linguistic flexibility is found in the dyslexic child's practice of carrying the sound of the letter name over to the pronunciation (or

TABLE 2.1

Naming Error Types

Error	Description
Circumlocution	A description of the function of the object rather than its name (for example, on presentation of the picture of a hat, responding, "What you put on your head").
Paraphasic-substitution error	A response in the right category but specifically wrong (for example, calling a wrench *pliers*, a mustache a *beard*, or an emerald a *diamond*).
Paraphasic part-whole error	An associate of the correct response (for example, calling a telephone a *dial* or a bicycle a *pedal*).
Half-right paraphasic error	(for example, *clotheshanger* for clothesline, *fireworks* for firecracker, or *sandglass* for hourglass).
Phonemic-sequencing error	(for example, "mindwill" for windmill, "horseshoe" for shoehorn, or "porthole" for pothole).
Perceptual error	(for example, "blocks" for dice, "paper" for envelope, or "jumprope" for stethoscope).

spelling) of words. They have difficulty shifting from the name of the letter to its sound, and vowels have potentially more sounds than do consonants. Most dyslexic children seen in the clinic cannot be characterized as either phonetic or whole-word readers, because most of them attach the first sound phonetically (particularly if it is a consonant) and then guess the rest, combining phonetic and visual aspects of the words but ignoring syntactic or semantic context. In addition, the word attack strategies and phonetic remediation techniques employed to help dyslexic children might in effect neutralize any attempts to characterize a dyslexic "reading style."

PROBLEMS OF SERIAL ORDER

Putting a word together phonetically or getting the gist of a sentence demands some proficiency with maintaining a serial order. The letters *o-n-e* have very different sound and meaning from *e-o-n* or *n-e-o*. The words "the boy kicked the horse" convey a very different picture if that subject-object order is reversed. Serial ordering is an integral aspect of language, and children who fail to learn to read adequately frequently confuse letter and word order. They even have trouble when language is not involved, as in tapping a sequence of blocks displayed in a random spatial array (Corkin 1974).

Children with reading disorders also lack the analytic capacity needed to fragment a word into component parts (or syllables) (Liberman and Shankweiler 1979) or to recognize whole words that they have been previously taught. They also fail to generalize to new words from the phonetic combinations they have learned; that is, knowing that *b-a-t* spells bat often does not help them read *m-a-t* or *s-a-t*. Even in a highly irregular language like English, there is enough regularity to generate a large reading vocabulary from phonetic roots, but these children have difficulty grasping and utilizing such principles.

The dyslexic child is the child with average or better-than-average intelligence who seems incapable of applying that intelligence to the task of decoding print into meaningful words or sentences. At the core of this disability there appears to be some disturbance in the functional language system—problems with articulation, word finding, naming, word analysis and generalization, verbal memory, and sequencing (verbal or nonverbal)—all skills which have been related to the integrity of the left-hemisphere language areas.

How (or why) is the speed and accuracy of naming objects related to the ability to read? Is there a cause-and-effect relationship? Research has correlated the naming deficit with reading disorder, possibly through cerebral proximity. The sites essential to reading and the sites essential to naming are adjacent in the cerebral cortex; if one is impaired, the other is likely to be impaired as well. It has been shown, through cortical stimulation of the left-hemisphere areas during adult craniotomies performed under local anesthesia, that naming and reading are affected at many adjacent sites (Ojemann 1975; Ojemann and Mateer 1979). There are other sites, around these naming-reading sites, where both sequential orofacial (tongue and mouth) movements and phoneme identification are affected by stimulation. In addition, an area that appears to serve verbal short-term memory surrounds the sequencing-phoneme identification system. All of these surround the fine-motor pathway for speech. Therefore, depending upon the extent and location of the disturbance in this peri-Sylvian language region of the left hemisphere, reading disability will be associated with deficits of any or all of the other related skills. Reading and naming are the most intimately linked, in terms of proximity in the brain; therefore, it is not surprising that a naming deficit is most readily elicited in children or adults with reading disorder.

Several researchers have attempted to distinguish subtypes of dyslexia (Mattis, French, and Rapin 1975; Boder 1970). However, the discriminatory power or remedial value of these subgroups, many of which tend to overlap and converge, is open to question. In fact, the dyseidetic (visual-perceptual) subtype, included by Mattis and Boder, has been omitted here; clinical experience has shown that this rarely poses a problem if the child is not retarded. Subtypes have been summarized as follows:

- *Articulatory-graphomotor type*. This was defined by Mattis, French, and Rapin (1975) and is congruent with Boder's (1970) dysphonic type; only articulation and fine-motor coordination, particularly graphomotor skill, are deficient.
- *Anomic type*. This type is usually characterized by slowness on word retrieval, with a tendency for circumlocution and paraphasic errors.
- *Repetition disorder*. This is characterized by short-term memory, poor initial information intake, and some missequencing of words (phonemic-sequencing errors).
- *Global mixed-language disorders* (Denckla 1979a). This type involves impairment in all aspects of language, especially phoneme discrimination, comprehension, repetition, syntax, and naming. Verbal IQ scores tend to be low, and there is often a rather dramatic history of late language acquisition.

As a group, dyslexic children tend to be slow on tests of repetitive and alternating movements and to show developmental "soft signs"; some, particularly those with histories of familial dyslexia, may be superior to normal controls on three-dimensional and spatial-configurational tasks.

LETTER REVERSALS

Up to this point, we have described the dyslexic child in terms of language and related sequencing deficits that consistently have been shown to be correlated with the disorder and, through clinical and electrophysiological studies, to be neurophysiologically related. Yet many would protest that this description has omitted the cardinal, idiosyncratic symptom identifying dyslexia—letter and word reversal (reading *d* for *b* or *saw* for *was*). Research has demonstrated that normal young children also reverse letters but rapidly outgrow the tendency once they have acquired a set of verbal mnemonic cues (for example, the letter with the balloon on the side of the hand I write with is the *b*; the other one is the *d*). Dyslexic children are slower to adopt mnemonic cues of any kind (Rudel 1981a) or to remember to use them (Corkin 1974), but letter reversal cannot begin to explain their problem. At best, this is an early correlate of the disorder and not a cause, for were *b/d* and *p/q* constantly misidentified, then the child's misreadings should be limited to words containing those letters. However, none of the examples culled from clinical files bears this out.

The fact that a child writes a letter backward or calls it by the wrong name (for example, *b* instead of *d*) does not mean that he or she sees it that way. Of course, this does not imply a perceptual problem: a primary deficit in perception is not consistent with normal intelligence. For the dyslexic child, the letters that are consistently misnamed and miswritten are all ones that differ in orientation. This is because differences in left-right orientation are arbitrary, and stable orientation is acquired relatively late. Actually, it is quite normal for beginning readers to mix up *b*, *q*, *p*, and *d*. However, by the age of seven or eight in girls and eight or nine in boys, such confusion should be resolved.

This mislabeling of letters may be just another aspect of the oft-demonstrated naming deficit of the dyslexic child, reflecting not what is seen but what is said. In other words, one cannot attribute to a deficit of perception what may be a deficit at the motor end of the reading input-output equation, in expressive language or in graphomotor skill. From a neuropsychological point of view, such a problem is likely to be associated with the output systems of the brain and, thus, is related to word-retrieval and sequencing tasks.

SENSORY INTEGRATION

Dyslexic children have neither the linguistic facility nor the flexibility to "see" sounds, words, or ideas that they readily "hear." One explanation, which has received considerable attention in research and remediation, suggests an interference with the process of integrating information from one sense to another. However, the dyslexic child's sensory integration problem, if he or she has one, appears to be selectively related to letters, words, and sentences and not, for example, related to the sights and sounds that make up his or her daily environment. In fact, various research studies have demonstrated that the critical factor in most investigations is not the intersensory nature of the task but keeping track of sequential incoming information, visual or auditory (Rudel and Denckla 1976). Dealing with sequences through some kind of internal encoding, not the difference in sensory modalities, is the critical difficulty for dyslexic children. The longer the sequence or the greater the number of sequences they are required to keep track of, the more poorly dyslexics perform. Earlier studies that implicated a deficit of sensory integration in children with dyslexia did not consider the possibility that the sequencing, not the intersensory, nature of the task produced the essential difficulty.

VERBAL IQ AND LANGUAGE DIFFICULTIES

The verbal IQ scores that we have cited are all one hundred or over, which would seem to imply these children have average to above-average language ability. Yet, research results suggest that their reading disability is related to language deficits. These two sets of findings are not irreconcilable: their difficulties with language are untapped by the verbal tests of the WISC-R. Dyslexic children, especially those from culturally advantaged environments, have no difficulty picking up facts, knowledge about the social world around them, or vocabulary. Questions on the WISC-R rarely require specific names, so a naming deficit would go unnoted. On the Vocabulary subtest, it is perfectly satisfactory to provide explanations and circumlocutions (rather than synonyms), and answers (except on the Arithmetic subtest) are untimed. Therefore, problems with word-finding or with long latencies of verbal response are not penalized in the test situation. The only subtest of the WISC-R that taps sequencing ability is the Digit Span, and dyslexics often do very poorly on this test (Rudel and Denckla 1974). In a recent study of sixty dyslexic boys with a mean verbal IQ score of 106.02, the mean Digit Span Scale score was 7.57, which is significantly lower than the mean of the scaled scores of the subtests that make up the verbal IQ score (Helfgott, Rudel, and Kairam 1986).

If, despite deficiencies in their language system, reading-disabled children have at least average intelligence, then they must have other skills at above-average levels. In fact, some children with reading disorders demonstrate superior abilities in tasks involving spatial configuration (Denckla, Rudel, and Broman 1980), three-dimensional information processing (Corkin 1974), or logical reasoning (Smith et al. 1977). These findings have significant implications for prognosis and education.

Unlike children with many intact or even superior skills who have been diagnosed as dyslexic, some children have low-average or even borderline levels of intelligence and few if any strengths. Although the discrepancy between their capacity and reading ability may at times be sufficient to warrant a diagnosis of dyslexia, their inadequate reading skills are generally consistent with most estimates of their abilities and should not be confused with dyslexia, where cognitive deficits are both more specific and limited.

SPELLING

Parallels between reading disorders in children and the effects of traumatically acquired alexia in adults are often evident—but not always. Adults who become alexic as a result of acute brain trauma may, with a restricted lesion, continue to be able to write, a condition known as alexia without agraphia (Geschwind 1962). Some may retain the ability to spell through dictation. There are no comparable disorders in children, who fail to develop either spelling or writing if they have failed to acquire reading skill. In fact, children who read inadequately usually spell even more poorly than they read, and a problem with spelling alone is often the residual effect of an earlier problem with learning to read. There have been attempts to characterize subtypes of dyslexia from the types of errors made by children with reading disorders. Children who were poor spellers without being (or even having been) poor readers were different from those whose spelling retardation was an aspect of their reading retardation (Nelson and Warrington 1974). A generalized language deficiency underlies at least some cases of spelling-plus-reading retardation, but the mechanisms underlying retardation in spelling only remain unclear. Since spelling is a serial-order and rule-dependent task, those children with only a spelling problem may simply "read for meaning" without focusing on individual words. Unless these readers meet with an unfamiliar word, they read efficiently and without making note of spelling patterns. A good reader with a spelling problem may simply focus inadequately on spelling rules and patterns. On the other hand, children with both reading and spelling problems, demonstrating an inability to apply spelling rules and patterns, may have more global problems with language and serial-order tasks. Dyslexic children who have a problem with maintaining serial order are likely to reverse letters even when they have fairly good phonetic and/or visual grasp of the words.

In a language like English, where so many words are not spelled phonetically, phonetic spelling produces errors. Retarded spellers who produced a preponderance of phonetically accurate misspellings performed much more like normal spellers on a variety of linguistic tasks than did another group of phonetically inaccurate poor spellers (Sweeney and Rourke 1978). Spelling, like reading, can be an index of the grasp of phonetic one-to-one correspondence. Where poor spelling is not accompanied by reading retardation, or where spelling errors consist of "good" phonetic errors, a generalized language deficit appears to be least likely.

One of the problems with characterizing some children as poor phonetic ("dysphonemic" in the Boder classification) and others as poor visual ("dyseidetic" in the Boder classification) spellers is that it is often difficult to tell which is which. Further, many poor spellers are unclassifiable (Boder 1973). The child who spells phonetically but incorrectly because he or she cannot recall how words look would be classified as a poor visual speller or "dyseidetic," according to the Boder classification. The child who spells nonphonetically ("dysphonemic"), however, is also a poor visual speller if he or she spells incorrectly ("dyseidetic"). Logically, a good "visual" speller would not misspell familiar words at all, even if he or she had no grasp of sound-letter (phoneme-grapheme) correspondence, for the "visual" speller would remember how words looked. Unless this child were tested with unfamiliar words or with nonsense syllables, the phonetic deficit (or dysphonemia) would remain undetected. In fact, for some adults who learned to read (and spell) primarily through visual, nonphonetic means, their deficit in sounding out words did not become apparent until they needed to learn a foreign language or a specialized professional vocabulary (Rudel 1981). In one case, a third-year medical student was referred for diagnosis because he was unable to remember names, "and in medicine everything has a name." He was a "terrible speller" and felt he had to look up all words. Despite his ability to read meaningful material (*Iowa Test of Basic Skills*) at the ninety-ninth percentile, he could not pronounce simple nonsense syllables and was totally baffled when faced with new medical terminology. Further, when a new word or name was incorrectly read, he had difficulty identifying it as the same word that he heard pronounced correctly in class.

34

In evaluating the phonetic or nonphonetic spelling errors of reading-disabled children, one must also bear in mind that by the time most of them are nine or ten years old, they have experienced several years of intensive phonetic training by parents, teachers, tutors, and resource room instructors. This gives them more opportunity not only to mix up words but also to confuse teaching methods and rules. One often sees bizarre "phonetic" errors that seem to indicate a serious lack of language ability and word-root information, as well as an inability to recall how words look. One eleven-year-old recently wrote that he was going with his parents "to the POKE INNOES" (phonetically perfect). A ten-year-old who certainly must have been familiar with the traditional beginning of stories: "Once upon a time . . . ," wrote "Ooce a pond a tym." (Note, incidentally, the elimination of the adverb "upon" and the substitution of a concrete noun, *pond*.) It seems likely that earlier in their school careers, these phonetic, dyseidetic spellers had difficulty with phonetic reading or spelling. A dysphonetic speller at age eight may, at age twelve, after four years of phonetic training, become "dyseidetic." One study suggests that these classifications are decreasingly sensitive with age (Pennington and Smith 1983). Before one can assume dyslexic subtypes from the differences between phonetic and nonphonetic spellers, however, longitudinal studies on this issue are essential. These differences may relate to age and training rather than to differences in brain organization.

Dyslexic children who try to spell phonetically perseverate the sound of the letter name and fail to make the essential transition to the sound or sounds of the letters. Thus, "cat" is often spelled *k-a-t* because the sound of the letter *c* is sibilant. The *q* is used for the initial letter of words spelled *cu*, as in "cute," which would be spelled *qut*, or "cucumber," spelled *qukumber*. Sometimes the *y* is used for the sound of *w*, since the letter *y* begins with the *w* sound. On the spelling portion of the WRAT, the word "will" is often spelled *yill* (or *yil* or *yel*). The soft pronunciation of the letter *g* probably accounts for the frequency with which *g* is substituted for *j* in words like "majority," spelled *majoraty* or some similar variant. This lack of linguistic flexibility may also account for the poor use of vowels. The letters *a*, *e*, *i*, *o* and *u* are often used alone, without application of contextual rules, for the long vowel sound. For example, "educate" or "fade" would be spelled without the final *e*, the word "brief" spelled *bref*, and "dirty" spelled with an *e* instead of a *y*.

Spelling phonetically requires not only the transformation of letter names to letter sounds but also the application of certain rules of pronunciation. Spelling involves more than learning the correspondence between sounds and shapes, phonemes and graphemes; the correct spelling of most words depends on orthographic regularities that cannot be ascertained from such simple correspondences. Dyslexic children fail to grasp word families: the consonant-vowel-consonant combinations with their short vowel sounds; the long vowel sound of the vowel–consonant–final *e* combinations, the *-ought, -aught,* or *-ight* words; the hard *th* versus the soft *th* sounds; the diphthongs; et cetera. One can use grapheme-phoneme correspondence only by first translating the letter name into its spectrum of possible sounds and then applying the rules for pronouncing letter combinations.

Dyslexic children sometimes omit sounds and whole syllables, spelling, for example, "material" as *matirell* or "equipment" as *equiment.* They sometimes include extra sounds, as in *equiptment,* or mishear sounds (or mistake them during writing), as in *ruim* for "ruin." Then there are inconsistencies in spelling that defy classification from one occasion to the next. For example, the same child made the following alterations in his spelling less than three months apart:

Word	First Spelling	Second Spelling
majority	mogoraty	moiger
institute	instatut	instartut
reverence	reveruncs	reverce

It would be very difficult to determine whether these misspellings were influenced more by the application of phonetics or word visualization, by some combination, or by neither. Clearly, the rules of word organization are unknown to him, and his errors appear almost random. In their inaccurate reading, as well as in their inaccurate spelling, the initial letters are almost always correct. The only exceptions occur when the sound of the letter name is erroneously substituted (*y* for "w" or *q* for "cu"). The beginning of each word is usually correctly read or spelled. Initial sounds are simpler because they are less subject to contextual or rule modification, and they are more easily isolated, both visually and auditorally, from other sounds. The initial letter is not surrounded on both sides by other letters and is sounded first. In the context of reading errors, they are also more often correctly spelled and read by adults with acquired alexia. Therefore, it is unlikely that there are dyslexic children who make exclusively phonetic or exclusively visual errors as, for example, in Boder's classification of dyslexic subtypes.

WRITTEN EXPRESSION

Just as their spelling is often worse than their reading, so too is the written expression of dyslexic children usually much poorer than their reading, and almost always much poorer than their oral expression. Although some of them draw pictures very well, their handwriting or printing usually is so impaired that they have difficulty reading what they have written. Figure 2.1 illustrates what some dyslexic children produced when asked to write on any subject for five minutes.

These examples were not selected for dramatic effect but constitute the first few cases taken from an alphabetic arrangement of case studies. These children all had average to better-than-average verbal IQ scores. Obviously, the skills involved in reading, spelling, and writing do not constitute especially strong factors on the WISC-R, the most commonly used test of intellectual potential. Only one subtest of the WISC-R— the Digit Span—taps verbal serial ordering and as noted above, dyslexic children usually score lower on the Digit Span than on other verbal subtests. A deficit of serial ordering, then, is characteristic of many dyslexic children, and it inevitably interferes with the requirements of clear exposition.

RESIDUAL EFFECTS IN YOUNG ADULTS

Young adults who were dyslexic as children often complain of difficulty with serial ordering in writing. In more than one instance, this difficulty has turned into a career obstacle. For example, a twenty-three-year-old "internal control analyst" with a verbal IQ score of 113 on the *Wechsler Adult Intelligence Scale* (WAIS) describes her work as follows:

In order to write or evaluate procedures I go over with the people who are actually doing them or people who would be effected by them what they are actually doing and test to see if they are doing it by looking at their work in detail and scheduling out (what I have looked at), redoing, and checking the things I did on a sample of their work.

FIGURE 2.1

Male, eleven years and seven months old, with a verbal IQ score of 119

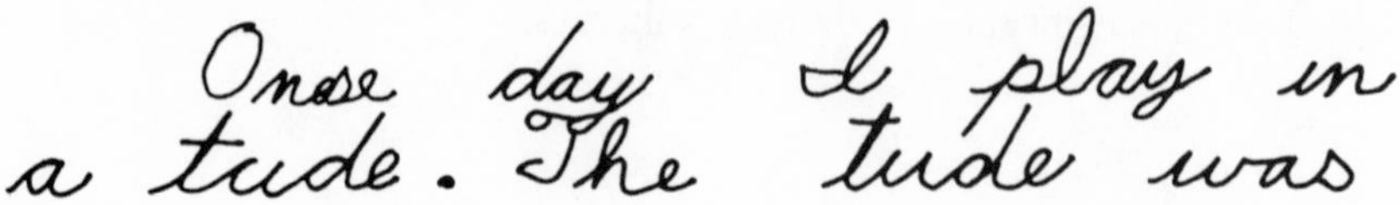

Once day I play in a tude. The tude was (handwritten)

Once day I play in a tude. The tude was

Male, eleven years and five months old, with a verbal IQ score of 103

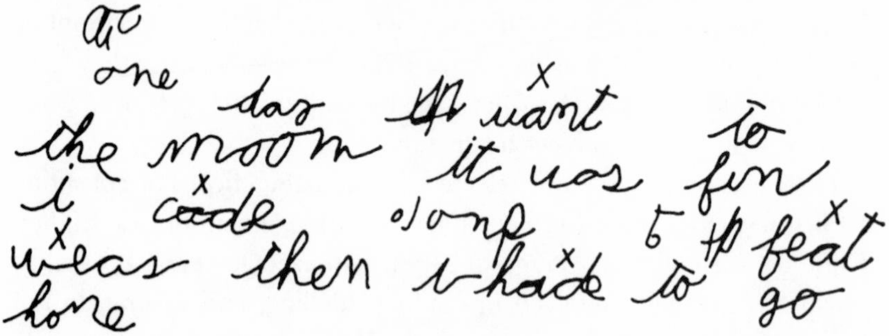

(handwritten sample)

one day [indecipherable] went to the moon it was fin i [indecipherable] aloup . . . feal wear then hade to go home

Male, thirteen years and ten months old, with a verbal IQ score of 117

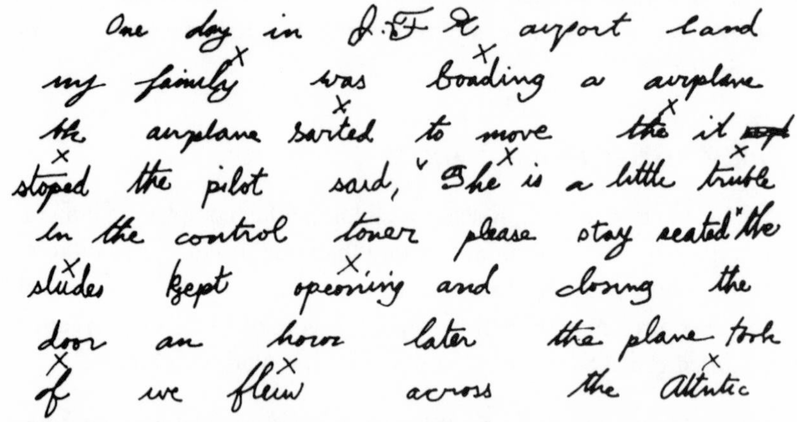

(handwritten sample)

One day in JFK airport I and my family was boarding a airplane the airplane sarted to move the it stoped the pilot said, "The is a little truble in the control tower please stay seated" the studes kept opeoning and closing the door an hour later the plane took of we fluw across the Altntic . . .

Learning Difficulties: Disorders of Symbolic Representation

Male, ten years old, with a verbal IQ score of 101

THE Cat is siting in his cha
he like drik Milk and he like int qLiv
but he dunt like goig out!

The cat is siting in his cha [last letter indecipherable] he like drik milk and he like [int 9liv] bur he dunt like goig out.

Male, nine years and four months old, with a verbal IQ score of 113

One day a nyght man got kilk buy
dragone. And the next day a night man
got kild buy a dragone and one day
the. King was riding his horse. He wanted
to go toe his cave. come out a show
Your self. Sad the King and his son
Went with him. and some night man went
with him. and hie shot the dragone.

One day a night man got kilk buy dragone. And the next day a night man got kild buy a dragone and one day the king was riding his horse. He wanted to go to his cave. come out a show your self sad the kind and his son went with him and some night man went with him. and hie shot the dragone. [One assumes the "night man" is a knight.]

I make comments on interral control weeknesses; Areas then an employee could take advantage of or an area that records are not adiquately kept on (so that if some one would like to go back and check on things, they can).

The comments I write up and I have to come up with plans of action to correct the problem. for example a person in purchasing should not have total control of items ordered, the person that orders things shouldnot also receive goods and keep the records of things received.

Many adults who were dyslexic as children never develop a firm grasp of phonetic rules and have difficulty reading unfamiliar words when they try to learn foreign languages or become involved in a new, specialized field like medicine, where many of the critical words have foreign roots. This phonetic flaw is often camouflaged in their reading of English because they have learned to compensate for the problem through meaning, but when they read nonsense words, the flaw becomes apparent. The young woman quoted above read a series of nonsense syllables as follows: "phume" as *phaon*, "tup" as *trip*, "relhime" as *releeme*, and "gaction" as *gatchton*. A twenty-four-year-old geophysicist read "jod" as *job* and "kit" as *kid*; and a twenty-nine-year-old medical student read "guig" as *gig*, "tup" as *tape*, "nepe" as *neypey*, and "thade" as *thad* (Bryant 1975). These are all high-achieving young adults with high verbal IQ scores.

COMPREHENSION OF ORAL/WRITTEN LANGUAGE

The critical factor in how much written or oral language dyslexics understand appears to be determined by *which* language factors are impaired. Dyslexic children, deficient in the capacity to decode written into oral language and oral language into written, have very specific and limited deficits of language; but, their language comprehension and reasoning may be quite good. They often understand what they have read despite the errors they make in reading, as if there is access to meaning at some level. This at least appears to be the case when direct questions are asked of them following their reading of text. In a study of sixty dyslexic boys (all reading at least 15 percent below the level expected for their age and IQ), reading comprehension was far superior to accuracy (Helfgott, Rudel, and Kairim 1986). Subjects read at a mean grade level of 3.12 for accuracy (SD = 1.41), but at grade level 5.34 for comprehension (SD = 2.7), a mean difference of two years, two months. The difference between accuracy and comprehension was significant ($p <$

0.001), despite the fact that comprehension scores are limited by reading inaccuracy. (Once the child has exceeded a certain number of decoding errors in a given paragraph, the test is terminated.)

In fact, the degree of difference between accuracy of reading and comprehension appears to be a function of intelligence. In this study, the children with the best comprehension despite the inaccuracy of their reading (that is, with the largest accuracy-comprehension discrepancies) had the highest IQ scores. In the general population, IQ scores generally correlate very well with reading ability (about 0.6). For the sixty reading-disabled boys under study, however, there were still positive correlations between IQ measures and reading, but the correlations were greater for comprehension than for accuracy: 0.3 for accuracy and 0.45 for comprehension.

This may suggest to some that these children would not be dyslexic at all if they were required to read silently for comprehension rather than aloud for word recognition, but that is an oversimplification. In this test, direct questions were asked at the end of each paragraph to measure comprehension. These questions helped to cue in the most intelligent boys to the (often) correct response. If they had been left to find the essential points of the text on their own, without the guidance provided by the direct questions, they probably would not have done well. Further, the reading material dealt with everyday events; if the readings had covered less familiar occurrences or an area (history, science, or social studies) in which the boys had little or no prior knowledge, their reading would have been much more inaccurate and they would have fared more poorly on the direct questions. Many dyslexic children do grow into fairly adequate silent readers, particularly when they have some familiarity with the subject matter; however, they often continue to have difficulty with reading unfamiliar material and words with unusual roots, as well as with spelling and writing.

In sum, children with reading disorders that affect their ability to decode print into spoken language fail to make the same sense when they read that they make when they speak. Whether reading by "sounding out" words phonetically, from the way words look, or (most frequently) through some combination of the two, they make phonetic, semantic, and syntactic errors that they would rarely or never make when speaking. Many of them may be capable of ignoring the errors made when reading, and, at least on direct questioning, are able to make sense of the text. These children are the ones usually referred to as dyslexic; and when their academic problem is restricted to reading and spelling, they are said to have a specific reading disorder.

In sharp contrast to dyslexic children with relatively good comprehension, some children, who may or may not have had difficulty learning to read, have trouble comprehending what they have read. The critical question here is how well they would understand the same material if it were read to them. If their comprehension of text that is read to them is significantly better than their comprehension of what they have read themselves, then, clearly, there is some interference between visual input and language processing. In some instances, such interference is nothing more than the unusually great amount of effort and time that the child requires to decode the written material: something is, literally, lost in translation. Alternatively, the child simply may read too slowly to allow for comprehension. In brain-damaged adults, a lesion confined to any part of the left visual (occipital) cortex will slow reading speed even if the printed message does not fall within the affected visual field (Poppel and Shattuck 1974). Some reading-disabled children have been reported to experience slow visual processing, leading to the conclusion that these children may have less direct access to, or some interference in, the transfer of visual information to language or motor areas. Those with oral language comprehension problems, as distinct from or in addition to reading comprehension problems, seem to have analogous difficulties with processing auditory stimuli. According to Tallal and Piercy (1973), the rate of auditory processing of sounds and receptive language scores are highly correlated ($r = 0.85$).

Those children with comprehension problems for both oral language and written text, however, cannot be said to have a reading disorder, since the problem is not specific to reading and, therefore, lies beyond a diagnosis of dyslexia. In fact, impaired oral language comprehension may be improved when these children learn to read, because one reads at a slower rate than one listens to spoken language and because written text can be reviewed repeatedly to aid comprehension. Unlike deficits in decoding written text, comprehension problems usually show up in low verbal IQ scores, though the child's individual potential may appear somewhat better on intelligence tests done with nonverbal instruments.

In practice, reading comprehension disorders are rarely referred for diagnosis in the early grades, when reading ability is measured primarily by the accuracy of text decoding. For the first four grades, at least, most texts are very explicit; that is, they demand very little implicit reasoning or association with previously acquired knowledge for comprehension. Here are two examples from the *Gray Oral Reading Test.*

Grade One:
> One morning a boy made a boat. "Where can I play with it?" he asked.
>
> Father said, "Come with me in the car! We will take your boat with us."
>
> Soon the boy called, "Please stop. I see water. May I play here?"
>
> "Yes," said Father. "Have a good time."

Grade Five:
> Hundreds of years ago, most of Europe was a very poor region. But China, a large country in eastern Asia, had many of the comforts of a rich, civilized nation. Only a few people from Europe had visited this distant region. One was the famous Marco Polo. He learned some of the languages that were spoken in China and served its great ruler for many years.

In addition to its more difficult vocabulary, the fifth-grade passage demands much more prior knowledge (What is Europe? What does the phrase "comforts of a rich, civilized nation" or the word "served" convey in this context?).

Reading comprehension problems, then, may be secondary to poor or extremely slow text decoding or a primary disorder not specific to reading. In the latter instance, a disorder involving oral comprehension is not necessarily related to reading and probably reflects some disorder of receptive language. Text comprehension is related much more closely than accuracy to measures of intellectual capacity and is more likely to become apparent in the later grades, especially if the child has not had an earlier problem learning to decode.

Comprehension and the Receptive Language System

Some recent studies of comprehension difficulties in children suggest some inflexibility of the receptive language system, much as problems in decoding text imply some inflexibility of expressive language. While children with decoding problems have difficulty shifting from letter names to letter sounds or using semantic or syntactic cues for word recognition, children with comprehension disorders have difficulty shifting from an initial premise or point of view. Thus, if the first sentence of a paragraph reads, "It is believed . . . ," children with a comprehension disorder will not absorb evidence contrary to that belief presented in the remainder of the passage. Instead of utilizing key words throughout the paragraph in recall, these children tend to cling to the initial sentence; therefore, they have difficulty understanding texts written in an inductive style, where more than one sentence leads up to the main point. Some children with comprehension problems rely too heavily on prior knowledge of the subject and tend to alter their recall of the text to suit what they already know. This, too, suggests inflexibility and perseveration, not so much of language, but of cognition, a constriction of thought. Reading comprehension, like all comprehension, demands association with what is already known but with sufficient flexibility to allow critical analysis and expansion or correction of that essential prior knowledge.

For the sake of clarity of exposition, I have presented the tasks of decoding and comprehending text separately; indeed, there appear to be some different skills involved in these two aspects of the reading process. In reality, however, the two are interrelated. For even the best readers, the decoding process is faster and smoother when the content is relatively simple and clear, and, conversely, meaning is more accessible when the phonetic and syntactic contexts are more familiar. Thus, one can more readily comprehend the familiar set of phonetic and grammatic combinations in one's native language than in a recently acquired, foreign language. A child who is having trouble decoding and who is reading words haltingly and inaccurately must have more difficulty with comprehension than the child who reads smoothly. Conversely, a child can recognize words, with faster phonetic unscrambling, when he or she has a firm grasp of the vocabulary and content. In still another sense, the decoding-comprehension relationship is reciprocal. The child with a persistent decoding problem tends to read less than his or her peers. This avoidance of reading eventually takes its toll by limiting acquisition of vocabulary and other information. Reading is not an end in itself, and all other learning that depends on the ability to read (social studies, science, et cetera), including comprehension, is adversely affected when the basic decoding skill has not been adequately acquired.

DECODING WITHOUT COMPREHENSION—SPECIAL CASES

There are rare cases of precocious (often by age three) and even superior rote reading skills in the almost total absence of comprehension among children who learn to read (or to decode) despite deficiencies of age and intelligence, that is, when they are very young and/or mentally defective. Often these are retarded or autistic children with oral language comprehension problems but with good repetition and naming skills. Their expressive language is mostly a parroting of what they have heard (some are echolalic), and many of them fail to use language for communication. Some have excellent visual-spatial and auditory perceptual abilities; at very early ages, they can distinguish letters of the alphabet and eventually whole word configurations. Such "hyperlexic" children are rare but startling to encounter. One six-year-old girl could "read" the *New York Times* but failed to comprehend simple sentences (read or spoken), and a three-year-old boy could read at least one hundred words (in upper-case printed letters only) but could not respond when asked his name nor follow one-step commands. He tended to repeat the questions or the commands. In these rare instances there is no facilitative reciprocity between decoding and comprehension, reading appears to be but one aspect of a very limited language system, with intact repetition and naming. These "hyperlexic" children are not learning disabled but represent an extreme example of a condition that, like learning disability, is not predicted by either age or IQ. These children are able to perform a particular, isolated skill that others with far greater capacities are unable to perform. However, this isolated skill is of dubious value; for in no way does it facilitate learning through the medium of the printed word. It is in no sense a form of communication.

Dyscalculia

LANGUAGE AND SYMBOL SYSTEM

Another critical symbol system that frequently causes learning difficulties is mathematics. Like *dyslexia*, defined here as unexpected difficulty in learning to read, *dyscalculia* refers to unexpected difficulty in learning to calculate. Arithmetic, like reading, depends upon a great many functional systems, and a problem with any one of them can interfere with some aspects of skill acquisition. Arithmetic shares with reading a dependence on language, serial order processing, as well as other cognitive skills. Like letters of the alphabet, which have not only names but also different sounds in different contexts, numbers have names that refer to both quantity and position in a series. Children who lack the linguistic flexibility to learn the sounds letters make in different contexts may have similar problems with numbers. Seven is more than six but less than eight—serial order here also connotes relative quantity, which can be achieved through a great many different mathematical operations, such as addition, subtraction, multiplication, and division. The number can be part of a larger whole or itself divided into parts. Just as many dyslexic children have difficulty segmenting words into syllables, so they may also have difficulty in grasping parts of whole numbers or in writing down one part of a number and carrying the rest. The capacity to automatically recall number names, number combinations, or multiplication tables may be as difficult for these children to achieve as the rapid recall of names for colors, objects, or letters (Denckla and Rudel 1976).

SERIAL ORDER PROCESS

Serial order, which is intrinsic to language, is also essential to maintaining the ordinal position of numbers, as in counting or in learning multiplication tables. Mathematical problems are often presented orally; solving them requires the rapid extraction of relevant elements. This may be difficult for children with language impairment, especially when the problems are presented in complex, inverted syntax or as a conditional (if . . . then). Arithmetic is presented in this way on the *WISC-R*. The Arithmetic subtest and the Digit Span subtest, which demands the maintenance of serial order, were two of the three subtests most poorly performed in a study of dyslexic boys (Symmes and Rapoport 1972). Problem solving involves not only the selection of the appropriate arithmetic operations but also the proper sequencing of these operations. Mathematics demands the ability to maintain serial order between and within procedures. There are, clearly, common skills involved in learning to read and learning to do arithmetic; therefore, most children who have trouble learning one also have trouble learning the other.

Early success in learning arithmetic, then, is clearly dependent upon language skills very similar to those needed in learning to read. The more global the language impairment or the short-term verbal memory deficit, the more likely that all initial learning will be affected. In a research study of dyslexia, sixty boys taking the WRAT had below-average scores not only for reading (prose or single words) but also for written arithmetic as well, that is, for solving nonverbal basic arithmetic operations (Helfgott, Rudel, and Kairam 1986). As a group, the boys' mean verbal IQ score of 106 was significantly higher than either the reading or arithmetic percentile rank. The WRAT single-word reading score placed the boys at approximately the fifteenth percentile. Their WRAT score for solving nonverbal basic arithmetic operations was in the fourteenth percentile. A significant discrepancy (a full standard deviation) is clear, not only between the IQ scores and the reading scores but also between the IQ scores and the arithmetic scores. Thus, although the subjects were referred for reading problems, the study found equal difficulty with written arithmetic.

Studies in adult neurology support the conclusion that the underlying difficulty may be some inadequacy in the language system. Language difficulties in aphasic patients interfere with performance in arithmetic through paraphasic substitution of one number for another (Benson and Denckla 1969). A more recent study of adults found a significant relationship between the presence (but not the type) of aphasia and acalculia (Basso et al. 1981).

LANGUAGE-RELATED DIFFICULTIES

Arithmetic, which involves so many complex skills, may also be a source of learning disability for children who have had little or no difficulty learning to read. These children generally have no problem with learning number names, serial order, or even number combinations, but their language, serial ordering, and rote memorization skills cannot help them with arithmetic reasoning or the application of basic operations. The vocabulary of mathematics ("less," "more," "greater than," et cetera) is sophisticated. Without an adequate level of language skill, these children have difficulty with simple word problems and basic number concepts. Children who have trouble drawing conclusions, making inferences, and detecting sequence in text find word problems particularly difficult. Therefore, language is a critical aspect of math competence.

The correlation between the relative position of numbers and meaning (units, tens, hundreds, et cetera) in arithmetic is very difficult for children with spatial problems to grasp. They have particular difficulty with subjects related to geometry, where rote learning of combinations will not compensate for the basic lack of spatial concepts. They have difficulty visualizing angles, distances, and part-whole relationships. To make matters worse, many arithmetic operations (for example, adding columns of numbers) are calculated from right to left, while reading requires the opposite direction (left to right). For a child with spatial difficulties, these seemingly contradictory demands are very confusing.

SPATIAL DIFFICULTIES

Some children with spatial problems have been identified as having a "developmental Gerstmann syndrome," which implies left-right confusion and finger agnosia (loss of ability to correctly identify individual fingers). They may also have difficulties with reading, though to a lesser extent than with arithmetic, and their writing (graphomotor skill) is seriously impaired. The syndrome relates to a condition in brain-damaged adults who, following some trauma to the left parietal region of the brain, develop acalculia (inability to do arithmetic), loss of left-right discrimination, and finger agnosia. Whether the syndrome really exists in this form in children has been called into question (Benton 1975). There have been few studies of its developmental form, though a large predictive study of dyslexia examined problems with finger identification (Satz et al. 1978). Whether or not the condition is called "developmental Gerstmann syndrome," some children lack number sense, specifically with place values, with carrying from one column to the next, and with number reversals in oral dictation.

Learning Difficulties: Disorders of Symbolic Representation

In contrast to children with spatial problems, dyslexic children, once they have learned to calculate or to use calculators, sometimes emerge as relatively good students of mathematics. If they are bright, as many of them are, their adequate or sometimes exceptional organizational and conceptual spatial abilities carry them through the more advanced stages of mathematical reasoning. Some dyslexic children are not only able to understand spatial concepts but also, after age ten, may exceed the performance of matched controls without learning disorders (Owen et al. 1971; Denckla, Rudel, and Broman 1980).

Very different populations of children, then, may have problems with mathematics at different stages of schooling. Following early difficulties with numbers, some fail to develop the necessary concepts for more advanced levels of mathematical achievement. These children tend to have relatively limited intellectual endowment and never get beyond the four basic operations, much like children who learn to read without comprehending beyond a certain basic level.

The evidence from diagnostic practice suggests that children with attentional disorders have difficulties with arithmetic for different reasons than those noted for children with language or spatial problems. Unless research groups selected to study arithmetic as a learning disability specifically include or exclude children with reading and attentional disorders, the results will be confounded. The diagnostician can assess the nature of the deficit in arithmetic only by determining the extent to which it relates to a language or attentional disorder.

SEX DIFFERENCES

Many girls who have early difficulties with arithmetic, possibly because of some sex-linked lag in a specific facet of brain development, tend to avoid number facts or manipulations, mathematics, science, statistics, et cetera. At the junior high school level, girls perform better than boys on computational skills, but boys perform better on mathematical reasoning (Benbow and Stanley 1983). This suggests that far from being discouraged by early failure, girls do better than boys at the beginning of arithmetic instruction but fall behind as mathematical concepts replace rote operations in their schoolwork. Certainly, the ratio of boys to girls (about four or five to one) among the reading disabled does not appear in research on underachievement in arithmetic. There has been far less research in this area, and therefore far fewer statistics on sex ratios are available.

TIME CONSTRAINTS AND PERFORMANCE

The amount of time required to perform arithmetic operations is, of course, critical. Given all the time they need, some children may eventually come up with correct answers even though they lack sufficient conceptual grasp of numerical manipulations or adequate knowledge of number combinations to make calculations within time limits. School and standardized examinations are usually timed, and in real life one doesn't have unlimited time to calculate how much money to leave for a tip, whether one's change is correct, or how many days remain until a certain date. Conversely, some children have difficulties with arithmetic because they fail to take the time afforded them. They sacrifice accuracy for speed. In problem solving or in just carrying out arithmetic operations, they may fail to note the instructions, to observe the signs, to work through to the end, or to use the time allotted to check their solutions. The time allotted for a task may or may not be adequate for task completion, depending on the effectiveness or power of the cognitive strategy chosen by the child.

On this seemingly simple dimension of deployment of time in the performance of arithmetic (or any other subject), Kinsbourne and Caplan (1979) have distinguished two aspects of learning: (1) *cognitive power*, the capacity to learn, and (2) *cognitive style*, the temperament, attention, and mood that relate to learning. In this chapter, we have delineated some of the deficits of cognitive power in children with learning disability. In chapter 3, we will describe children with deficits of cognitive style: those children with an attentional deficit disorder (ADD), with or without hyperactivity, whose failure to deploy attention effectively inhibits their adjustment at school. The time dimension discussed above is a critical variable in understanding and assessing their problem.

Chapter 3

Disorders of Attention

RITA G. RUDEL

Attention Deficit Disorder

DEFINITION

The term *attention deficit disorder* (ADD) is used in the *DSM III* to describe a variety of generally maladaptive behaviors formerly subsumed under "hyperactivity" or the "hyperkinetic syndrome." Motor restlessness is the most obvious symptom in this complex pattern of behaviors, and it initially received most of the research and clinical attention. This symptom is characterized not so much by its excessiveness but by its lack of goal directedness: motor activity is not necessarily more frequent in hyperactive children than in their peers, but the activity appears to be aimless, constantly shifting from one thing to another. Minimal brain damage or dysfunction (MBD) is also symptomatic of hyperactivity, indicating some lag in or dysfunction of the child's cerebral development, rather than caused by the environment.

According to the *DSM III*, ADD is said to occur with hyperactivity, without hyperactivity, or residually (that is, when hyperactivity was an aspect of the syndrome at earlier ages but is no longer). Many children who were hyperactive until about age ten finally get their motor restlessness, but not their mental restlessness, under control: the mind continues to wander while the body remains still. Denckla quotes an adolescent with ADD: "My mind is like a television set in which someone is always switching the channels" (1979a, 576). This description reflects several key indicators of the disorder:

1. "Someone" other than the child switches the channels, a vivid characterization of the drivenness for which the self is neither responsible nor, indeed, in control.
2. The constant "switching" of channels attests to some inner need for novelty, for continually changing stimulation, and serves as the counterpart to this need.
3. The "channels" represent the difficulty in sustaining attention to one type of problem or to one stimulus for any length of time.

DEVELOPMENTAL MODEL

From birth onward, children differ enormously in temperament, sleep patterns, motor activity, and exploratory behavior, as well as in their response to parental guidance or discipline. For the child's safety, at least, parents have to say no to potentially dangerous activities, and to attain some peace and quiet for themselves, they may also discourage excessive restlessness. Just as children differ in activity levels, parents also differ in their thresholds for what they consider excessive and in their disciplinary effectiveness. Many insist that hyperactivity in children is the product of parental permissiveness or of inadequate limits set by those in authority. To some extent, child-rearing practices do affect behavior, but the consensus among researchers and clinicians finds that the motor problem is only the most dramatic or obvious symptom in a syndrome characterized by maturational deficiencies of sustained attention, impulse control, concentration, planning, and response to discipline (reward and punishment)—all or any of which are severe enough to interfere with functioning. Once a child is part of an organized group, for example, preschool or first grade, the behavioral demands are likely to be much more affected by immaturity than the demands at home. In predicting academic success or failure in the preschool child, the clinician looks first at the child's ability to pattern behavior on the standards of the group. The child who is unable to adapt at age four or five is likely to have many problems, of which motor restlessness is only one possible aspect.

From the earliest weeks of life, the infant will immediately turn toward a new stimulus in the environment until, having mastered it, that is, having taken in its attributes, he or she will attend to it less and less. Habituation sets in, and the stimulus is no longer attended to at all. A new stimulus, or some variation of the first, will then be required to once again hold the infant's attention. The more similar the second stimulus is to the first, the less attention it will receive and the more quickly the infant will become accustomed or habituated to it. The fact that the infant spends less time fixating on the second, similar stimulus indicates that the redundant features of the two stimuli have been recognized as the same, as already known and, therefore, not requiring further attention.

Researchers have demonstrated certain adaptive aspects to these early orientation-habituation responses with very ingenious research methods (Kagan and Lewis 1965). The orientation response, the immediate turning toward the new stimulus that has invaded the infant's environment, is clearly an important survival mechanism. Further, the infant's attention to that stimulus until it is discriminated for its various attributes (or learned) is clearly the beginning of object recognition, and the turning away from the identical stimulus when it is reintroduced measures how well the stimulus was learned in its first presentation. The relatively briefer period of attention paid to a minor variation of that stimulus reflects the development of an inner continuum that weighs familiarity. Habituation, the turning away from a stimulus once it is learned, is also adaptive; otherwise, the infant would not seek out new stimuli or be alert to their introduction into the environment. Instead, the infant would remain focused on what it already knows. Habituation that is too rapid, that occurs before the stimulus is fully apprehended (or learned), on the other hand, will make it impossible for the infant to distinguish that stimulus adequately from its variants, so that similar stimuli will be treated as totally new or as identical, not as different forms of something previously encountered. Such overrapid habituation can have a negative effect on learning, and on establishing object dimensions, differentiations, and generalizations. At the very least, these processes will take a longer total time than in the normally habituating children: the child will require more trials with each new stimulus or variant to accomplish the same degree of stimulus differentiation. Overrapid habituation can lead to negative patterns of behavior as well. The infant who turns away from a stimulus too rapidly will require a greater number of novel stimuli to keep his or her attention focused; lacking these, he or she may engage in maladaptive, restless, stimulus-seeking behaviors. For example, hyperactive children quickly tire of new toys: "He is very excited about getting a new toy," related one father, "but barely are the wrappings off when he is already bored with it and wants something else." This attitue toward toys may extend, later in life, to friends, teachers, jobs, and spouses.

DISTRACTIBILITY

There is, then, no problem in getting the attention of the attentionally disordered child (that is, in getting the child to orient toward a stimulus); the problem arises in getting the child to sustain that attention over time (that is, in preventing the child from habituating the stimulus too quickly and seeking another). In the past, these children often were characterized as distractible, or stimulus driven, and their learning environments were kept as free of distraction as possible. However, such efforts failed, largely because hyperactivity sometimes *increases* when these children are obliged to work in stimulus-reduced environments. Distractions do not necessarily deflect their attention from a task any more than for other children. Some studies indicate that hyperactive children may perform *better* in the presence of extraneous stimulation; for example, background music sometimes improves their performance. The evidence, therefore, suggests that the distractibility seen in hyperactive children must be the product of uncontrolled stimulus-seeking behavior generated from within, not of extraneous stimuli in the environment.

Distractibility refers to the ease with which attention can be diverted from one thing to another or the completion of a specific task can be disrupted. In that sense, what is relevant to the task at hand must be attended while what is irrelevant must be ignored. Freedom from distraction requires the ability to distinguish relevant from irrelevant stimulation; however, what is relevant in one situation is entirely irrelevant in another. Hearing car horns honk is very relevant, and certainly must be attended to, when one is crossing the street, but it is totally irrelevant, and ought to be ignored, when one is studying indoors. Researchers have not found distractions in the environment that disrupt the performance of children with ADD, casting doubt on assertions that these children have defective filter systems and cannot distinguish task-irrelevant from task-relevant stimuli. In fact, most research studies show that children with ADD do filter out irrelevant stimuli and are not necessarily distracted by them.

In these experimental situations, children with ADD do not behave differently from controls; however, two important points require consideration. First, tasks that examine distractibility in the laboratory rarely continue long enough to induce fatigue or boredom. They don't, for example, go on for the length of time it takes a child to do arithmetic homework, write a composition, or listen to a teacher giving a lesson in class. Therefore, these experimental tasks do not provide an investigative analogue for the conditions that in real life make the child with ADD vulnerable to external distractions. Second, while children with ADD can filter out external task-irrelevant stimuli, there is no evidence that they can filter out self-generated, task-irrelevant stimuli. Distractibility in these children may take the form of intrusions of fantasies, feelings, thoughts, and ideas unrelated to the task at hand. It is in this sense that children with ADD may have deficient filter systems. While they can ignore task-irrelevant stimuli in the environment, they may lack the attentional controls to filter out, or hold in abeyance, intrusions from within.

COGNITIVE CONTROL

Steadily increasing orientation toward information from the external environment is an essential part of a child's normal development. Cognitive control enables the child "to keep a distance from or to remain insulated from internal information (e.g., emotionally laden fantasies, memories, and wishes)" (Santostefano 1978, 220). Not all internal information, however, is task irrelevant. As the child's development proceeds, he or she must check information from the environment or associate it with information held in memory; the child thereby becomes capable of shifting back and forth between cognitive processing of external stimuli to inner thoughts. For example, as noted in chapter 2, the child must associate information held in mind with what is explicitly stated in texts in order to understand and retain the new material. Stories, dramas, or poetry would be dreary word exercises were it not for the contact they make with the inner emotions and fantasies of the reader. What is known as well as what is felt must be brought to bear on what is seen, heard, or read for the experience to be meaningful. The essential difference between the immature and the mature use of an internal reference system, of course, is that the latter provides a task-relevant association while the former represents a task-irrelevant intrusion.

Before the child can achieve the essential flexibility between internal and external reference systems, however, he or she must first control his or her attentional focus on incoming information and learn to filter out internally generated irrelevant thoughts or emotions. The child with attentional problems may be late in achieving either the capacity to focus exclusively on external stimuli or the flexibility to shift between external and internal processing. Some may never achieve either capability. This inability to maintain attention free of the flood of internal intrusions has a devastating effect on concentration and, therefore, on learning.

IMPULSIVITY

Attention deficit disorder is also manifest as impulsive behaviors: (1) responding to a stimulus without taking the time to await the appropriate signal, (2) failing to organize materials effectively, or (3) taking action without planning ahead. Such behaviors would lead one to expect, therefore, that children with ADD react more rapidly to a stimulus than other children their own age, but again, they do not. Several studies have shown that their reaction time (RT) is slower and more variable than other children's (Cohen and Douglas 1972; Firestone and Douglas 1975; Parry 1973). These unexpected results must be interpreted in the context of the specific experimental conditions and of the probable underlying deficiency common to slower RT and greater response variability (from very slow to very fast). In experimental studies, stimulant medication seems to reduce both RT and the variability of response speed, which suggests that children with ADD are underaroused and/or have unstable arousal levels. Their restless, often aimlessly hyperactive behavior is seen as a stimulus-seeking reaction to their underarousal; further, neither underarousal nor overarousal is conducive to sustained, focused attention to a task. While a low dosage of stimulants improved the performance of hyperactive children on a memory recognition task, a high dosage resulted in a poorer performance (Sprague and Sleator 1976). Left unmedicated, many of these children may shift from underaroused to overaroused states, which may account for their variability, excitability, disorganization, and moodiness. At least in some cases, the deficit may reflect poor modulation of the attentional system (or of arousal) rather than a deficiency.

RESPONSE TIME RESEARCH

Although simple RT studies fail to show unusually rapid response in hyperactive children, experiments that include a "vigilance" period (when a preparatory signal precedes the critical reaction signal) reveal an impulsive, jumping-the-gun phenomenon. On such delayed reaction time (DRT) tests, children with ADD are slower to respond to the critical signal and are more variable than controls. They also respond more frequently during the interstimulus interval after the warning signal but before the appropriate reaction signal. This would suggest that once children with ADD are primed to respond (by the preparatory signal), they are less able than controls to inhibit responding prematurely. Experiments and diagnostic tests that make use of a preparatory signal followed by a response stimulus set up a period of vigilance during which the subject (or patient) expects something to happen. He must, during that period, inhibit responding but remain alert to the imminent onset of the critical target.

In some of these experiments, the preparatory signal may be followed by a neutral, noncritical signal. Children with ADD not only respond to the preparatory signal itself, before the onset of the next stimulus, but also respond inappropriately to whatever noncritical stimulus follows the preparatory signal. At times, they respond to the critical or target stimulus when it has not been preceded by the preparatory signal. All of these "false alarm" responses in delayed reaction or vigilance tests indicate inadequate inhibition of response, or impulsivity: that is, a failure to restrain behavior. In addition, children with ADD fail to respond more often than controls when the critical stimulus follows the preparatory signal. Such omissions of response appear to reflect instability of attentional focus, of maintaining vigilance.

During such experimentally designed vigilance periods, one can record an electrical waveform called the contingent negative variation (CNV) in the vertex region of normally functioning children. However, this variation is reduced in older children with learning disabilities (Dykman et al. 1971) and absent in those under eight-and-a-half years of age (Cohen 1976). As noted earlier, researchers rarely screen experimental groups of learning-disabled children for attentional disorders; therefore, the children under study may, in fact, have difficulties that are primarily attentional rather than learning.

These vigilance studies, incidentally, also lend further support to the conclusion that distractions are not usually environmental. When researchers added distracting voices to a tape containing the signals for the test, the distractions did not disrupt the performance of children with ADD any more than it did that of controls. However, in addition to making more errors of commission (false alarm responses to noncritical stimuli) and omission (neglecting to respond to a critical target stimulus), hyperactive children also failed to sustain their own level of response (as compared to controls') over an extended period. As the task continued (for fifteen minutes), the error rate of hyperactive children went up. Thus, reaction time and other tests of vigilance reveal not only impulsivity (poor inhibition of response) but also slowness, instability, distractibility, and poorly sustained effort.

SEARCH STRATEGIES

There are other ways of looking at impulsivity. As noted earlier, the infant orients toward a novel stimulus until he has discriminated it from previously encountered like stimuli, before habituating his response. With increasing maturation, the child is able to take into account an increasingly large number of features at one time. He continues based on preceived similarities and differences to establish hierarchies of classification, looking before he leaps. The impulsive child fails to use effective search strategies for extracting the most productive information from the surrounding stimuli in order to establish hierarchies of classification. In other words, the impulsive child is most likely to "leap" at stimuli that are least effective. Without adequate search strategies and with poor feature selections, children with ADD generally fail to establish the most basic modes of extracting and organizing information.

The search strategies of a small child exploring the surrounding environment are haphazard and disorganized, often centered on a single aspect without reference to the broader, relevant context. Piaget spoke of the need for the young child to "de-center" his or her explorations from a single salient feature to other available cues. Impulsive children tend not to de-center; they fail to keep the goal in view (or in mind) during exploration, and the features fixated are not necessarily critical ones. Goal-oriented search strategies are essential in most comparative behavior: for finding whether two or more things are the same or different or for making a choice from a series of possibilities where all the features have to be examined systematically. If the child's exploratory behavior continues to be haphazard and inadequately goal-oriented, then he or she cannot systematically compare and eliminate features. The child's decisions, then, are bound to be based on single, very salient details.

Impulsive children may not only fail to develop perceptual search strategies but also may fail to develop logical search strategies and may lag behind more reflective children. Without an adequate perceptual search strategy, impulsive children may overlook relevant features of the environment and ignore essential aspects of a logical problem when they fail to examine its component parts. Trial-and-error approaches are time-consuming, difficult to keep track of, and ultimately boring. Research studies have compared impulsive children with reflective children (otherwise matched for age and IQ) on the use of systematic strategies to solve problems. In games like "Twenty Questions," the child can test hypotheses about the correct answer by guessing, by focusing on one attribute at a time, or by focusing on common attributes so that as many as half of the items can be eliminated with a single question (Mosher and Hornsby 1966; Neimark and Lewis 1967). Researchers found that while impulsive children understood and retained the instructions of the game, they were more likely to try to solve the problem in a random fashion rather than by first discovering the logical cues inherent in the array of stimuli. When they didn't guess, their focus was too narrow to encompass the total game situation (Cameron and Robinson 1980).

COGNITIVE STYLE

Despite their problems, children with ADD do learn and need not fall behind grade level at school. They have sufficient "cognitive power" to compensate for their inadequate "cognitive style" (Kinsbourne and Caplan 1979). Many studies have shown that, in contrast to children with reading disorders, children with ADD have little difficulty with

59

retrieval tasks in formal assessment situations. Their Digit Span scaled scores on the WISC-R usually are not deficient; and they can repeat meaningful sentences, learn lists of unrelated words, nonsense syllables, or paired word associations, and retain what they have learned after a delay as well as other children. A problem with memory becomes apparent only under research conditions that tap into their inadequate search and organizational strategies, for example, when what they have learned in a list format is elicited in a multiple-choice format of more than two choices (Hoy et al. 1978) and when there are too many items to learn by rote without the self-generation of mnemonic cues or prior rearrangement or classification of the material to be learned. Children with ADD can equal the performance of controls in learning lists of words with meaningful associations (fruit-pear) but fall behind when the pairings are meaningless (soup-pencil). Learning meaningless associations demands a conscious and deliberate effort to relate the words through self-initiated cues. Children without attentional problems can spontaneously rehearse the material, but children with ADD rarely can. Thus, children with ADD have the capacity to absorb and recall at least equal amounts of material as controls, but they are likely to fail at higher levels of academic training where rote learning is less important than the organization of material into hierarchical structures and where associations are subtle or implicit rather than explicitly given.

The diagnostician often evaluates many very bright young adults in college or even in professional graduate schools whose histories suggest earlier attentional problems. These students still have difficulties with taking multiple-choice tests, with knowing how to study, or with relating what they have read to previously acquired information. Many high school students score far lower on the SATs than on IQ tests. Many of them develop formidable rote memories in the course of their schooling and, therefore, do quite well with basic skills material—to a certain point. However, they tend to do less well or even to fail when the curriculum demands self-generated cognitive strategies. One sixteen-year-old boy reported that his academic performance varied according to the type of examinations he was given: he could do very well on fill-in-the-blank questions or on short essays when the questions were very specific, but he could not deal with multiple-choice tests or with what he called "vague" essay questions where the required information did not come directly out of the text. He saw these tests as "unfair" and "confusing." The symptoms of ADD do not disappear when the children outgrow their hyperactivity or restlessness; rather, the effects persist and may even be exacerbated as heavier demands are made on contextual thinking, complex structural hierarchies, and independent, self-initiated study—all of which require high-level organizational skills.

GRAPHOMOTOR FUNCTION

Children with ADD are not necessarily learning disabled; they often learn to read, write, and do arithmetic with consummate ease. However, they may be identified as production disordered, because their problem with basic academic skills is most likely to be manifested in poor writing, that is, impaired graphomotor skill. One epidemiologic study by Busch* found that signs of motor immaturity in preschool children predict attentional rather than learning disorders (Busch). Another study (Denckla and Rudel 1978) demonstrated significant motor slowing, relative to controls, on timed repetitive and alternating movements of the hands, fingers, and feet of dyslexic children unscreened for attentional disorders but not of dyslexic children without attentional disorders. (Note again the paradoxical slowing in children often characterized as hyperactive.) The unscreened group also exhibited more overflow (mirroring or other extraneous) movements. Poor graphomotor skill undoubtedly arises from a combination of poor fine-motor coordination as well as from a failure to take the time to adequately copy shapes. For reasons that are not entirely clear, difficulties with the mechanics of writing often translate into very deficient, immature written expression. Children with ADD display a "block" to writing, in the form of delaying tactics and difficulties with self-initiating behaviors, and they write (or type) at much lower conceptual, semantic, and syntactic levels than one would expect from their oral expression. Researchers have not yet determined whether this problem stems from the earlier graphomotor impairment.

* Reference unknown. See page *xiii*.

School-Related Problems

Aside from this specific problem with writing skills, children with ADD are often referred for evaluation because of behavioral disorders. In the earliest grades, they lack the inhibitory controls to sit still, stop talking, or remain in line when required to do so. They often have difficulty copying from the blackboard, which is a task of tracking information from one place to another. As they advance in school, their problems take on new dimensions: they may sit still in class, but their minds wander; they fail to heed instructions; they forget to bring necessary books to school; they forget homework assignments or have trouble getting started (that is, initiating a task either in school or at home). They sit in front of blank sheets of paper for hours, failing to begin and always finding new distractions. Children with ADD routinely leave reports unwritten for weeks and cram for tests far into the night before the exam (if, indeed, they remember the upcoming test at all). This is not due to any fault of memory but, rather, to a failure to note what is going on in the classroom.

RESPONSE TO REINFORCEMENT

Under certain conditions of medication, structure, and reward, children with ADD can perform more like normal controls, and understanding these conditions helps us understand the nature of the disorder. As noted above, stimulant medication often improves their attentional focus, possibly by raising or stabilizing arousal levels. However, these children need structure in order to overcome their lack of self-initiation for starting or completing work. They need someone to work with them and to help them to maintain a steadier state of effort. Yet children with ADD respond differently to reward (or reinforcement) in the learning environment. In experiments that demonstrated improved performance with positive reinforcement for every correct response, there were no differences in performance between hyperactive children and controls; however, when a partial reinforcement schedule was employed (that is, when only some of the correct responses were rewarded), the number of trials required to reach a solution was much higher for the hyperactive children, many of whom failed to reach a solution at all. Information feedback could not take the place of positive reward, nor could punishment for incorrect responses. In some trials, nonreinforcement, or inconsistent rewarding, had a frustrating effect on children with ADD but not on controls, who did equally well with a partial reward condition. While response to environmental stimuli is overrapidly habituated by children with ADD (that is, they fail to sustain interest or effort and are easily bored), their response to reward does not habituate at all, and in fact, their performance depends significantly upon the consistency of rewards. Therefore, can one conclude that children with ADD are less involved in learning for its own sake or in doing things for their intrinsic interest?

TASK INVOLVEMENT

Research has shown that whether a task is challenging and interesting or repetitive and dull does affect the performance of children with ADD. Although they may initially respond poorly to challenging tasks, their performance improves with repeated exposure; on the other hand, their performance on dull, repetitive tasks deteriorates over time. In sum, their level of attention and effort (and, therefore, their performance and learning) depends to a greater extent on extraneous factors than does the performance of normal controls. The presence of someone to structure the problem and to re-ignite interest as it flags; the consistency, even constancy, of reward for every correct response and the challenge or stimulation of a repeated problem; all of these factors strongly affect the performance of children with ADD. Research suggests that children with ADD experience impaired self-initiation and self-monitoring as well as a curious passivity during problem solving, which, again, seems paradoxical. The experimentally demonstrated need for constant positive reinforcement demonstrated in research clarifies the clinical observation that children with ADD have difficulty accepting delayed gratification or contingent reward. The promise "If you do this now, then . . ." usually is ineffective for them, just as it often is for a much younger child.

SOCIAL ADJUSTMENT

Socially, impulsivity can have serious negative consequences. Very young children may blurt out unflattering remarks to others and appear to be charming, but if they continue to do so at school age, they quickly find themselves without friends. Lacking adequate search strategies, or failing to first employ any, impulsive children fail to size up social situations accurately and react inappropriately to isolated features or facts rather than to their context. In class, they frequently shout out responses or volunteer answers before adequately considering the questions; in other words, they leap before they look. In playing games, they fail to stay within the rules and often, to the chagrin of their playmates (and even their parents), alter the rules as they go along. Because they lack the capacity to plan ahead, they may fail to develop adequate strategies to compete with their opponents, so they tend to lose without grace. Children so dependent on positive reinforcement cannot bear to lose, and they become very angry and frustrated when they do. They terminate games, especially when they are losing, because without positive reinforcement, they are unable to sustain their attention to the end. As a consequence of their social behavior, children with ADD often find younger children more suitable as playmates.

CONTINUUM OF BEHAVIORS

Most people can recognize something of their own behavior in the spectrum of difficulties that characterizes children with ADD. Writers who are extremely well motivated to produce words, for example, also experience "writer's block"—sitting in front of blank sheets of paper for hours or days on end while they find "essential" things to do elsewhere. Delaying tactics are known to us all. Most of us have also experienced what seems like excessively rapid boredom when trying to accomplish certain tasks and, on occasion, have failed to heed what we say, check our answers, size up social situations, or carefully consider all the possibilities before responding. At least as frequently as we have groped unsuccessfully for the fitting retort, we have responded impulsively and then regretted it. We discover, suddenly, that our attention has drifted from a text or speaker. We are all occasionally distractible, impulsive, easily frustrated, and impatient. At times, and for certain tasks, we need constant positive reward in order to continue effectively. The underlying characteristics of attention are measured on a continuum: up to a certain point, such attentional difficulties are common. After a certain degree of persistence and pervasiveness, a disorder of attention is indicated. When these difficulties interfere with normal functioning, they become more than just an intermittent annoyance.

Just as children with ADD may or may not be hyperactive, they also may or may not have all of the other symptoms associated with the disorder. How many symptoms must they have and how severe must these symptoms be to constitute a deficit? This question can be answered only in the context of the child's needs and the behavioral demands made on him or her. Clearly, a child who is being educated in a one-to-one situation by a private tutor will not have as much interference from a deficient attentional system as a child with the same disorder who is trying to learn in a class with thirty-five or forty other children. Just as the discrepancy between capacity and achievement necessary for a diagnosis of dyslexia depends upon the tolerance of the school system, the degree of deficiency that constitutes an attentional disorder also depends upon the permissiveness of the environment, the type of educational setting, and social or parental expectations.

One occasionally encounters children with ADD who would seem impaired in almost any setting. Some parents perceived an impairment from the day their child was born, while other parents described their child as having been perfectly normal until teachers, fellow students, and the world at large began finding fault. For example, according to the mother of a boy whose severe attentional disorder was painfully apparent, her son was a nonconforming genius who was misunderstood and maligned by others. Some children have very subtle disorders of attention, and their problems can be magnified by excessive parental and academic demands. Even though structure is essential to learning in these cases, arbitrary rules, authoritarian discipline, and punishment can prove counterproductive.

As a rule, though, an attentional disorder must interfere with normal functioning before it can be diagnosed as such. Therefore, the severity of attentional problems required for diagnosis depends largely upon what is required of the child. The diagnostician must evaluate the parental, social, and scholastic demands on the child in order to understand the stresses and strains on his or her attentional system.

Excessive Slowness to Habituate Stimuli

The basic elements ascribed to attention—orientation toward stimuli in the environment and habituation of response to these stimuli—are also measured on a continuum; too much of either is not necessarily a good thing. Consider the infant who habituates response very slowly, that is, continues to fix attention on one stimulus. He or she may continue to do this beyond the point where any new information can be extracted and thereby fails to note the introduction of new stimuli into the environment—a very maladaptive contingency. Although children with this type of attentional disorder are not as common as overrapid habituators, diagnosticians see several for evaluation each year. One ten-year-old boy, for example, was described by his parents, both extremely capable professionals, as having "skewed development," brilliantly capable in some areas and only average or below average in others. They noted a "tendency to become obsessively involved with things or ideas" and to react poorly to changes in routine. He rarely initiated new activities or spontaneously expressed interest in something. He could never think of a new toy or game he might want, but when he received one, he could go on playing with it ceaselessly. He was rarely bored but very often boring. Some time before he was seen in the clinic, he became interested in trading baseball cards: he learned everything there was to know about them and would talk about them endlessly, boring everyone, including his classmates, without noticing that he had lost his audience. This is a perfect example of an inability to accurately assess a message communicated in a social setting. This boy was clearly unable to gauge the degree to which his intense interest in baseball cards had come to bore his friends and family. Although of superior intelligence (his parents noted), he failed to pick up cues that other children picked up very easily.

His history revealed an early tendency to obsessiveness. For example, at age two, he became absorbed in looking at and saying the letter O; at age two-and-a-half, he began to read but did not speak words or phrases (except for *ma-ma* or *da-da*) until he was three. Thus, he might read the word *cookie* aloud, but when he wanted one, he would only point in the appropriate direction. Language was a visual-verbal exercise for him before it became a means for communication. He was "hyperlexic," but once he developed language comprehension, he could also read for meaning and continues to do so very well. His concentration was described as "fantastic." His resistance to changes in routine was also apparent very early in life, and in the course of a testing session, he resisted a change in the position of his chair in relation to the examiner: he kept returning the chair to its original position. Yet, as his parents had reported, he possessed very superior intelligence in spite of an attentional system that resisted response to new stimuli and failed to habituate the old.

From this child's history, it is apparent that he has a problem with the modulation and deployment of attentional controls. Unlike most children with ADD, however, this ten-year-old is an overfocused child, at the opposite end of the attentional continuum. He is not distractible; rather, it is almost impossible to get him to shift his orientation. He is not impulsive; he rarely initiates new behavior or does anything spontaneously. His concentration and attention span are formidable, and he is well-behaved. He continues at tasks without positive reinforcement and even in the face of negative reinforcement. He has no learning disability, but he has difficulties with certain types of conceptualization—in dealing with more than one dimension of a problem at a time, with inferential reasoning, with getting the point of a joke (except for puns), and with initiating ideas.

Another such overfocused child, a very intelligent eight-year-old girl, became so absorbed in something she was doing in class that she failed to notice when all the other children left the room. She remained in her seat, alone in the room, while some of her classmates stood at the open door and laughed at her. Many such children become scapegoats and the butt of jokes. They are often described as "blocking out the world" or "out of it."

MECHANISMS OF ATTENTION

The frontal lobe mechanisms that monitor the things that we pay attention to stay in touch with the outside world through the cognitive, exteroceptive system and with the internal world through the limbic, interoceptive system. Clearly, maintaining a balance between these two attentional systems is crucial not only for academic success but also for maintaining social contact with the world around us. The frontal cortex, through a subcortical relay, the caudate nucleus, is also an essential part of the reward system of the brain, instrumental in experiencing pleasure and in learning. If these areas are less well developed or dysfunctional in children at either end of the ADD continuum—from impulsive, distractible children who require positive reward for every correct response in order to maintain a normal level of learning efficiency to the overfocused child who sticks to tasks or orientations beyond the point at which they cease to be fruitful or adaptive without any reinforcement—one could thereby account for their atypical response to reinforcement.

Both of the overfocused children discussed above were so bright that, despite some weaknesses, they were not learning disabled; at least, they had no difficulty acquiring basic academic skills. However, like most children with attentional disorders, they, too, had problems with planning and organizing their efforts. They would put off getting started on activities (writing compositions, homework, or reports) until the last moment and then often failed to overcome their inertia. The causes of these difficulties, however, may differ for the two types of attentional disorders. While children with the more common type of ADD might procrastinate by finding other, more attractive things to do, overfocused children seem unable to shift attention from what they are doing to what has to be done, particularly if the competition is between something well known and routine and something new and still untried. Overfocused children also procrastinate because they have inordinate difficulty initiating new actions or coming up with new ideas for compositions, stories, or even a paraphrase of something they have read: their capacity for fantasy and creativity is very limited. Once they get going on a project or an idea, they tend to be extremely slow and to have great difficulty completing the work on time. They obsessively go over and over their work without necessarily changing or improving what they have done.

COMPENSATORY MECHANISMS

Both of the overfocused children briefly described above were referred for diagnosis because of their slowness, their inability to begin or to complete work, and their social problems at school. Their case histories indicated that they always had been overfocused, somewhat obsessive, and intolerant of changes in routine. However, such characteristics are not restricted to children with these early case histories. Children with the more common form of ADD, with or without hyperactivity, may develop obsessive behaviors in the course of growing up and in their striving to overcome their limitations. A child's obsessive attention to detail, or learning everything there is to know about a subject, may protect him or her from overlooking something essential; saying everything known about a subject may spare the child from leaving out the correct response; preparing everything that could possibly be needed prior to tackling an assignment makes it unnecessary to keep getting up for one thing after another; and rewarding oneself after each phase of a task may replace the need for constant external reinforcement. These compensatory mechanisms, which are found in older children and young adults with histories of attentional disorders, are often as maladaptive as the original disorders. The child's equal attention to all details precludes any hierarchical organization of the material and, even more disabling, often becomes obsessively repetitive. The child can waste as much time through repetition as with aimless searching. One twelve-year-old boy, and several young adults, displayed amazing memories and could, with repetition, absorb almost anything without really learning it. However, learning implies the capacity to distinguish the essential from the unessential and to organize new material so that it relates to previous information. This can rarely be achieved with rote memorization.

A young medical student who was having difficulty relating the names of syndromes to their symptoms showed us the texts from which he studied: virtually everything was underlined. When asked, during testing, how an orange and a banana were alike, he responded, "Alike in color, edible, grow on trees, skins" but failed to note that they are both fruits. When asked how north and south are alike, he included the correct response, "directions," in a lengthy list of nonessential details, such as: "English-language words; both have *T*s in them; usually spelled with small letters; usually adjectives that denote . . . ," et cetera. The correct response was almost lost in the litany of task-irrelevant details about the two terms. This obsessive attention to all details and the obsessive inclusion of all known facts may be maladaptive adjustments to ADD. The child who shifts from total disorganization in approaching a task to total organization may turn the means, the preparation, into a ritualistic end. After all, when is one ever *totally* prepared to begin a task? The child's delaying tactics may be different and, on the surface, may appear to be constructive, but they are no less disabling. Similarly, the child's transfer of the need for continuous external reward to self-reward with sweets, drinks, or cigarettes may lead to overindulgence. Further, the amount of work that merits a reward may shrink while the amount of reward increases. After all, children (and adults) with attentional problems characteristically fail to monitor themselves.

The "cognitive style" (to use Caplan and Kinsbourne's term) is impaired at either end of the ADD continuum, and the effects are usually equally counterproductive. Impulsivity and obsessive behavior coexisting within the same child may be contextual—certain situations may elicit one type of response and others, the opposite. Thus, there are impulsive, distractible children with ADD who can spend apparently limitless amounts of time with a particular game or favorite activity. One boy, who was intolerably impulsive in school, spent almost every waking hour out of school playing "Dungeons and Dragons." When told that their child has a short attention span, parents often will protest that at home it is impossible to drag the child away from a favorite pursuit. Occasionally, an impulsive child can harness this capacity to fixate attention and concentrate effort on a single interest to develop unusual skills in music or art.

ADD with Learning Disability

Neither overfocused nor underfocused children with attentional problems necessarily have learning disorders as such; that is, the subject matter at school is well within their grasp (Keogh 1971). The statistics on this issue are few and contradictory, but diagnostic experience indicates that many children with learning disabilities also have attentional disorders (Safer and Allen 1976).

If selection (or diagnostic) criteria for ADD include hyperactivity, however, then the incidence of mixed types (ADD with learning disability) is reduced. In a study of 241 hyperactive children, only 22 (9.1 percent) were also reading disabled, whereas 36 (15 percent) had reading scores more than one standard deviation above age expectation (Halperin et al. 1984). Cantwell and Satterfield showed that a significantly greater proportion of hyperactive children than controls performed below predicted grade level on reading, spelling, and arithmetic on the WRAT, but fully three-fourths were above, at, or less than a year below grade-level expectation (1978). In attempting to contrast the performance of hyperactive children with and without learning disabilities, Ackerman et al. had difficulty finding, when using very stringent discrepancy criteria and matching for IQ, hyperactive children with learning disabilities (1982).

Whatever their incidence in the general population, "mixed" types do exist. In diagnosis (as contrasted with research), where one is concerned with disabling effects and possibilities for remediation, the interaction of the ADD and even a mild or moderate learning problem may be very significant. Thus, while the degree of severity of either the learning disorder or the attentional disorder may not be sufficient to qualify the child for a research study of "mixed" types, in real life, the combination may be more devastating than either condition alone.

Children with learning disabilities *and* ADD do not always exhibit secondary reactions. Some children have characteristics of both from the beginning. This is particularly apparent in children with preschool attentional problems along with delayed and/or aberrant language development. These children are very likely to have attentional problems at school as well as trouble learning to read. This combination of ADD with dyslexia (or dyslexia plus ADD) is often predictable from the child's preschool developmental history. Children with ADD, whether or not they are dyslexic, usually have poor visual-motor integration, which results in impaired graphomotor skill, which is manifested as difficulty with copying forms and difficulty with learning to write. This deficiency is undoubtedly yet another aspect of their poor fine-motor coordination and inadequate motor control. As noted earlier, difficulty with the mechanics of writing often translates into very deficient, immature written expression. Just as dyslexic children are unlikely to accept as language the nonsense words they read, these dysgraphic children (even when they are not dyslexic) are unlikely to speak the nonsense words they write.

Difficulties with arithmetic also may develop as another aspect of the language inadequacy that is at the root of reading impairment for many of these children. In others, however, difficulties with arithmetic may be secondary to their failure to pay attention to instructions and signs, to keep columns of numbers straight, or to monitor solutions for reasonableness.

At the opposite end of the attentional continuum, overfocused children do not entirely escape problems with learning. Even when they are unusually gifted intellectually and are performing at or above grade level on basic skills, overfocused children often encounter academic difficulties. In their narrow focus on details, they often fail to take into account the whole situation and have difficulty inferring the presence of the whole from only a part. Similarly, they have difficulty making inferences from what they read. The two overfocused children described above were overdependent on what was explicitly stated and lacked the flexibility to follow a shift in point of view, despite their very high IQs.

SEX DIFFERENCES

An overwhelming proportion of children with learning disorders are boys. Among children with dyslexia, boys outnumber girls by a ratio of about four or five to one, and the proportion of boys to girls among hyperactive children is estimated as between ten or twenty to one. Diagnosis of ADD without hyperactivity is still too recent for any good epidemiologic evidence to be available. In diagnostic services, though, it is clear that more girls have ADDs without hyperactivity than with hyperactivity, but their number, relative to comparably affected boys, is still small. Boys do appear to be at greater risk for developmental disorders that appear early in childhood or during school years.

Sex differences that have been demonstrated in research and diagnosis are only relative, for there is always considerable overlap. Still, these differences may provide important clues to the underlying neurological deficits, since brain organization and rate of maturation also differ in boys and girls. Girls, for example, generally learn to speak earlier, retrieve words more rapidly, and are less likely to develop reading disorders. Perhaps the earlier maturation of language and more accessible lexical store are essential to reading. When girls have reading problems, they appear to have somewhat different correlated symptoms. In normative studies, the demonstrated decrease in cognitive functioning and learning during preadolescence or early adolescence occurs earlier in girls than in boys. As yet, however, there are insufficient data on differences between attentionally disordered boys and girls. When they become available, they may provide important clues for biochemical differences in the brain and, ultimately, may aid in remediation.

PART TWO

EVALUATION AND NEURO-PSYCHOLOGICAL ASSESSMENT

Chapter 4

Developmental History and Evaluation

RITA G. RUDEL

Evaluation

To paraphrase the oft-quoted (and perhaps too often unheeded) caution that the conduct of war should not be entrusted to generals, the testing of children for learning disabilities should not be left to test administrators. All testing, like all research, provides a cross section (or, in longitudinal studies, a series of cross sections) of behaviors in a moment of time; therefore, it is essential to obtain certain genetic, historical, and social facts about the child to provide a more expanded time frame for the particular samples of tested behavior. The examiner obtains this information from rating scales and developmental history forms filled out by the parent(s) and from interviews of the child and the parent(s). Whenever possible, the examiner should also obtain previous assessments of the child, for these provide a measure of stability or the direction of change. Occasionally a parent balks at providing previous test results and may

75

even fail to mention any; but the child sometimes will bring up the subject in the course of the test sessions, or the child's familiarity with the standardized tests may betray previous assessment. Parents who withhold such information generally claim they wanted to prevent bias in the current evaluation. Such parents are really testing the tester; they tend to take their child from one examiner to another in hopes of finding the perfect solution to a problem they only dimly understand and are not prepared to face.

OBSERVATIONS

In this chapter, we will briefly discuss various rating scales, developmental history forms, and interviewing methods and how this information relates to diagnosis. There is another essential data source for which no precise measures or rating scales are available, however: the examiner's observations throughout the encounter with the child and the parent(s). The neuropsychologist must be an alert, efficient observer; he or she will rarely capture a glimpse of the child at home, at school, or at play, but he or she can gain valuable insight by sampling behavior in the waiting room and in the course of testing.

Observation begins with the initial telephone inquiry for a diagnosis. The examiner can draw the first clues about the child's environment and the emotional climate in which he or she lives from the reason given for having the child tested, the attitudes toward evaluation, and, most important, the description of the child and the problem. These attitudes conveyed in the telephone inquiry often form the starting point for an eventual interview. Although the examiner's observations of the child proceed from this background of information, he or she should not be prejudiced, negatively or positively, at this point. The examiner's own observations sometimes differ from those of the parents, but that constitutes only a discrepancy to be reconciled. Often, the examiner needs additional data or must question the child or the family further. In some cases, however, the behavioral discrepancy is typical, and the child who has a behavioral problem at home or at school may be easy to work with in the structured, one-to-one setting of the test situation, where he or she is at the center of attention, where no single task goes on for very long and approval (reinforcement) is frequently given. In contrast, a child who is not considered to have a behavior problem at home or at school may appear distracted and restless during testing, a condition that suggests poor adjustment to and some fear of new situations. The examiner observes how well the child is dressed, groomed, and prepared for the day, which may reveal something about the care he or she receives at home. The child's reticence, cooperativeness, friendliness, or nervousness must all be gauged in terms of whatever other data are obtained.

Behavioral changes during the day are important to note. Does the frightened child finally relax? Does the fidgety child become more or less restless as the day wears on? Is there a big improvement following the lunch break? Aside from the information provided by such alterations in behavior, the examiner must be sensitive to conditions that may affect the child's performance. Observations of mood changes sometimes can be supported by the simple repetition of certain tasks; for example, a child who scored very poorly on Digit Span or Coding subtests of the WISC-R early in the test session may improve later, when he or she is more relaxed. Indeed, if a child is noticeably restless or anxious, it is a good idea to defer tasks that depend heavily on focused attention. Careful observation of the child, then, is critical not only for assessing the way he or she relates to others but also for the best possible sequence of test administration.

At times, it is necessary for the examiner to observe the child through the parent's eyes. This is particularly true when a parent makes extravagant claims about a child's ability despite apparently severe limitations. If a child does not learn very much in the school setting but is said to know "many songs by heart," "the entire prayer book," or "every event he has ever been to," then the examiner should allow the child to perform or to relate some episodes from the past with the parents present. There are no standardized norms by which to assess such special skills, but the performance allows you to judge the validity of the claim, the degree to which the child is dependent upon cuing from the parents, the coherence of what is related, and the meaning (if any) the child appears to derive from what he or she is saying, singing, or drawing. I have seen parents suddenly (and sadly) lose their illusions about the child's "special gifts" when they see a demonstration in the presence of a friendly but objective observer. On the other hand, a child's mimetic, musical, or graphic skills may be present (if rarely) in the context of other limitations; as there are no "tests" of these abilities, they must be observed, informally but carefully, as part of the total assessment.

Adopted Children. The following sections of this chapter, involving the genetic prenatal and perinatal history of the child, are rarely part of the assessment of adopted children. Adopted children seem to constitute a larger proportion of patients than their numbers would indicate. In northern New Jersey, from 1970 to 1977, adoptees constituted about 30 percent of Martha Denckla's neurological service (largely dedicated to children with learning problems), although only 10 percent of children in that area were adopted (Denckla, personal communication). Many children given up for adoption are born to high school dropouts, who may have been learning disabled and/or have had behavioral problems, which suggests genetic links to deficits of both learning and attention. Further, many of these young mothers receive little if any prenatal care, and they are more likely to deliver premature and high-risk (poor Apgar) babies. Low hormone levels and poor nutrition in these "child-mothers" could also contribute to the high incidence of developmental problems in this adopted population. Therefore, although the examiner usually can obtain little or no information on the adopted child's family history, there is some likelihood that learning disorders may be implicated.

GENETIC FACTORS

Studies suggest a constitutional basis for dyslexia (Critchley 1970) and hyperactivity or ADD (Wender 1971). Research also links specific reading disorders to familial patterns. Thomas often observed a "congenital word blindness" in more than a single family member (Thomas 1905). Since then, a number of studies have shown that the unaffected siblings of dyslexic children are often inadequate spellers (Owen et al. 1971), that parents of dyslexic children have similar patterns of information processing (Gordon 1980), and that parents and siblings of dyslexic children perform less adequately than controls when reading under experimental stress (Finucci 1978). Some studies relate subtypes among reading-disabled children to subtypes in their families (Finucci et al. 1982; Decker and DeFries 1980), and another study reports that a gene identified as chromosome 15 may play a role in one form of reading disability (Smith et al. 1979).

In a diagnostic setting, the examiner cannot go so far as to test the families of children with reading problems, but through questionnaire and interview, he or she can establish the presence of a familial factor and can diagnose a constitutional basis for dyslexia with that much more certainty. Simply asking the mother whether she or the father are able to read or had difficulty learning to read can be awkward and is generally met with a categorical no, from which it is difficult to proceed. Besides, as research has shown, parents and siblings of dyslexic children often can read but have other related language or learning problems. Thus, for example, one mother who denied ever having had reading problems proceeded in malaprop fashion to mispronounce half-a-dozen words in the course of five minutes of conversation. A more discrete approach is preferable; the parent(s) can fill out, alone and unobserved, the questionnaire that includes questions concerning learning difficulties as part of the family medical history (see Developmental History Form at the end of this chapter) (Gardner 1986).

There are certain difficulties with this method as well. The mother usually completes the questionnaire, and she may not know what, if any, learning problems the father or others in his family may have had. When discussing the responses on the questionnaire in a later interview, the examiner should ask the respondent parent to check with the other and to provide the information before the test data are evaluated. In these days of divorce and small families, the amount of information generated by questionnaire and interview sometimes is inadequate for a valid genetic assessment. The examiner should note the quality of the respondent parent's writing and spelling, as well as the overall competence with which the questionnaire was completed.

With some positive histories, the examiner must be cautious. When the parents have separated or divorced acrimoniously or even, occasionally, when they are living together, one parent may try to place all "blame"—genetic and behavioral—on the other. Confidences involving recently discovered idiot relatives, learning problems, psychotic uncles—all "on the other side"—will abound. In these instances, it is very important, if possible, to call the other parent in for an interview and to subtly set the record straight without reference to the previous information. Problems with spelling and/or arithmetic in parents or siblings are of particular interest. One physician father admitted that he could never spell, and a writer father said that he was unable to balance his checkbook. As noted in chapter 2, many of the same skills required for reading are also involved in spelling and arithmetic, and a more subtle deficit may impair the latter skills without affecting reading.

It is sometimes more difficult to reconcile a young patient's learning problems with the behavioral problems that the parent(s) indicates in the rest of the family. Some parents will deny that there was ever a learning disability, a grade repeated, or extra help required to get through school, but they will reveal that the father, mother (or both), or a sibling had histories of conduct problems, were kept after school, often had to go to the principal's office, were threatened with expulsion, et cetera. Such a family history, even without recollections of concentration problems or excess distractibility, raises the possibility that the patient has an attentional disorder to which the learning problem is related only secondarily through impaired attentional processes (Keogh 1971).

The genetics of ADD are not as well established as the familial prevalence of reading disorder. The issue is still controversial, with a higher reported incidence of alcoholism, depression (unipolar or bipolar), and neurotic anxiety in one or both parents of children with ADD, with or without hyperactivity. The very nature of the associated problems in parents of children with ADD raises questions about discipline and structure in their households. Even when the examiner can establish a constitutional basis for ADD in a child through neurological examination and/or EEG findings, he or she must factor the interaction of an impaired attentional substrate and parental discipline into the evaluation. In children without such positive signs, the effect of parental discipline (or the lack of it) in producing the attentional disorder is a critical issue.

Behavioral interaction between parent(s) and child often can call into question the competence of a parent(s) in providing structure and limits for the developing child. For example, the mother of one wildly hyperactive four-year-old boy sat on the floor in the corner of the testing room and whimpered into her knees while the clinician tried to subdue her son into some sort of testable condition. The genetic connection here was tenuous, but the passive disciplinary neglect was very real. A great deal of research remains to be done on the genetic factors in ADD, but the diagnostician need not be limited to an either-or conclusion. The testing situation will never provide a comprehensive measure of consistency in discipline. Thus, any conclusions about the degree to which genetics or environment determine the severity or type of the child's problem must be evaluated with the utmost of care. An absence of conduct or behavioral problems in families of children with ADD does not disprove a genetic factor; rather, there is simply inadequate information on the nature of that link. A parent's or sibling's substance abuse, emotional problems, or previous behavioral problems provides a possible genetic link but also indicates familial instability and poor or inconsistent discipline. When siblings (who, presumably, have had the same type of upbringing, structure, stability, and discipline) have no conduct or attentional problems, one can, with somewhat greater certainty, attribute the patient's attentional problem or hyperactivity to constitutional factors, with or without evidence of genetic link.

PRENATAL AND PERINATAL "AT RISK" FACTORS

There is no conclusive evidence linking learning problems with prenatal or obstetrical history, although some studies relate the mother's use of alcohol, barbiturates, cigarettes, even coffee to the heart rate and birth weight of the newborn. Prenatal conditions that contribute to lower birth weight place the child at risk for later difficulties. (See Developmental History Form on pages 103–11.) If the mother had a great many complications of pregnancy and delivery, the likelihood of a prenatal predisposition for developmental anomalies is increased (pages 104–5). This predisposition should be reflected in postpartum information, with lowered Apgar score and possible jaundice, poor suck, et cetera (page 105). In clinical experience, such postpartum histories are rare in learning-disabled children but more frequent in children with congenital brain damage. The same is true for the incidence of miscarriages or prior still births (page 110).

INFANCY PERIOD

The only true occupation of the infant is to eat, sleep, and occasionally seem to take note of the presence of a human face or the sound of a human voice by smiling. There may be considerable information on the adequacy of adaptation (the basis of all learning) in how well the child, with the help of a parent, establishes these patterns. The child's birth weight and the adequacy of his suck are important factors in determining the frequency of feeding; however, given that these factors are within normal limits, the infant should take in enough sustenance at each feeding to last about three to four hours. Usually within a matter of weeks, the infant establishes a regular feeding pattern. During the night, when visual and auditory stimuli are at a minimum, sleep periods should increase as feedings decrease. In a matter of months, the infant may be down to four or five feedings a day and may sleep through most of the night. In retrospect, regular sleeping and eating patterns appear more difficult to establish in children who are subsequently diagnosed as being hyperactive or as having attentional problems. Their restlessness was often first apparent during sleep periods: they would awaken at night without provocation or at the slightest noise. Their eating schedules often differed from one day to the next, and many had been colicky. Some studies attribute their apparent digestive troubles to the large amounts of air they swallowed during feeding (Caplan and Kinsbourne 1979).

There are no data on the responsiveness of these colicky, difficult-to-manage infants to the sight or sound of others, but some parents report that, compared to siblings, these children were not responsive to cuddling and rarely stopped crying when picked up, they were difficult to calm or soothe, and their restlessness sometimes extended to head banging.

Clearly, in their inability to establish regular eating and sleeping habits and their lack of social responsiveness, hyperactive children often can be identified during infancy. However, there are no identified patterns of infant behavior that consistently characterize children with other learning disabilities. Such patterns, if they appear at all, occur later in childhood with a delay in acquiring certain skills.

DEVELOPMENTAL MILESTONES

When a parent boasts that the child is precocious or complains to the pediatrician that the child is slow, the child is being measured against some implicit standard: neighbors' children, older siblings, a schedule of development reported in a journal or book, or the statements of older relatives (usually grandmothers). The standard for comparison also involves an age gradient, for the child who seems cute and bright at ten months when he or she says "da-da" to every adult male would seem somewhat retarded if the behavior continues until the age of two. Therefore, in assessing the normalcy of certain behaviors, the examiner also looks for the dropping out of certain earlier behaviors. In fact, by age two, "da-da" should be supplanted by "daddy" or some other suitable name. The two-year-old who begs "Pick you up" when he or she wants to be held is making a perfectly acceptable pronominal reversal, but a child would be suspect for language and/or socialization problems if he or she is still doing this at age four.

The age at which certain behaviors appear, then, is usually a good index of future development. The pediatrician may reassure a worried parent by noting that Albert Einstein also failed to speak until he was three, but a single such exceptional instance does not weigh heavily against the more common finding that late onset of speech, or the failure to use phrases or sentences between the ages of two and three, often predicts later deficiencies of oral and/or written language. Milestones in speech and language development are probably most regularly perceived as "late" by parents of dyslexic children (pages 106–7). Late speech onset, in the absence of other signs and in the presence of normal language comprehension, does not predict intellectual retardation nor, for that matter, does early speech onset necessarily indicate intellectual superiority. Rather, an early discrepancy between apparently normal intelligence and the somewhat slow mastery of language seems to foreshadow developmental dyslexia, which translates into a discrepancy between IQ and reading ability later in childhood.

LANGUAGE DELAY

The child who is slow to acquire the ability to comprehend what is being said is more likely to have deficiencies beyond learning or attentional disorders. Language comprehension delay may be the first sign of dysphasia (globally poor language development), intellectual retardation, autism, or some combination of these disorders. Typically, the learning disabled child fails to use sentences or phrases at the usual time (age two to four), and continues to speak in single words. Many of these children also have articulation problems so that only their immediate family can understand what they are saying. This may persist to school age and, of course, can be socially handicapping. The ability to name colors or coins (page 106) as well as other objects is often delayed; the child seems to speak a great deal, but he or she lacks precision (for example, "Gimme the thing that is over there sometime"). This delay and/or imprecision of language is often carried over to learning the letters of the alphabet and to reading.

MOTOR COORDINATION

Children with learning disabilities are not usually slow to sit, stand, walk, or run. Children with delayed milestones in these gross-motor activities are more often brain damaged and/or intellectually retarded. Occasionally, one sees learning-disabled children with mild athetosis (involuntary twitchings and tremors of hands and feet) and a history of gross-motor delay, but then they are more likely to be globally impaired even if they score within the normal range on IQ tests. A sort of general clumsiness sometimes characterizes the performance of learning-disabled children. One mother tried to describe it in this way: "I spent his childhood crying over and wiping up spilled milk." In contrast, dyslexic children tend to be slower than average in achieving skills that involve fine-motor coordination (buttoning clothing or tying shoelaces), and their writing is often characterized as poor (pages 106–7).

Although toilet training certainly involves a measure of learning and an even greater measure of control, learning-disabled children rarely are slow in this regard. Rather, hyperactive children, with or without learning disabilities, are more often delayed in toilet training; some fail to achieve control at night and remain enuretic well into childhood. This is another "paradox" of children with attentional disorders: they fail to awaken when necessary during the night despite the restlessness of their sleep.

SOCIALIZATION

Infants prefer to look, for the longest periods of time, at representations of the human face (Fantz 1965). The presence of a real person who will smile or coo, sing or talk, is often all that is necessary to keep an infant occupied and happy. From the earliest days of life, therefore, social attachments are important, providing an index of the "normalcy" of the infant's development. Infants who would rather attend to objects than to people, who are not soothed by contact, and who make no effort to imitate (by exchanging smiles or coos, for example) are at risk for later problems with social learning. One eighteen-year-old girl, whom Martha Denckla followed for ten years, failed to form infantile or childhood attachments. Although her IQ scores are borderline, she still has to be "taught" the meaning of social interactions that are taken for granted by normal four-year-olds, and she fails to "read" facial expressions or to understand differences in tones of voice (Denckla, personal communication). A somewhat less impaired (with superior IQ scores) but still socially obtuse ten-year-old boy was more intrigued by blocks, letters, or toys than by people (Denckla, personal communication). Despite the substantial difference in the IQ scores, both of these children have particular difficulty learning anything new, making inferences, or shifting from one point of view to another. One can conclude, then, that some common impaired substrate appears to affect both socialization and flexibility of adaptation or thought.

FRIENDS AND PLAY

A child who has never had friends must be considered at risk for disorders related to learning, that is, for failing to acquire any social coping skills. In these cases, it is important to ask the following questions:

1. Did the child have normal opportunities for meeting and playing with other children?
2. Did the child desire the companionship of other children but fail to form attachments?
3. Did other children reject this child?
4. Did the child fail to show any interest in other children?

Given normal opportunity, the failure to make friends suggests some underlying autistic or schizophrenic adaptation. Given opportunity and the desire for peer play, social rejection suggests a failure of social learning, poor adaptation to group rules, and, possibly, poor language comprehension.

Social behavior later in childhood also provides essential information. Jansky and DeHirsch (1972) note that the child's ability to model behavior on others or to adapt to group norms is the essential first predictor of school performance. In order to learn in a classroom setting, in contrast to the often one-to-one situation at home, the child has to sit still and focus attention when others do so and not only when he or she is ready. This degree of adaptation to social requirements is a prerequisite for learning. While the developmental history form asks only about the child's current behavior, it is important to determine whether these behaviors were a problem earlier in the school experience (page 108).

Most often, the inability (or unwillingness) to model one's own behavior on that of the group is characteristic of the immaturity, disinhibition, and distractibility that characterize the child with attentional problems and/ or hyperactivity. Many of these children adjust better socially with younger playmates than with those their own age (or older), primarily because they have not achieved age-appropriate, rule-governed behavior. Since they seek immediate and constant reward, losing a single turn in a game often leads them to break up the game or alter the rules. One five-year-old boy described a hyperactive friend who, he said, "changes the rules as he goes along." Playing an entire game as simple as "Candy Land" still requires sustained attention over a protracted period of taking turns. The child must keep the object of the game and the rules themselves in mind: they guide the play and serve as the basis for short-term gains and the long-term outcome, that is, whether one wins or loses. Such games make precisely the demands that hyperactive children find difficult or impossible to meet. Therefore, whenever the occasion to play games arises, these children are out of the social picture.

Children whose problems are not attentional but involve understanding and manipulating symbols, counting, carrying through a series of goal-oriented moves, or maintaining the appropriate spatial direction, will have very similar difficulties with such games and, therefore, with socialization, if for very different reasons. The effects will be more circumscribed and circumstantial. Dyslexic children are sometimes described retrospectively as having failed to sit still or pay attention during storytelling (at home or at school), although at that stage they were not required to read. It is likely that dyslexic children are slow to develop enough of a grasp of language to follow the complexities of a story but their comprehension may be adequate for shorter sequences. Again, the problem is not one of paying attention but, rather, of sustaining attention through an activity that is only vaguely or not at all understood. Inattention during storytelling is more likely to be noted as a problem at school, where the child cannot easily see illustrative pictures or ask questions. Parents of dyslexic children, however, usually will admit that they rarely read to their children at home because they did not appear to enjoy or demand it.

SCHOOL VERSUS HOME

Some developmental difficulties may emerge differently in school than at home. Children described as devils at school may be angels at home, or vice versa (pages 107–9). When assessing the pervasiveness of behavior problems, the examiner must be careful to determine whether the conflicting reports are really situational or the product of very different tolerance thresholds in the two environments. "I don't understand the complaints at school; he's [she's] always been wonderful at home" is often heard from parents. If a child is the center of attention at home, receiving constant praise and reward, then problems of inattention, hyperactivity, and a low frustration threshold do not emerge as frequently as in school or are benignly overlooked. This is particularly true of only children of employed mothers who share day-to-day problems with an indulgent housekeeper during the work week and with fathers on weekends. This pattern is common also in children with relatively mild attentional problems whose capacity for sustained activity and concentration are not challenged in the home but who lack the flexibility and maturity to function in the more demanding group situation of a classroom. "Situational" behavior problems at school, reported as part of a developmental history and without the usual preschool pattern, may signal an inability to learn that the child has been covering up by acting as if he or she didn't *want* to learn. Some very competitive children find it easier to suffer the consequences of a conduct disorder than to admit that they do not understand school activities that others seem readily able to grasp.

Children who have a history of poor behavior at home but who do well at school are more likely to be responding to unsympathetic parents, lack of structure and consistent discipline, or conflicts with siblings and other members of the household. School provides them with a less stressful setting, more even-handed discipline, greater consistency, clearer and more reasonable expectations, and a regular program of activities—all or some of which may be lacking at home. At times, the parent's desire for perfection makes school appear to be a haven of attainable goals. Children who are not allowed to entertain friends at home because they make "a mess" or "too much noise" find the opportunities to socialize at school just what they need to keep home-cultivated temper tantrums at a minimum. With competitive siblings no longer physically present, some children suddenly seem to "grow up" at school and manage to save their angry outbursts for home. In fact, such children are brought in for diagnosis when their conduct disorders become exacerbated at home or when the contrast between their two sets of behavior, one for school and another for the home, becomes painfully apparent to the mother or father. Such histories of situational hyperactivity, attentional problems, or conduct disorder rarely point to underlying constitutional problems except in their milder forms. Instead, these behaviors are generally reactions to stress and, once again, point to the critical relationship between innate temperament and discipline.

BEHAVIOR PROFILE

In evaluating the pervasiveness of hyperactivity or ADD, the examiner needs data from both the child's home and the child's school. Conners (1973) has developed rating scales (long and short forms) for parents and teachers. The individual items of the long form are grouped into the four following factors: (1) conduct problems; (2) hyperactivity factors; (3) inattention/passivity; and (4) a hyperactivity index. The "hyperactivity index," in contrast to "hyperactivity," represents a broader cross section of behaviors that are characteristic of hyperactive children but are related to more than just excess restless motor activity. However, hyperactivity and the hyperactivity index are so highly correlated that one rarely finds a child who can be characterized by one and not the other.

The factor scores are derived by assigning weighted points for each answer, adding the points, and dividing the total by the number of items in that factor. A score over 1.5 for any factor is considered within the range of the ADD and is the cutoff used in research studies. In diagnosis, the grouping of individual ratings provides the examiner with a behavioral profile. Is the disorder most manifest in the child's conduct, motor restlessness (hyperactivity), or dimension of attention, or is the distribution almost equal? The examiner cannot always obtain teachers' ratings and, therefore, must consider the nature of complaints from the school (which are often the reason for referral for diagnosis) and/or the parent's report of the child's behavior in school through the years. Rating scale scores are adequate for research purposes, but diagnosis requires an interview to clarify the parent's frame of reference: what behavioral standards guided the scores?

Interviewing the Parent(s)

The primary purpose of the interview is to clarify and amplify the parent's responses on the developmental history form and rating scale. The interview also provides the opportunity for a closer look at the parent-child relationship, not only for what is said about the child, but also for how it is said—the tone of voice and the means of expression. Developmental history forms and rating scales provide the content but not the expression of how the child and his or her problems appear to the parent. A view of the parent's attitudes toward the child and of the family constellation also yields some ideas on the possibilities for remediation. In my practice, I have found it useful to conduct the interview after the forms have been completed and, if possible, after some objective estimate of the child's academic achievement (if that is the problem) in the context of his or her intellectual potential has been made.

Looking through the developmental history form also affords a glimpse of the parent's basic skills. Did he or she understand the questions, answer them to the point, and spell correctly? Was the handwriting legible or childish? Familial tendencies for poor acquisition of basic skills are sometimes apparent in the completion of these forms. The examiner can make such a judgment only when the parent completing the forms has had the necessary educational opportunity. If one parent does not read or write English, however, the other (absent) parent should fill out the forms, and the interview can be postponed until after the information is complete. When neither parent speaks English, a real problem emerges for the examiner. A translator usually can be found, but this method is cumbersome at best. When possible, one can translate the developmental history forms for the parent(s) and then translate the responses. Bilingual parents should choose the language with which they are most comfortable—if a translator is available. In any event, interviewing a parent without a common language is extremely limiting; therefore, it is often useful to get in touch with the child's teacher or other professionals who are familiar with the case. Failing all else, the observations the examiner made in the course of testing become all that much more important.

RECALLING DEVELOPMENTAL MILESTONES

A mother who insists that she cannot recall any of the child's developmental milestones, even approximately, is saying something very important about her relationship with the child (unless, of course, the patient is neither the first nor the last child born in a very large family). Someday, a father's claim to little or no information about the child's birth and early development may be as fraught with significance as a mother's similar claim, but at present this is still quite common and, therefore, not apparently deviant from the norm. In this instance, the mother will have to complete the forms and reschedule the interview for a later date. The examiner sometimes can elicit information that the forms cannot by providing a time frame for developmental milestones; for example, "Was he [or she] walking on his [or her] first birthday?" If this fails, the examiner can discuss family history (moves from one city to another, vacations, or visits to relatives) and, by estimating the child's age on these occasions, can relate developmental data to these events. "Was he [or she] toilet-trained when you visited your in-laws? Did you have to change diapers en route? Did he [or she] speak to your mother when he [or she] met her? Do you recall what they said? Was your mother surprised that he [or she] was not talking in sentences at that time?" By providing an event-related context, the examiner sometimes can obtain a fairly reliable estimate of the child's developmental history. (The examiner should note, however, that in filling out the forms, the parent failed to provide a similar event-related context for reconstructing the child's history. Similarly, the child, in attempting to learn or to recall, may fail to actively construct [reconstruct] contexts as metamemory aids.) When efforts to reconstruct developmental milestones fail, however, it is reasonable to assume that the child's development had been fairly normal: had it been unusually deviant, either very fast or very slow, it would not likely have been forgotten.

Rarely, but occasionally, one encounters parents who willfully withhold this sort of developmental information because they feel it will have a negative impact on assessment of the child. This is especially common when a school or district board demands an evaluation for the purpose of removing the child from a regular school or classroom. Usually there is nothing else the examiner can do to elicit the information once he or she has tried to impress upon the parent(s) how important the information is for arriving at an effective diagnosis of the child and, in the broader view, to our understanding of these developmental problems.

In any event, however complete or incomplete the information on the developmental history forms, the examiner will require further clarification and amplification. The object of collecting all this information is to determine whether or not there is a constitutional component to the child's learning or attentional problem. This does not imply an either-or situation, however; the fact that a child clearly had previous problems suggesting constitutional factors does not rule out improper or inadequate care or upbringing as contributing factors. Rather, the amount of structure and the consistency of discipline in the child's home interact with his or her constitutional endowment to produce the syndrome, particularly with ADD. Similarly, a child with a constitutional predisposition to learning problems probably will be even more affected by a stressful home situation than a child without such a predisposition. Just as diabetes, ulcers, and other physical problems are known to be exacerbated by stress so, too, is the capacity to learn. Children with learning problems are more dependent than others upon help from parents willing and able to provide it. The developmental history forms, rating scales, and interviews help us put together a total picture of the situation in which the child is developing, the parent's attitudes toward the child, and the nature of the help the child will need in order to function more adequately. Help may have to come in the form of altering the parent's view of the child and making suggestions for establishing an environment conducive to more productive learning.

REASONS FOR SEEKING A DIAGNOSIS

The first area covered in the interview is the parent's reason for obtaining the diagnosis. This is particularly important when the parent has sought the diagnosis for his or her own information or when the diagnosis is being sought against the parent's own wishes. Conflicts between parents ("He [or she] was dead set against my having this done"), between parent(s) and the child's therapist ("His [or her] psychiatrist keeps telling me the problem is emotional, but I don't believe it anymore"), between parent(s) and pediatrician ("The doctor says he's [or she's] slow but will outgrow it"), or between parent(s) and school ("They say he [or she] has trouble learning, but he [or she] is smart as a whip at home"). All of these conflicts over the issue of having the diagnosis done are possible areas of tension and stress in which the child is trying to function. Fortunately, only the very rare (but unforgettable) parent seems to loathe his or her own child and makes statements like "I don't know why they want this evaluation; he's just an idiot and has always been." Also rare, but to be reckoned with, are parents who clearly have unrealistic or even foolish reasons for wanting assessments: they want to know whether their child is as bright as a neighbor's child who has been put into a class for the "intellectually gifted," or they want their child advanced a year in school. One mother wanted to know whether her son was brain damaged because he was taken out of the "intellectually gifted" group. Often the answers to these questions are less important than the fact that their children have to live with these parental pressures to perform. A "diagnosis" in these instances may include referring the parent(s) for counseling. From time to time, one of these seemingly inane excuses for a diagnostic workup masks a real (and sometimes justified) concern that something is wrong with the child, a concern which emerges during the interview or in consultation after the results have been evaluated.

Occasionally, the "real" reason for referral will lead directly to the parent's concerns about a hereditary "flaw": whether the illiteracy of an aunt, the retardation of a cousin, or the aberrant behavior patterns of a grandparent may be part of a child's immutable legacy. Whether or not this is the reason given for seeking a diagnosis, the interview provides the opportunity to determine how relevant the indications are for a genetic component to the child's problems (pages 110–11). When the parent indicates that a blood relative also had problems in school, the examiner should inquire about the distance of the relationship, what the problems were, and so on. There is no question that some parents tend to magnify these possible genetic connections (particularly when they occur "on the other side" of the family) and some parents tend to minimize or deny them. Therefore, the examiner needs to explore these questions in order to give the information the appropriate weight and perspective.

AMPLIFYING THE MEDICAL HISTORY

Almost all children hit their heads at one time or another during childhood, but they rarely experience adverse consequences as a result. Periods of unconsciousness or convulsions following a blow to the head often suggest trauma, so it is important to establish the length of any such periods, the number of seizure episodes, and the use of anticonvulsants. It is also important to establish how the accident occurred and whether the parent was negligent, for this may indicate a pattern of poor judgment and/or inattention to the child. Alternatively, the head injury may have resulted from the child's own restlessness and recklessness, which points to a possibly premorbid ADD and/or hyperactivity. In this case, the history antedating the accident is pertinent. If the child has a history of ear infections with fluid in the ears at varying times, the examiner should try to establish whether the child also experienced associated periods of deafness. If hearing problems occurred during critical times of language acquisition, then there may have been some damage to the developing functional system. Research suggests a positive relationship between dyslexia and the incidence of ear infections, and although the negative evidence (incidence of temporary deafness due to ear infections in normal readers) has never been adequately evaluated, it is important to track down the severity of the complaint, frequency, the age of the child when the ear infections occurred, and the type, if any, of language delay. For example, a fourteen-year-old girl who had required a mastoid operation following a left-ear infection at age five appeared to have some invasion of the left hemisphere. Until a diagnostician found subtle language difficulties and established poor processing of incoming auditory information (with dichotic listening procedures), the early medical history and subsequent problems with written language were never related. Instead, the girl had suffered the usual accusations of laziness and poor motivation.

CLARIFYING BEHAVIORAL PATTERNS

Information on the child's behavioral development is the most difficult to obtain during interview with the parent(s), primarily because different parents have different thresholds of tolerance overall and often different expectations for boys than for girls. For example, within the same family, hyperactivity will be better tolerated, and even excused, in boys. Birth order in the family may also make a difference. Thus, a boy following one or two girls into a family may seem hyperactive in contrast. The examiner needs to establish some more objective standards during the interview by asking questions about "short attention span," "temper outbursts," and "poor self-control" (page 109). If the parent(s) indicates that the child does not listen when spoken to or does not follow directions as well as others, then the examiner must determine whether the child simply fails to comprehend what is being said (pages 107–9). For example, when asked to put the bread and butter on the table after putting the milk back into the refrigerator and feeding the cat, a child who can process only part of that multiple command may appear to be inattentive even though, in fact, he or she has not understood the entire set of instructions. Instructions often have to be repeated to these children, not because they are not listening, but because they are not processing all of the information. Of course, this deficiency can be ascertained in testing, but it is useful to pin down when and how often the inattentiveness occurs. Asking the parent(s) to compare the patient with siblings or other children (cousins or neighbors, for example) or to estimate the frequency of occurrence and the situations in which the inattentive behaviors occur may clarify the behavioral evaluation and, incidentally, the parent's feelings about the child and his or her problem. A parent can be at wit's end and sympathetic over the behavior of a child, or a parent can be at wit's end and hostile. A parent may also be more concerned about his or her own problems than over the child's aberrant development. These varying parental attitudes provide incidental clues to the child's home environment.

The parent's knowledge of the child provides another glimpse of his or her objectivity and feelings toward the child. The developmental history form asks the parent(s) to rate the child's overall level of intelligence as well as school performance (page 107). The degree to which these ratings conform to the facts is important; during the interview, the examiner should try to determine the basis for the parent's rating. (It is at this point, incidentally, that we sometimes learn of previous assessment[s] earlier denied.) The parent(s) who overestimates the child's intelligence is often trying to avoid the real problem and/or pushing the child to perform at levels beyond his or her capacity. Parents also sometimes underestimate the child's scholastic achievement, while overestimating the child's intelligence. It is as if the parent(s) are expressing the hope that the child is stubbornly refusing to live up to an imagined greater potential. The parent(s) who overestimates both intelligence and achievement may simply lack objectivity or any real insight into the child's problems. When intelligence is underestimated, the parent(s) may be comparing the child to brighter siblings or expressing anger and hostility toward the child. If the child is in fact below average in academic achievement, the parent(s) may simply be accepting school performance as an indicator of the child's intelligence. In any case, it is important that the examiner try to determine the basis for parental judgments.

EVALUATING SOCIAL SKILLS

The child's socialization is to some extent circumscribed by the parent's mobility, preferences, and own social interactions. For example, the child whose mother shuns the neighborhood playground, has no friends of her own, and makes no after-school dates for him or her, is less likely to have a flourishing social life than the child whose mother actively seeks appropriate friends. Therefore, the examiner needs to establish not only whether or not the child has friends (page 108) but also the parent's attitudes toward other children in the school and in the neighborhood and the level of effort the parent(s) makes to foster social relationships for the child. It is only when the parent(s) has failed in a sincere effort to have the children socialize and when the child's developmental history indicates a lack of desire for bonding to others that a congenital or acquired avoidance of socialization is implicated.

The failure to develop social *skills* in the presence of a desire for and availability of social contacts is a learning problem and must be distinguished from disinterest in socialization. As noted in chapter 3, children with ADD, with or without hyperactivity, often have difficulties with socialization because of their low frustration thresholds, poor goal orientation, or lack of rule observance at play. Therefore, the examiner should explore the basis for social failure as completely as possible during the interview, at least to determine the parent's view of the child's problem. Sometimes a child clearly lacks interest in socialization or any social skill, but his or her parent(s) nonetheless perceives the problem as the result of unjustified persecution: "This kid in her class just turned all the others against her." The parent's lack of social perception, especially when the pattern of social rejection has been recurrent, is in itself informative. The parent's paranoia about the child appears to be defensive, a means of coping with an unacceptable, unpleasant reality.

PARENTAL OBJECTIVITY

Some parents complete the developmental history forms and rating scales with such thoroughness and consistency that there is only minimal need for additional information or clarification. Many parents know their children and their problems extremely well and with great objectivity. In these cases, the diagnosis may become a statistically categorized, detailed confirmation of the parent's initial complaint, which does not necessarily make it less important or necessary. In such cases, the interview with the parent(s) may lay the groundwork for future consultation on means to overcome or at least ameliorate the child's problems.

Do parents who see their children with painful clarity love them less than do those who see their children in a kinder light? Although research is lacking on this issue, based on clinical experience with a great many parents and children, I have found no such relationship. Recognizing a child's limitations or difficulties does not necessarily diminish the parent's emotional response to that child. Perhaps the parent who sees his or her child with the greatest clarity is the one who has tried to help and, therefore, has experienced the child's problem firsthand. Ignoring or rationalizing the child's problems is not necessarily evidence of greater love but may, in fact, be the reaction of a parent who refuses to love an imperfect projection of himself or herself. ("He is my child, why can't he be like me? I was such a gifted student.") Parental love takes many wonderful and varied forms, and it is not diminished by the cold light of objectivity. For this reason, a diagnostic service should be open to referrals by parents themselves and should make information about their children freely available to them. Reports to parents, however, should be written somewhat differently (though not less objectively) than reports to professionals.

DETERMINING FREE-TIME ACTIVITIES

The ways children spend their free time may also place limitations on opportunities for socialization. The child who is taken from one after-school activity to another—gymnastics, swimming, choir practice, ballet, or art lessons—will not have the time for the ordinary give-and-take of play in such highly constrained, adult-guided activities. The examiner needs to determine whether the child's inadequate peer relationships drove the parent(s) to involve the child in a multitude of extracurricular activities or whether the child selected these activities independently. When different activities are scheduled almost every day but fail to add up to a coherent pattern of interests, we can be fairly certain that the parent(s) is substituting these activities for children to play with and is distressed about the child's lack of social skill. Alternatively, the persistent pursuit of "interests" may be the parent's way of trying to find something special at which the child can excel. The examiner can clarify these issues by studying the parent's answers to questions about the child's interests, observing the child's attitude in the interview, and comparing the parent's and the child's views about these outside interests—they are not always the same.

The parent(s) who insists that the child has no time for homework or essential tutoring because of a fascination with games like "Dungeons and Dragons" is conspiratorially committed to avoiding the real issue of the child's learning and/or attentional problems. One mother argued that the game gave free reign to her son's imagination and ultimately would be more important to his development than "playing stickball with the boys" or "completing his asinine assignments." In such instances, the child's main hobbies and interests can be a destructive force, especially if the parent(s) believes that they somehow bestow a stature and distinction that the child seems unable to attain at school. On the other hand, a genuine talent or interest is extremely important to the learning-disabled child, both for future vocational planning and for self-esteem.

It is, therefore, extremely important to nurture special abilities in learning-disabled children. The examiner should make a point of inquiring whether these avenues of possible accomplishment have been investigated. Some dyslexic children, whose handwriting and copying of forms are often very poor, have a talent for drawing pictures, as in the case of a seventeen-year-old dyslexic from a disadvantaged, bilingual community who had dropped out of school. His artistic ability was discovered during a diagnostic workup; as a result, he was referred to and obtained a scholarship for a school of applied arts. He learned to read in his sign-painting class. The important issue with free-time activities is whether the child's interest is genuine: Does the child have some special skill or interest in this activity? Does it provide a healthy outlet and positive counterweight to poor academic achievement? If the child is consumed by this special interest, then this passion may explain the child's apparent inattentiveness at home and at school. Since tests are unlikely to reveal these special skills or interests, the examiner should try to achieve some perspective on their importance to the child, at present and in the future. Cases of total absorption with special interests are extremely rare; unfortunately, parents' most frequent response to the question of what their children enjoy doing most is "watching TV."

Even when watching TV is the child's favorite activity, it is important to determine the amount of time spent in front of the TV and the types of programs the child watches. The child who is allowed to watch as much TV as late as he or she wishes may be incapable of concentrating at school the next day because of sleepiness and the anxiety impact of programs unsuited to the child's age and level of maturity. The child who will watch anything on TV is quite different from the child who loves to watch TV newscasts and cultural programs. The latter child may experience TV as a vital source of information and not as a pacifier. Therefore, until the examiner can make this qualitative distinction, "watching TV" is not necessarily a negative activity.

CONCLUDING THE INTERVIEW

The examiner generally concludes interviews by asking parents if they would like to add anything that has not already been covered; occasionally, further questions will follow. Additional information often centers on intrafamilial conflicts: the effect they may be having on the child and whether or not they are not the central cause of the child's difficulties. This type of question is impossible to answer until the testing has been completed, but the examiner should bear in mind that if such conflicts are mentioned, then the child probably has a stressful home situation. Accounts of this type are more prevalent among divorced or separated parents who believe that visits to the "other" parent are somehow destructive. "He just buys him all the candy and toys he wants and lets him get away without doing his homework, so I'm always the bad one" is a typical remark. Usually, there is nothing the examiner can do about these life situations except to be reassuring and sympathetic and, possibly, to suggest counseling. One mother suspected that her daughter always displayed more hyperactive behavior after having dinner at her in-laws'. Subsequent medical tests proved that the child was allergic to tomatoes.

Thus, the problem was not that everyone at dinner "spoiled" the child but, rather, that dinner invariably included pasta with a tomato sauce, and the child's allergic reaction triggered her hyperactivity. The problem was alleviated by changing the menu rather than declining invitations.

Interviewing the Child

The entire time spent with the child is, in a sense, an interview since the child's responses to questions often contain information beyond what is asked, though children differ in this regard. Some tend to be monosyllabic and rather reticent with information, while others find something personal to add at every opportunity. It is difficult to keep some children focused on the task at hand; they prefer to use the time to talk about friends, siblings, and outings. Obviously, the child who volunteers little or no information requires more direct questions; further, this is more likely to be necessary, the older the child. While questions must be geared to the child's age, the information covered in the interview is, to some extent, the same as for the parent(s). The examiner must ascertain the child's views of the problem, school, friends, sports, after-school activities, and special skills or interests; however, the child's developmental history is not covered in the interview unless the child brings it up. A learning-disabled ten-year-old once told the clinician, "I have an uncle who never made it through school, and my mother says I'm just like him." Here the unfortunate effect of the mother's statement on the child's self-image and motivation is more important than the possible genetic "at risk" factor. In this type of situation, it is best to assure the child that inheritance of complex characteristics is not proven, automatic, or inevitable. The interview serves not only to get the child's view of the problem but also to establish rapport, to put the child at ease, and to gain some insight into his or her style, poise, humor, and social skill.

SCHOOL-RELATED QUESTIONS

The examiner should try to set a friendly, relaxed tone for the child before testing has begun; therefore, he or she should avoid questions or issues that may set the child on edge. Various lines of questioning can be pursued, if possible, during breaks in the testing or at the end of the day. After arithmetic testing, for example, one may ask, "Is this your favorite subject in school?" or "Have you started work on fractions in school?" The examiner should try to cover the various areas originally outlined by the end of the day. Does the child know why he or she is being tested (or, for younger children, playing these games) here today? This type of question may shed some light on the child's awareness of his or her own problem, though it is a question *never* asked of children with known brain damage, head trauma, or psychiatric disorders. If the child with a learning problem simply states that he or she has trouble in school, then the examiner should ask about the nature of that trouble and explore the child's attitudes about school—the teachers, the subject matter, the other children. If the child simply responds with "Okay," "All right," "Pretty good," or something similarly evasive or uninformative, the examiner should try to get specific examples: "Who's your favorite teacher?" "Why?" "Which one do you dislike the most?" "What subject do you like best?" "Why?" "What was the worst time you ever had in school?" "Who is your best friend in school?" If these more specific questions fail to elicit information, the examiner could try talking about an unhappy incident in his or her own school experience and then ask the child whether anything like that ever happened to him or her. If the child just answers no despite all this effort, then it is best to go on to other areas; obviously, the child does not want to talk about school or the problems there.

If, according to the parent(s) or another source, the child has attentional difficulties, the examiner shouldn't ask whether he or she has a short attention span or is impulsive but, rather, should explore his or her awareness of any difficulty in keeping track of what is going on: "Do you get the homework assignments from one of the other kids?" "Do you get bored listening to your teacher explaining things?" "Does your mind wander a lot to other things?" "Do you have trouble copying from the blackboard?" If the answer to all these questions is a noncommittal "Sometimes," then the line of inquiry is not worth pursuing.

Developmental History and Evaluation

Probably the most important areas to explore are those that the child is most likely to be willing to discuss—after-school activities, sports, friends, hobbies, and other special interests. The child's responses should help fill out the picture of what goes on in the child's life outside of a failure to live up to expectations at school. They also should reveal the extent to which the child's views confirm or conflict with the parent's views. Differences between the child's and the parent's reports are important and require further exploration, though without indicating to the child that the parent(s) said something different. Sometimes, for example, a child will ask about the parent's responses: "Did my mother tell you I just loved those darned swimming lessons?" It is better to avoid the obvious conflict and ask a tangential question, such as, "Don't you like swimming?" This type of question usually will evoke a response from the child's view without mentioning what the mother said or whether, indeed, she said anything at all. If the child insists upon airing a conflict with his or her parent(s) before testing, it is best to defer the topic, saying, "Let's talk about this later; we should get on with this." Since the interview with the parent(s) is usually scheduled later in the day, the examiner generally can quite honestly tell the child that he or she hasn't spoken to the parent(s) yet and request that the child talk about this particular problem later. If the child insists on relating the story immediately, the examiner should listen as dispassionately as possible but should calmly try to change the subject. It is important here to reduce test anxiety with an interview and not to air topics that may be anxiety-provoking.

If the child's life outside of school is also fraught with defeat, then it may be advisable to abandon further questioning until the end of the day. The child who sees himself or herself as a "loser" on all counts—failing at school, at play, and at sports, and lacking friends and particular outside interests—provides a much grimmer picture than the child whose learning problem is a relatively isolated one. The prognosis for the former child is poorer, and this child may, in fact, suffer from depression. For the child who says almost nothing in response to questions or who appears to require a more indirect approach, a sentence-completion test may be used to elicit information or attitudes where direct questions fail (Forer 1967). Even if the child has no problem with reading, I have found it preferable to administer the sentence-completion test orally. This method seems to provoke more spontaneous, less inhibited responses and, incidentally, doesn't limit the child's responses to words he or she can spell. These responses may then form the basis for more direct questions.

EVALUATING THE CHILD'S ABILITIES

In evaluating the child's responses, the examiner should bear in mind not only what the child says but also how he or she says it. The examiner needs to be attuned to any problems with expressive language—not only on tests but also in conversation. Similarly, the examiner should note whether questions have to be repeated, explained, or simplified. Occasionally, during the interview, "naming" problems appear in children with disorders of written language. Children who declare that their favorite activity is watching TV, for example, are often unable to name a single specific show they watch: "I watch cartoons" is a typical response but, on questioning, not a single name emerges except for the ubiquitous "Sesame Street." One ten-year-old boy spoke proudly of his violin lessons but was unable to name a single composer or composition he was learning or had learned. He described the piece he was currently studying as having "two of those number sign things," by which one assumes he meant sharps. The child's ability to maintain syntax in sentences also contributes to the examiner's final assessment.

Conclusions

Whether employing direct questions or completed tests to get a picture of the child's life and adjustment, we should never lose sight of the fact that language is the medium we use. The parent's skill with language plays an important role in the evaluation and is as much at issue as the child's. Without being patronizing, the examiner gears interview questions to the parent's educational level, just as questions directed to the child are geared to his or her age. After all, the purpose of the evaluation process—the forms, the questionnaires, and the interviews—is to create a coherent portrait of the child. This cannot be achieved with responses to test questions or test scores alone. The consistency with which that picture emerges is critical, for if it remains unfocused, some vital information is lacking. It is impossible to tell what that missing piece in the jigsaw of diagnosis might be without the life history, a sense of the child's environment, parental attitudes, and the stresses and constraints under which the child is obliged to function.

DEVELOPMENTAL HISTORY FORM*

Child's name _____ Birth date _____ Age ____ Sex ____
                last   first
Home address _____
                    street   city   state   zip
Home telephone number _____
                            area code   number
Child's school _____
                    name   address

Present placement of child (place check in appropriate bracket):

	Column A Adults with whom child is living	Column B Non-residential adults involved with child
Natural mother	( ) ____	( ) ____
Natural father	( ) ____	( ) ____
Stepmother	( ) ____	( ) ____
Stepfather	( ) ____	( ) ____
Adoptive mother	( ) ____	( ) ____
Adoptive father	( ) ____	( ) ____
Foster mother	( ) ____	( ) ____
Foster father	( ) ____	( ) ____
Other (specify)	_____	_____

Place the number 1 or 2 next to each check in Column A and provide the following information about each person:

1. Name _____   Occupation _____
            last   first
    Business name _____   Business address _____

    _____   Business tel. No. _( )_____

---

* Reproduced with the permission of the author and publisher from: Gardner, R. A., *The Psychotherapeutic Techniques of Richard A. Gardner*, Cresskill, New Jersey: Creative Therapeutics, 1986.

2. Name _____   Occupation _____
           last   first

     Business name _____   Business address _____

     _____   Business tel. No. __( )_____

Place the number 3 next to the person checked in Column B who is most involved with the child and provide the following information:

3. Name _____   Home address _____
                                                         street

     _____   Home tel. No. __( )_____

     Occupation _____   Business name _____

     Business address _____   Bus. tel. No. __( )_____

     Source of referral: Name _____   Address _____

     _____   Tel. No. __( )_____

Purpose of consultation (brief summary of the main problems): _____

_____

_____

_____

_____

PREGNANCY

     Complications:

         Excessive vomiting _____ hospitalization required _____

         Excessive staining or blood loss _____

         Threatened miscarriage _____

         Infection(s)   (specify) _____

         Toxemia _____

         Operation(s)   (specify) _____

         Other illness(es)   (specify) _____

     Smoking during pregnancy _____ average number of cigarettes per day _____

     Alcoholic consumption during pregnancy _____ describe, if beyond an occa-

         sional drink _____

     Medications taken during pregnancy _____

     X-ray studies during pregnancy _____

     Duration _____ weeks

Developmental History and Evaluation

DELIVERY

Type of labor: Spontaneous _____ Induced _____

Forceps: high _____ mid _____ low _____

Duration of labor _____ hours

Type of delivery: Vertex (normal) _____ breech _____ Caesarean _____

Complications:

cord around neck _____

cord presented first _____

hemorrhage _____

infant injured during delivery _____

other (specify) _____

Birth Weight _____

Appropriate for gestational age (AGA) _____

Small for gestational age (SGA) _____

POST-DELIVERY PERIOD (while in the hospital)

Respiration: immediate _____ delayed (if so, how long) _____

Cry: immediate _____ delayed (if so, how long) _____

Mucus accumulation _____

Apgar score (if known) _____

Jaundice _____

RH factor _____ transfusion _____

Cyanosis (turned blue) _____

Incubator care _____ number of days _____

Suck: strong _____ weak _____

Infection (specify) _____

Vomiting _____ diarrhea _____

Birth defects (specify) _____

Total number of days baby was in the hospital after the delivery _____

INFANCY-TODDLER PERIOD

Were any of the following present—to a significant degree—during the first few years of life? If so, describe.

Did not enjoy cuddling _____

Was not calmed by being held and/or stroked _____

Colic _____

Excessive restlessness _____

Diminished sleep because of restlessness and easy arousal _____

Frequent headbanging _____

Constantly into everything _____

Excessive number of accidents compared to other children _____

DEVELOPMENTAL MILESTONES

If you can recall, record the age at which your child reached the following developmental milestones. If you cannot recall, check item at right.

	age	early	I cannot recall exactly, but to the best of my recollection it occurred at the normal time	late
Smiled				
Sat without support				
Crawled				
Stood without support				
Walked without assistance				
Spoke first words besides "ma-ma" and "da-da"				
Said phrases				
Said sentences				
Bowel trained, day				
Bowel trained, night				
Bladder trained, day				
Bladder trained, night				
Rode tricycle				
Rode bicycle (without training wheels)				
Buttoned clothing				
Tied shoelaces				
Named colors				
Named coins				

Developmental History and Evaluation

Said alphabet in order _____

Began to read _____

COORDINATION

Rate your child on the following skills:

	Good	Average	Poor
Walking			
Running			
Throwing			
Catching			
Shoelace tying			
Buttoning			
Writing			
Athletic abilities			

COMPREHENSION AND UNDERSTANDING

Do you consider your child to understand directions and situations as well as other children his or her age? _____ If not, why not? _____

_____

How would you rate your child's overall level of intelligence compared to other children?   Below average _____ Average _____ Above average _____

SCHOOL

Rate your child's school experiences related to *academic learning*:

	Good	Average	Poor
Nursery school			
Kindergarten			
Current grade			

To the best of your knowledge, at what grade level is your child functioning:

reading _____ spelling _____ arithmetic _____

Has your child ever had to repeat a grade? If so, when _____

Present class placement: regular class _____ special class (if so, specify)

_____

Kinds of special therapy or remedial work your child is currently receiving

_____

Describe briefly any academic school problems _____

_____

_____

Rate your child's school experience related to *behavior*:

	Good	Average	Poor
Nursery school			
Kindergarten			
Current grade			

Does your child's teacher describe any of the following as significant classroom problems?

Doesn't sit still in his or her seat _____

Frequently gets up and walks around the classroom _____

Shouts out. Doesn't wait to be called upon _____

Won't wait his or her turn _____

Does not cooperate well in group activities _____

Typically does better in a one-to-one relationship _____

Doesn't respect the rights of others _____

Doesn't pay attention during storytelling _____

Describe briefly any other classroom behavioral problems _____

_____

_____

PEER RELATIONSHIPS

Does your child seek friendships with peers? _____

Is your child sought by peers for friendship? _____

Does your child play primarily with children his or her own age? _____

younger _____ older _____

Describe briefly any problems your child may have with peers _____

_____

_____

Developmental History and Evaluation

HOME BEHAVIOR

All children exhibit, to some degree, the kinds of behavior listed below. Check those that you believe your child exhibits to an excessive or exaggerated degree when compared to other children his or her age.

Hyperactivity (high activity level) _____

Poor attention span _____

Impulsivity (poor self control) _____

Low frustration threshold _____

Temper outbursts _____

Sloppy table manners _____

Interrupts frequently _____

Doesn't listen when being spoken to _____

Sudden outbursts of physical abuse of other children _____

Acts like he or she is driven by a motor _____

Wears out shoes more frequently than siblings _____

Heedless to danger _____

Excessive number of accidents _____

Doesn't learn from experience _____

Poor memory _____

More active than siblings _____

INTERESTS AND ACCOMPLISHMENTS

What are your child's main hobbies and interests? _____

_____

What are your child's areas of greatest accomplishment? _____

_____

What does your child enjoy doing most? _____

_____

What does your child dislike doing most? _____

_____

MEDICAL HISTORY

If your child's medical history includes any of the following, please note the age when the incident or illness occurred and any other pertinent information.

Childhood diseases (describe any complications) _____

_____

Operations _____

_____

Hospitalizations for illness(es) other than operations _____

_____

Head injuries _____

_____ with unconsciousness _____ without unconsciousness _____

Convulsions _____

_____ with fever _____ without fever _____

Coma _____

Meningitis or encephalitis _____

Immunization reactions _____

Persistent high fevers _____ highest temperature ever recorded _____

Eye problems _____

Ear problems _____

Poisoning _____

PRESENT MEDICAL STATUS

Present height _____ Present weight _____

Present illness(es) for which child is being treated _____

_____

Medications child is taking on an ongoing basis _____

_____

FAMILY HISTORY—MOTHER

Age _____ Age at time of pregnancy with patient _____

Number of previous pregnancies _____ Number of spontaneous abortions

(miscarriages) _____ Number of induced abortions _____

Sterility problems (specify) _____

School: Highest grade completed _____

Learning problems (specify) _____ grade repeat _____

Behavior problems (specify) _____

Developmental History and Evaluation

Medical problems (specify) _____

Have any of your blood relatives (not including patient and siblings) ever had problems

similar to those your child has? If so, describe _____

_____

_____

FAMILY HISTORY—FATHER

Age _____ Age at the time of the patient's conception _____

Sterility problems (specify) _____

School: Highest grade completed _____

Learning problems (specify) _____ grade repeat _____

Behavior problems (specify) _____

Medical problems (specify) _____

Have any of your blood relatives (not including patient and siblings) ever had problems

similar to those your child has? If so, describe _____

_____

_____

SIBLINGS

	Name	Age	Medical, social, or academic problems
1.			
2.			
3.			
4.			
5.			

LIST NAMES AND ADDRESSES OF ANY OTHER PROFESSIONALS CONSULTED

1. _____

2. _____

3. _____

4. _____

ADDITIONAL REMARKS

Please use the remainder of this page to write any additional comments you wish to make regarding your child's difficulties.

Chapter 5

The Context for Assessment

JANE M. HOLMES

The framework for developmental neuropsychological assessment as described here is a theory of brain-behavior relationships in children that
emphasizes the systemic nature of the interaction between the child and
his or her environment. This theory draws heavily on knowledge of the
developing neural substrate for behavioral competence at different ages.
The goal of the assessment process is to construct a Child-World System
that "characterizes the reciprocal relationship of the developing child
and the world in which he functions." (For a fuller discussion of this
systemic theory and its applications to evaluation, diagnosis, and management of learning disorders, see Holmes and Waber [in press].) We
emphasize *learning disorder*, rather than *learning disability*, with a neuropsychologically based learning disorder defined as "a failure to adapt
successfully to the learning environment that is best understood in the
context of a developmental neuropsychological theory" (Holmes and
Waber, in press). The wide range of potential behavioral disturbances
this involves contrasts with the more restricted use of *learning disability*,
which typically refers to disorders of symbolic representation.

The *neuro* part of the developmental neuropsychological theory described in Holmes and Waber (in press) is modeled initially in terms of three brain axes whose workings are elicited by, and modify, the environment in which they find themselves. (*Environment* should be understood in the widest sense: basic sensory inputs; the products of learning; individuals and institutions in the world; and structural and hormonal changes in the inner environment attendant on normal growth.) All observed behaviors reflect the dynamic interplay of these three axes as the individual responds to his or her world, the impact of the brain-world interaction being modified by developmental change as the individual matures.

The three neuroanatomic axes are (1) the anterior/posterior axis, involving executive and control (output) processes, as opposed to the input, or reception/processing, of information; (2) the lateral axis, involving the two hemispheric systems and their contrasting information-processing styles; and (3) the cortical/subcortical axis, involving complex feedback relationships between higher-order planning systems and the extensive subcortical systems mediating life-support, arousal, drive responses, and the regulation and execution of behavior in general. Although the anterior/posterior axis may well be the most functionally important, the lateral axis has been discussed most in both neuropsychological and popular contexts. Therefore, we will describe its contributions to behavior first.

The Lateral Axis

Of the three neuroanatomic axes, the lateral axis is most well known to the general public; its fashionableness has led to some oversimplified views of hemispheric functioning. The initial work in delineating hemispheric differentiation within the brain was done with patients who had sustained unilateral brain lesions. Early neurologists and neuropsychologists were able to describe repeated relationships between certain types of "damaged" behavior and specific types of damage to the brain. Such research resulted in models of brain action that relate given (damaged) psychological functions to a given (damaged) area of brain.

As early as the turn of the century, John Hughlings Jackson warned of the dangers of strict localization (Taylor 1931), arguing that disruption of a psychological behavior because of specific local damage does not mean that the intact behavior is either a unitary psychological function or necessarily located "in the hole." However, subsequent discussion of functional models of brain organization proceeded as though localization (strict or otherwise) were essentially the case. With the investigation of different brain lesion groups and of subjects without known brain damage, it became clear that functional models of brain-behavior relationships were limited.

A new generation of models stresses the information-processing capacities of the two hemispheric systems, arguing that they have contrasting modes of processing that make one more efficient than the other when dealing with different types of information. This results in the mobilization of the more efficient system for the type of information to be tackled. Within this type of model, the brain-behavior relationships appear to occur all things being equal; in other cases, it would appear that certain behaviors are so critical that, given a young enough animal, they can be acquired by systems other than those predicted on the "standard model."

The best example of this capability is found in the group of children studied by Maureen Dennis in Toronto (Dennis 1980; Dennis and Kohn 1975; Dennis and Whitaker 1976; Kohn and Dennis 1974). These children had either hemispherectomy or hemidecortication in connection with Sturge-Weber disease and thus function with either an isolated left hemisphere or an isolated right hemisphere. Although surgery was completed prior to the onset of language in Dr. Dennis' population, in both groups of children, both groups of children acquired language post-surgery. In spite of the well-documented relationship between left-hemisphere brain systems and the use of language in the majority of the adult population, the "isolated right hemisphere" group of children learned to communicate effectively for day-to-day functioning. It would thus appear that in the present stage of human evolutionary development, language is so important a part of "humanness" that it can, and will, be acquired by any means possible—at least when the child is young enough to find alternative brain pathways to mediate the skill.

Within the context of information-processing models of hemispheric functioning, the customary (though not necessary) aspects of brain-behavior relationships as they relate to left- and right-hemisphere brain systems can be described as follows:

FIGURE 5.1

LEFT-HEMISPHERE SYSTEMS
Preferentially involved with
  • the building blocks of language
  • parts of complex materials
  • temporally processed information

RIGHT-HEMISPHERE SYSTEMS
Preferentially involved with
  • spatially represented information
  • the relationship between parts
  • configurational aspects of
    complex materials

I emphasize the preferential involvement of left-hemisphere brain systems for the "building blocks of language," rather than with language itself, because I have witnessed many examples of differences in language behaviors that do not cluster with the usual patterns of language-processing deficits. These differences occur in behavioral clusters that, from the psychological point of view, reflect discontinuities in the organization of complex materials and, from the neurological point of view, are associated with left-sided motor findings (which argues for the relative weakness of right-hemisphere brain systems).

An example of this type of difference in language skills can be seen on the Vocabulary subtest of the *WISC-R*. This subtest taps the child's ability to demonstrate knowledge of vocabulary in response to a single word offered by the examiner. The child who offers the response "an animal" to the target word *donkey* is given full credit (two points), according to the standard scoring for the task. Similarly, the child who responds, "A donkey is a . . . , a . . . , a . . . , well, he has four legs. . . . He's a . . . , he has two long ears (with accompanying gestures) . . . er! . . . and a tail. . . . He's a . . . , ah . . . an animal!" is given full credit. The behavior in offering this information, however, is clearly very different from that of the previous child and raises the hypothesis that word-retrieval difficulties are present and are being compensated for by a circumlocutory strategy.

The third example is quite different from the others: "A donkey is an animal. He has four legs and two long ears and a long tail with a bunch on the end, and they have them in Mexico, and they carry things, and they carry things up mountains that are very heavy, but they don't fall over because they're very surefooted, and my aunt rode on a donkey when she was in Mexico, and they went over a hill, and somebody fell off, and they had to take them to the hospital . . . ," and so on. This child clearly understands what a donkey is but does not so evidently understand what the nature of the psychological task is. His or her problem is at the level of discourse relationships: the basic building blocks of language (sound segments, grammatical units, and vocabulary items) are easily available, but the ability to organize them into a cleanly focused response is not evident. Although the child's difficulty is seen in the language domain, the underlying processing problem would appear to be one of organizing the language knowledge, rather than manipulation of the language structures. This is the child who, where asymmetric performance is seen on the formal neurological examination, typically presents with left-sided motor findings, as noted above. The implication of right-hemisphere brain systems in the difficulty is entirely consistent with what we know about their role in brain-behavior relationships: they are important for appreciating relationships between parts of complex materials of all kinds and, thus, for grasping the overall organizing principle of such materials, verbal and nonverbal.

Another example of the need for great care in describing the actual behavior of a child or adult emerges through more careful consideration of the "configurational aspects of complex materials" noted under "right-hemisphere systems" in figure 5.1. The word *configurational* tends to call forth some sense of visualness (presumably related to the *figure* at the word's center). This connection may be even more seductive because right-hemisphere brain systems are thought to play a major role in visual processing. However, configurations can also occur in the auditory domain, for example, the information provided by intonational contour in normal speaking. There is no single segment or set of segments in the prosodic line of an utterance that unequivocally reflects that the speaker is mad, glad, or sad. Rather, the intonational contour of the whole utterance is what reveals the speaker's state of mind. Although intonational contours always operate over language elements in normal conversation, it is the disruption of right-hemisphere systems that interferes with the ability to process and/or produce the information carried by prosody (Ross 1985).

These examples highlight the fact that a given psychological function such as language not only can be understood in terms of psychological subfunctions (word retrieval, verbal formulation, language comprehen-

FIGURE 5.2

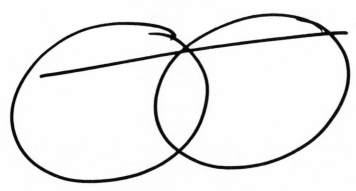

A: Left-hemisphere lesion

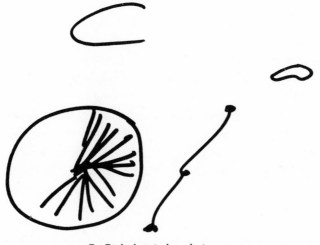

B: Right-hemisphere lesion

sion, and so forth) but also can be broken down in terms of the underlying brain-based processes that need to be mobilized to mediate the activity in question. They also serve, however, to highlight another critical feature of the model with which I approach neuropsychological assessment in general, that is, the "complementary contribution" model characterized by Edith Kaplan (1976). Kaplan demonstrated the importance of the complementary contributions of the two hemispheric processing systems in the context of visually represented materials. It has long been recognized that patients with unilateral brain lesions tend to draw anomalous figures and that patients with lesions in the different hemispheres are

117

likely to draw different types of anomalous figures. The examples above represent the types of behavioral breakdown that can be seen in the presence of a left-hemisphere or a right-hemisphere lesion. The examiner's instruction in both cases was "Draw a bicycle." In example A, one would be hard pressed to recognize "bicycleness" in a rather blobby reproduction of the overall shape. In example B, "bicycleness" is easier to recognize because of the representation of the parts that are critical to the category (wheel with spokes, pedals, handlebar, seat). Actual case examples of these types of deficits can be found in McFie and Zangwill (1960) and Warrington, James, and Kinsbourne (1960). Kaplan's interpretation of these types of data emphasized the role of the individual doing the drawing, rather than the lesion; for example, she realized that the atypical behavior was not a product of a left-hemisphere lesion but of an individual with a damaged left hemisphere and an intact right hemisphere—or vice versa. Thus, example A, which appears in the presence of left-hemisphere damage, can be seen as the product of the *intact* right-hemisphere systems doing their best in the absence of their mates, whereas example B can be seen as the product of the intact left-hemisphere systems doing their best without the appropriate input from the other side. Intact right-hemisphere systems contribute a sense of the overall configuration of the material, and intact left-hemisphere systems contribute a sense of the individual, categorizable parts. Thus, Kaplan has demonstrated that complementarity of functioning is a critical variable in normal brain performance. Presumably, we need two working hemispheres to produce any normal ongoing behavior.

The complementary contribution model is not the only important notion to come from Kaplan: she has also changed our working model of brain-behavior relationships from one based on *pathology* to one based on *intactness*; that is, what we see in behavior can be attributed not only to the disruption of normally cooperating systems but also to the intact contribution of specific brain systems lacking their usual cooperative counterparts. This shift from pathology to intactness is very valuable for clinicians working with children in whom actual brain damage is neither known nor necessarily to be assumed. The complementary contribution model allows clinicians to explore cognitive functioning in terms of the relative balance of skills involved in mediating a given behavior. As we shall see, differential input from critical brain systems—*intra*-individual differences in overall ability—appears to be the hallmark of the risk for learning problems and is independent of the absolute level of cognitive ability overall.

Clear recognition of both the potential role of multiple brain systems in mediating a given psychological function and complementarity of that input is very important for educators. It is crucial to retain a separate understanding of the information-processing differences of the hemispheric systems and the information-processing models used in pedagogy with respect to learning-disabled children. The possibility for confusing the two is very strong, however, if hemispheric differences are conceptualized as simply "auditory" and "visual"—the typical basis for pedagogical models of information-processing differences. Although neuropsychologists recognize that the hemispheric dichotomy cannot be simply superimposed on an auditory-visual dimension, this is not the case for many educators. Thus, a variety of children with known hemispheric dysfunction have been educated solely within the "classic" learning-disabilities model based on information-processing differences—under the assumption that, given, for example, a right-hemisphere insult, the child will learn better in an auditorially based program, the undamaged left hemisphere being best addressed by means of the auditory modality. Unfortunately, within such a context, a child with significant right-hemisphere dysfunction may have just as much difficulty in dealing with configurations in the auditory as in the visual domain, a difficulty that is unlikely to be addressed within the psychologically based information-processing model.

A second problem we see in this population of children is an apparent confounding of lateralized neuropsychological deficit with a specific learning disability: "The right hemisphere is visual; therefore, the child with the right-hemisphere dysfunction will have a visual learning problem." Unfortunately, such a (false) syllogism may obscure the fact that the child's primary diagnosis should be "neurological impairment" and that other aspects of the neurological condition may render a strictly learning-disabilities model of remedial education insufficient to deal with the full range of a given child's behavioral needs. One child, whose parent was desperate for him to be categorized as "learning disabled," suffered neurological damage that included not only the effects of a right-hemisphere stroke but also major motor control and visual problems following an extensive period of coma. Specific recognition of the motor difficulty and the visual problems were not initially part of the child's overall remedial program; everyone had focused on the "right-hemisphere deficit" within the learning disability construct.

Before discussing the other two axes of the brain within our assessment model, it is important to emphasize that the complementary contributions of the two hemispheric systems (in terms of what can be loosely called their "information-processing capacities" with respect to complex materials of all types) are not the only roles they play in behavioral output. Left- and right-hemisphere systems have direct control of their contralateral motor systems, of the contralateral space, both on the body and in the world. The pediatric motor examination is used to demonstrate motor-system asymmetries in children referred for learning problems. Findings from the motor examination have proved especially valuable in supporting hypotheses based on other aspects of behavior with respect to the brain systems contributing less efficiently to overall behavior. There is, of course, essentially nothing that a psychometrically based model can do with lateralized findings on motor examination or asymmetries of body use in the course of standardized tests. Since such asymmetries are not part of the psychometric model, they have not been described within psychological assessments (at least, not in nonmedical contexts). However, once the value of the neuropsychologically based model for assessment is recognized, such asymmetries will become important behavioral markers for the clinician. Indeed, a striking number of children demonstrate systematic differences in the use of their bodies or the side of space in which they work, apparently unrecognized prior to the neuropsychological assessment.

Differences in the use of space that can be attributed to differential hemispheric input also can be seen with complex materials of different types. The following examples using the *Rey-Osterrieth Complex Figure* (*ROCF*—Osterrieth 1944; Rey 1941) show differences in the representation of the two sides of a complex design, as well as in the placement of the design on a page. Figure 5.3 illustrates the figure. Figure 5.4 is the copy of the *ROCF* drawn by a twenty-one-year-old man with average cognitive ability. The stimulus card was in full view at all times; the figure was completed in free field. The patient proceeded through the design in the left-to-right, top-to-bottom fashion characteristic of the mature adult. The left side of the design is notably distorted as compared to the right, which is essentially perfect. Yet the young man was satisfied with his product. He proved to have a small calcified lesion, about the

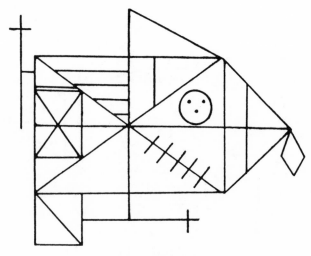

FIGURE 5.3

size of the tip of one's little finger, located near the midline in the right-central area.

Figure 5.5 was drawn by a male aged nine years, three months, with left hemiparesis, right-sided slowing on EEG, and decreased density in the right anterior capsular area. His overall cognitive ability was within

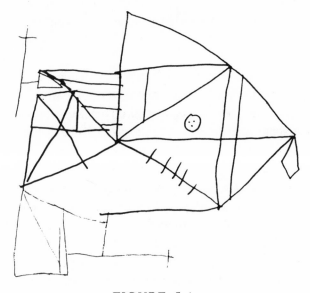

FIGURE 5.4

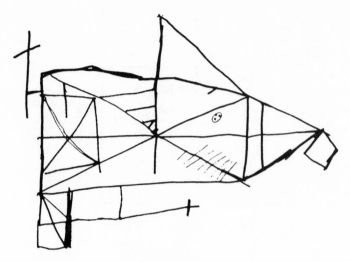

FIGURE 5.5

the normal range. The patient proceeded from left to right through the design, failing to attend to the left side of space in his organization of the overall figure on the page and "crowding" the right side of his figure into the remaining space, necessitating a new piece of paper and tape.

The Anterior/Posterior Axis

The importance of the anterior/posterior axis cannot be overestimated in the study of children. Frontal brain systems in particular are crucial to our understanding of developmental change: in adults, we take for granted the ability to express the knowledge mediated by the hemispheric brain systems; in children, however, the appreciation of incoming information and the ability to demonstrate knowledge in a useful form depend heavily on maturational competence. Thus, those brain systems heavily involved in the input and output of information are the focus of developmental neuropsychologists' interest.

The back of the brain can be considered its "storehouse of knowledge," or lexicon. Posterior brain systems are mainly involved in receiving, encoding, and storing information. Primary receiving areas route their information to the complex interactive systems of the association areas of the brain. Once appreciated, evaluated, and integrated, useful knowledge can be stored in memory. In contrast, frontal brain systems are involved in the selection, control, modulation, and general fine-tuning of ongoing behavioral responses of all types, and are crucial for independent action and goal-directed planning. They are engaged to deal with novel situations that require immediate high-level analysis and response. Indeed, when situations become routine, frontal brain systems appear to relinquish their primary control to more automatic subroutines mediated by other brain systems (see Mazziotta and Phelps 1986). Our ability to anticipate, select, plan, and monitor actions integrating the inputs from functional systems elsewhere in the brain depends on frontal systems, which are also critically involved in self-awareness (Stuss and Benson 1986). It is useful to think of these systems as the interface between what we know and how we use that knowledge in the real world: they guide our behavior, observe its impact, and relate changes in the behavioral domain back to the internal knowledge systems for further evaluation, appreciation, and association with other information already available. (It is important to note that the frontal systems are also part of the internal evaluators, appreciators, and integrators of information.)

In trying to understand the nature of frontal system functioning, a computer metaphor is useful in characterizing one aspect thereof, which is rather difficult to capture in clinical assessment or in the laboratory but is immediately recognizable by another competent human animal, notably the "on-line" capacity of the brain. By this I mean the ability to make a decision, then another based on that decision, then another based on the two previous ones and the sum of their parts, and then another based on that plus new information, and so on. This ongoing decision-making capacity is a large part of what is considered to be basic judgment in everyday situations. The intact individual takes this capability for granted; however, it is highly sensitive to damage to the brain, and its loss can be totally devastating.

The issue of on-line competence emerges in the context of late adolescents/young adults who have been injured in motor vehicle accidents. These patients are typically a problem for psychologists, because behavioral differences that are clearly apparent in ongoing interaction with other people can be difficult to document in formal tests. In these cases, formalizing the clinician's observations of the patient can make a major contribution, going well beyond quantification of behavior by test procedures. In many ways, the problem lies in the nature of testing itself. Often, the psychological testing situation itself provides maximal support for frontal system functioning, inasmuch as it is undertaken in a highly structured setting with minimal distraction, with maximal interindividual support, using highly focused questions or problems. Hence, a brain-damaged individual's competency in the testing situation may be totally irrelevant to his or her real-life capabilities. Typically, individuals who have sustained major brain damage (particularly of the acceleration-deceleration type) return to essentially their premorbid functioning on tests like the *Wechsler Intelligence Scales* and the *Wechsler Memory Scale* even when family, friends, and the psychological examiner recognize that the individual is "not quite right." Neuropsychologists working with brain-damaged patients have addressed this problem by developing specific tasks that are sensitive to frontal system functioning (Stuss and Benson 1986).

The "complementary contributions" described above for the lateral axis are also important in the interaction of the front of the brain with the back; no part of the brain ever really operates alone. Nor does the brain itself function as an independent unit, but is in a complementary relationship with the outside world. As noted above, frontal systems are the interface between learned knowledge and its application. This interactional principle goes one step further, however: without a world to function in or interact with, the brain does not develop normally. The specificity of response of visual cells initially described by Hubel and Wiesel (1962) in their Nobel Prize–winning work requires specific input from the external world within a certain time frame (the sensitive period). For these cells to commit themselves as specific feature detectors, however, they need concurrent correlated input from an animal's movement (Held and Hein 1963). Apparently the animal needs to "know" it is interacting with the environment for connections within the brain to be made.

If the relevant experience is not obtained within the appropriate time frame, those cells that would otherwise have responded to, say, vertical alignments are likely to simply die or be subverted to other functions in the competition for neuronal connectivity that is part of normal neural development in the young animal (Rakic and Goldman-Rakic 1982). Structural change in the brain (apparently reflecting increased connectivity) has also been demonstrated by Diamond et al. (1972); differences in environmental experience led to differences in brain weight in young rats from the same litter. Relevant data also comes from the use of eye patching to maintain visual function in amblyopic children until surgery can be performed, and from the potential impact on language development of compromised hearing after chronic ear infections at sensitive periods in language acquisition. Even more severe and pervasive disruption of languages is seen when a child is deprived of normal social and linguistic interaction beyond the age when language is normally acquired (Curtiss 1977).

Such examples provide powerful support for the concept of an interactive, dynamic model of neuropsychological functioning, not only within and between different brain systems but also in brain-environment interaction. The latter concept is critical for understanding how brain structures develop, for interpreting behavior in the context of a clinical assessment, and for devising effective intervention strategies.

The Cortical/Subcortical Axis

The third axis of the brain provides an important framework for evaluating the performance of developing animals, and especially the human animal who is of concern here. The cortical/subcortical axis is related to the anterior/posterior axis inasmuch as the cortical modulation of the output of subcortical systems is associated with anterior brain mechanisms. Behaviorally, the primary interest here is the child's developing ability to "put out" various behavioral competencies at all levels. The ease and fluency with which the child can do so changes as he or she matures, along with potential deficits seen in relation to this axis.

The significance of the cortical/subcortical axis is not surprising. "Ontogeny recapitulating phylogeny" has been an attractive notion for behavioral science, and this axis most clearly reflects the evolutionary additions to the brain postulated by MacLean (1973) in his concept of the "triune brain." The cortical/subcortical axis encompasses fine-tuned modulation and control (the cortical component) of three primary categories of behavioral output (the subcortical component): (1) arousal, alertness, attention (the "attentional matrix"; Mesulam 1985); (2) motor skill, motor activity level; and (3) basic drives crucial for maintaining the organism and the species. Anterior cortical systems orchestrate the arousal/alert state of the organism, the motivational salience of and/or emotional response to a given activity, the input from more posterior "knowledge" systems, and the specific motor response—evaluating the impact of the behavior on the world and integrating this new information into the total store of knowledge on an ongoing basis.

Although these different aspects of subcortical contributions can and must be distinguished in theory, they are closely related, if not essentially inseparable, in practice. Only an alert animal interacts with the environment; the awake animal is always in some sort of motion; all behavior has a continuo of emotional investment. This is particularly true of the young, whose primary developmental task is to learn to modulate the "excesses" of arousal, motor, and emotional responses, in conformity with adult expectations. In this regard, they can be seen to exemplify Edelman's model of brain-world interaction at the cellular development level: it is the environment that drives the immature brain (the stimuli to be perceived select the cells to perceive them, Edelman 1978); for the brain to be in charge of its environment requires experience, learning, and structural maturation.

In the clinical context, so-called hyperactive children are perhaps the best example of difficulty associated with the cortical/subcortical axis and, indeed, demonstrate the close interplay of different subcortical inputs. Changes in the diagnostic labels given to this group highlight the relationship of motor to arousal/attentional variables in their performance. The diagnosis of "hyperactive child syndrome" gave way in the *DSM III* to "attentional deficit disorder" in 1980. Clinicians had observed that the overactivity of the body characteristic of this group of children in their early childhood years "went underground" as they got older but that the attentional problems (overactivity of the mind?) did not, and, indeed, became more salient in the face of the increased demand for independent and challenging work expected of older youngsters. Accordingly, the diagnosis now emphasizes the attentional difficulty.

Neither of these diagnostic formulations, however, captures the entire cortical/subcortical axis input related to the overall behavioral presentation of these children. In an extended assessment, discontinuities that can be associated with anterior *cortical* systems are always manifest—and often not fully appreciated by parents and teachers. The missing concept is that of "organization": these children can be best understood as having an underlying organizational difficulty that renders them at risk for poor focusing of attention, poor modulation of motor activity level, difficulty in achieving appropriate responses to environmental expectations, and poor conceptual organization in the face of complex problem-solving activities (academic and otherwise)—all of which come under the purview of the frontal organizing systems of the brain (see also Barkley 1981).

Children with impulse control disorders may also benefit from analysis within a neuropsychological framework. The children I have seen have had test profiles very similar to those with hyperactive behavior or attention difficulties. They also proceed in a disorganized fashion when tasks require organizational skills, and they typically do better in terms of both general behavior and specific task performance in situations with inherent structure. To the extent that the difficulty for these children with impulse disorders involves the frontolimbic interplay of the cortical/subcortical axis, they should have organizational problems similar to children with attention disorders: frontal system input to general thinking skills is common to both groups. They differ, however, in terms of historic variables and behavioral presentation, a difference that underscores the importance of the tripartite assessment model discussed below.

Deficits in the modulatory interplay between cortical and subcortical systems are not the only type of problem associated with this axis. Children can also demonstrate dissociation of the "up" and "down" components thereof. In this regard, we need to differentiate specific motor deficits with respect to problems in programming the relevant segments (arguably involving higher-order cortical organization) as opposed to problems in maintaining rate, fluency, amplitude, and so forth (engaging subcortical mechanisms). Figure 5.6 highlights the dramatic impact of a severe and rapidly progressive ataxia of unknown origin on a twelve-year-old child's copy of the *ROCF* (Osterrieth 1944; Rey 1941).

The question for the examiner was "Is this child dementing 'behind' the ataxia?" The answer was negative, on the basis of the following observations:

1. Careful documentation of the child's actual organization of the lines in
    the figure yielded an organizational score and style of approach appropriate
    for his age (Waber and Holmes 1985).

FIGURE 5.6

2. A delayed recall of the figure was also scored at an age-appropriate level (Waber and Holmes 1986).

3. Although the young man's utterances were painful to observe (each sound segment was programmed separately with enormous effort) and clearly exhausted him, his spontaneous language revealed a good range of linguistic structures and vocabulary. He was able—and willing—to offer age-appropriate knowledge on the Information and Vocabulary subtests of the *WISC-R*.

4. He was unable to complete the Block Design task on his own because he could not hold the blocks steady. However, he was able to tell the examiner exactly how he wanted them placed, and he obtained an appropriate score for the task on this basis.

Further testing was not considered necessary given the level of the child's fatigue and the fact that the basic clinical question could be answered.

We have a less dramatic but equally interesting example of motor deficit in figure 5.7, drawn by a nineteen-year-old woman with a history of learning difficulty from the beginning of her school career. Although she reported that the easily observable sudden jerks of her hands and body had been with her as long as she could remember, no one had connected these to her learning problems. Neurological examination formally documented a striking choreiform movement disorder (Prechtl and Stemmer 1935). The movement disorder can be seen on the *ROCF* in regular "beats" of the pen, which are especially noticeable on horizontal

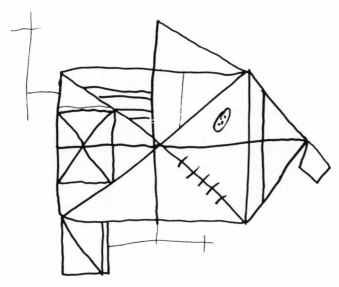

FIGURE 5.7

lines (requiring fine control of distal musculature). In many instances, the "beats" are evident at the point when the "begin to stop" message to the motor system must be initiated in order to end the line in the required place. Although the regularity of the anomaly in the lines probably would signal a specific deficit (rather than a developmental difference) to most observers, the drawing is clearly not that of a younger person with an immature motor system: the overall organization of the figure is that of an adult.

Measurement

THE MEDICAL MODEL

Up to now, assessment of cognitive functioning in children has had a psychometric context, psychological or educational. The relevant measurement instruments have reflected constructs derived from cognitive or educational psychology (and from the performance of adults with mature brains), and thus they emphasize discrete psychological functions presumed to underlie more complex behaviors. In applying such tools to clinical situations, rather than research populations, practitioners have fallen prey to the dangers of hypostatization. If, for example, a so-called diagnostic label, such as "auditory sequential memory deficit," were used simply as a descriptor, then it would be of little concern; but at the point that such labels also form the basis of remedial strategies, this is no longer the case.

The problem has serious theoretical implications. Let us consider a "worst case" scenario, but one I have actually observed and that serves as a frequent underlying model: A child with academic problems is given a WISC-R as part of the general assessment of learning ability. On the test he or she obtains a relatively depressed score on Digit Span. The tester has been taught that Digit Span measures "auditory sequential memory"; the low score is thus interpreted to mean that the child has an auditory sequential memory deficit. If this is so, then he or she needs training in auditory sequential memory. Given that Digit Span is an auditory sequential memory task, then the recommendation is made to train the child on Digit Span. Such reasoning involves a double abuse: first, of psychological tests, which are not intended as teaching instruments; second, and more important, of the child, since there is no real-world task of which Digit Span is an exemplar. The nearest is remembering telephone numbers, but their "chunking" (to beat the limitations of "the magic number seven plus or minus two"; Miller 1956) makes it very different. Inasmuch as there is no real-world task of Digit Span, the child who is asked to work on it is simply wasting time and energy. This is particularly pernicious since the child would not be in a clinician's office if he or she did not have a problem, and thus cannot afford to waste time or energy in any fashion. Furthermore, a child who can appreciate that the task has no real-world relevance is also likely to lack respect for the person doing the teaching, a result antithetical to the whole educational process.

There is a more appropriate model for clinical assessment, time-honored in the medical evaluation of behavior. The clinician assumes that an individual's performance on a given test must be viewed in light of observation and a detailed personal history, including symptoms. On the basis of this combined information, he or she then generates a diagnosis or diagnostic formulation, the diagnosis then generating the recommendations/treatment plan. In essentially the same way, a psychologist conducts an assessment, taking a personal history, observing the patient carefully, and administering tests. The psychologist utilizes the information from the test profile, along with the personal history and observations, to generate a diagnostic formulation, which guides the treatment plan. There is thus no direct relationship between the psychological tests and the recommendations for treatment.

THE DIAGNOSTIC BEHAVIORAL CLUSTER

Accepting this broader assessment model, we are still faced with the primary problem for behavioral measurement since the first efforts to develop formal measurement tools: any single behavior is as likely to be a random event as to have diagnostic significance. In neuropsychological terms, no one datum tells us anything about the brain.

Over the last several decades, the discipline of psychometrics has addressed this problem in great depth, developing well-tested techniques for estimating the probability of behaviors occurring by chance and providing standardized measurement tools for a wide variety of psychological endeavors. Where these techniques have been applied appropriately, they have proven invaluable as a baseline to "anchor" observations of behavior. They have been most useful in the study of groups—especially those examined in experimental paradigms, comparing the behavior of population to population. However, this is not the case for the practicing clinician, who always evaluates the individual and applies group-derived data to the single case, where the possibility always exists that a given performance falls outside of the expected range for the group.

To address this problem, most clinicians utilize a "behavioral cluster" assessment strategy. This usually means looking for other behaviors in the individual's overall performance that are congruent with the first observation(s) and thus support a specific diagnostic formulation. The greater the number of congruent behaviors from different domains, the less the likelihood that the difficulty experienced by the individual is occurring by chance.

A behavioral cluster strategy is particularly useful in the neuropsychological assessment of children because it employs knowledge derived from adult populations to form hypotheses about what one might expect to see in children; observations are carefully evaluated in light of such hypotheses, keeping in mind the developmentally determined capacities of children of different ages. The clinician proceeds on the basis of circumstantial evidence—circumstantial in that damage or dysfunction in

131

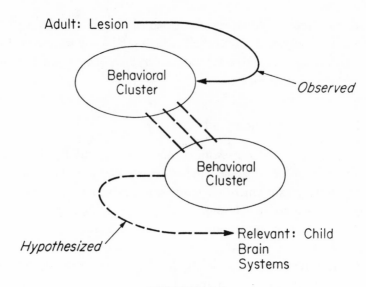

FIGURE 5.8

the child is not directly inferred on the basis of damage in the adult. Hypotheses about the child's neuropsychological status are based on comparable behavioral clusters in child and adult populations found in extensive neuropsychological tests tapping the same range of behavioral skills. This model is illustrated in figure 5.8.

The behavioral cluster model sets up the hypothesis that information about the brain systems known to be involved in the adult may be relevant (1) to understanding the child's overall behavior; (2) to explicating the nature of the specific difficulties that brought the child to the clinician; and (3) to setting up strategies for remediation and/or management. To reiterate: the model does not entail brain damage/dysfunction in the child, although this may prove to be the case. Instead, it highlights the neuroanatomic axis/axes critical for explication of the observed behaviors and the direction of the "imbalance" in the complementary contribution model of neuropsychological functioning.

The model demonstrated in figure 5.8 is only a very basic representation of the relationship between the adult's and the child's performances. Figure 5.9 below extends the behavioral cluster model to emphasize the full range of clinical skills the trained clinician always brings to bear on any observation of behavior. Note that the trained clinician's expertise is not (and cannot be) confined to clinical applications of neuropsychology alone. Relevant data comes from all branches of neuroscience and psy-

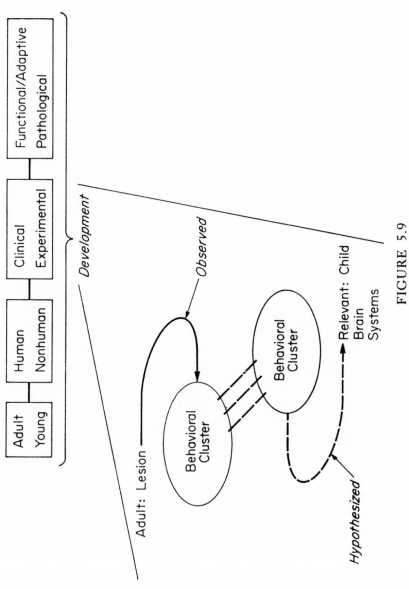

FIGURE 5.9

chology and includes adaptive as well as dysfunctional behaviors in both humans and nonhuman species.

Within a behavioral cluster approach to assessment, then, what constitute the relevant behaviors for the neuropsychological assessment of children? What are the sources in the overall clinical arsenal for the observations that will speak to the three neuroanatomic axes?

We can speak here of three primary sources: (1) the patient's history; (2) observation of the patient, reported or direct; and (3) actual test performance. Within each of these domains, we have different normative standards of comparison (Lezak 1976). Data from an individual's history, especially where children are concerned, are critical for documenting the acquisition of specieswide performance expectations. We can also evaluate information derived from observing the patient against such standards. Performance on formal tasks will respond to a normative comparison standard, developed according to rigorous psychometric principles. Within the context of appropriate test instruments, we must undertake close observation of the "process" by which the patient solves the problem posed by the examiner (Milberg, Hebben, and Kaplan 1986). The nature of a given individual's solving strategy provides further information about the underlying brain processes that he or she mobilizes to solve a given problem. Information, both quantitative and qualitative, from the personal history, from direct observation of the patient, and from his or her performance on formal tasks is evaluated in terms of its contribution to understanding an individual's given "brain style," in light of the complementary contribution model outlined above.

Within this model it is important to note that behavioral clusters include both positive and negative data. Historically, the fact that a child does not have primary evidence for oromotor apraxia is in itself a piece of evidence for another type of language output problem; observationally, the lack of any data speaking to a hearing impairment is another piece of evidence for a diagnosis of right-hemisphere deficit in a child with anomalous intonation contours. The lack of right-hemisphere-implicating errors on a visual motor task is part of the evidence allowing the hypothesis of "left-hemisphere impairment" to be proposed. In the course of a full neuropsychological evaluation, it is the confluence of these various types of data, all speaking to the same brain system or systems, that allows us to make the diagnostic formulation in neuropsychological terms. The progress of the clinician through an assessment is one of hypothesis generation: starting with the observation of a given behavior, we search for other observations. Together they will form a behavioral cluster coherent in its implications for the involved brain systems and with clinical significance when evaluated against the examiner's total knowledge of his or her field.

The assessment approach presented here requires a minimum amount of data. The clinician needs enough information from a sufficiently large number of behavioral domains to be sure that critical sources of knowledge are not missing. For most neuropsychologists, the basic requirement is to tap enough domains to speak to the three major brain divisions (the three axes outlined above).

It is instructive to compare the neuropsychological assessment of learning difficulty with the type of assessment undertaken within a more traditional psychoeducational construct. For example, it is not uncommon for a speech and language clinician to make valuable remarks about a child's functioning in the language domain without the psychoeducational team as a whole recognizing that the very same strategies and/or deficits are being played out in all of the child's thinking. In such a case, instruction geared simply to the language domain is likely to be less than optimal. I have also seen several children whose obviously atypical language use prompted a speech and language evaluation, which in turn documented specific deficits in language. The clinicians did not realize, however, that the child's overall thinking skills were quite seriously depressed, arguing (in most instances) that the "classical" learning disability teaching model was not appropriate. (The classical learning disability teaching model is a discrepancy model: it assumes average or better-than-average ability in most skill areas, with a specific domain of deficit.) Unfortunately, by age fourteen or fifteen, when these children turn up for skills assessment regarding employment/vocational choices, they not only are limited to a third- or fourth-grade reading level (in spite of years of "learning-disabilities" support in this area) but also (because of their limited cognitive capacities) often lack important real-world, functional skills.

The development of such skills in an instructional program matched to their thinking abilities would have enabled these children to fulfill their own potential, to enjoy a sense of mastery in relevant skill areas, and eventually to have the satisfaction of being productive members of society. At fourteen or fifteen, however, they have lost valuable years for developing the skills in question and often have a great deal of negative experience with learning. The advantage of the neuropsychological perspective in these instances comes precisely from the fact that the neuropsychologist is trained to think not only in terms of the skills the individual will need in the academic context but also in terms of general situations, personal, social, and vocational, at the time of assessment and in the future.

DEVELOPMENTAL CONSIDERATIONS

Perhaps the most important thing to recognize in the neuropsychological evaluation of children is that the developmental variables must come from at least three sources: (1) changes in the neurological substrate; (2) changes in cognitive ability; and (3) changes in socioemotional status. Although these three aspects of individual functioning are intertwined, they have different impacts at different times and in different situations. The increasing competence presumed of the maturing individual will also entail greater environmental demands.

It is thus important to explore the degree to which a given child can respond in all domains. Cognitive and socioemotional capacities may not develop in tandem. The major stress points in a child's educational career (Holmes 1987) highlight not only the positive relationship between the developing competence of the individual and the increasing amount of content material he or she is expected to tackle in the academic context but also the fact that an increasingly mature individual is expected to assume more and more responsibility for self. Thus, a child's progress through the school years entails not only an increase in *content* but also a decrease in *context*; that is, in the support offered by the school environment in terms of a homeroom, a single teacher, supervised instruction, and so forth. This means that evaluating the child's precise difficulty in the academic context requires close examination of the cause: is it the actual academic content or the conditions under which mastery of that content must be demonstrated? For example, a child may be quite capable of seventh-grade work without necessarily having the socioemotional competence/maturity to handle the work load in a typical junior high school environment, with different teachers teaching a variety of subjects in different classrooms, and with a substantial demand for independent work in the guise of homework assignments. Whether a child can respond to such demands as he or she develops can be related to the maturity of different underlying brain systems.

A clear appreciation of the impact of developmental change on interpretation of test performance is crucial. Although standardized tests may be appropriate for documenting a child's progress relative to children of the same age, they may not be helpful in evaluating personal developmental progress. This does not mean that standardized tests are inappropriate or unnecessary; however, they cannot be regarded as sufficient: we must clearly recognize their limitations for the intra-individual assessment that is the crux of neuropsychological work. The *WISC-R* is a good example. In constructing the test, Wechsler and his associates generated a set of normal curves for each subtest of the overall battery. This was done for each four-month cohort of children from six years to sixteen years, eleven months. Given the structure of this test battery, the mean score at every age is ten; thus, a line joining each age's score to the next would be straight. However, developmental psychology teaches us that, in reality, development is anything but linear.

What does this mean in the clinical context? Take, for example, a nine-year-old boy with academic problems. He completes the Block Design activity and obtains a scaled score of 11. This score is solidly in the average range and would not suggest difficulty for the child. However, in observing the qualitative aspects of performance, the clinician notes that he proceeded to the correct solutions in a highly disorganized fashion, utilizing almost all of the time allowed in an unsystematic trial-and-error manner. This lack of organization is not reflected in the score. At this age, the test gives little credit for speed; a correct solution is sufficient to demonstrate performance in the average range. With increasing age, however, the amount of time it takes to arrive at correct solutions becomes more important. Hence, for the older child, the score depends not only on accurate problem-solving but also on efficient organization of the problem-solving process.

This change presumably was necessary to allow Wechsler to measure the increasing competence of older children, part of which lies in the continuing maturation of frontal brain systems, thought to be related to changes attendant on puberty. To the extent that a disorganized child has relatively inefficient/immature frontal-system functioning, he or she can be expected to proceed on a somewhat different developmental trajectory than those children without such difficulties—whose performance forms the basis for the normative data of the standardized test instrument. Therefore, the clinician should not be surprised if the child previously identified as disorganized loses IQ points at or around puberty, especially on timed tests. Of course, the child does not lose intelligence but merely fails to take advantage of developmental change in the same manner as the normal population—reflected in changed performance as compared to the standardization cohort. In clinical neuropsychological practice with children, it is very important to make such a distinction, since loss of points on a standardized intellectual battery like the WISC-R can also reflect actual erosion of brain tissue, a possibility that demands prompt and aggressive intervention. In terms of the theoretical approach to assessment, the example highlights the importance of understanding the demand characteristics imposed by the construction of a standardized test instrument, in addition to those involved in the test activity and the interpersonal transactions that surround it.

Another important aspect of developmental change is what Goldman-Rakic has called the "heterology" of brain structure/function relationships in infants and adults (Goldman 1974). The available evidence supports the view that different brain structures mediate what appears to be the same behavioral function at different points in the maturation of the individual. This limits research paradigms using level of performance alone as a window into the maturation of brain structures. Analysis of the strategies used by the subject in solving the task then become critical. In the psychological sphere, Carey and Diamond (1980) provide an elegant example of this principle. They have demonstrated that the strategies used by children below the age of ten for solving a face recognition task are very different from those used by older children. Their data imply that, prior to the age of ten, the task is solved by evaluating discrete components of the pictured materials: the children rely on features of clothing, hairstyle, and so on to make the necessary discriminations between individuals. After the age of ten, however, children appear to be able to use recognition of the face as the basis for discrimination, with the result that they can recognize a given face irrespective of any confounding accoutrements with which it might be surrounded. (Interestingly, children gain this face recognition skill at a price, being no longer able to recognize the upside-down face. See Carey and Diamond 1980.)

The implication of these and similar findings is that specific brain-behavior relationships derived from the study of brain damage in adults may be irrelevant for identifying involved brain systems in children. Such data provide strong support for an approach to developmental neuropsychology that incorporates principles derived from both developmental neurobiology and developmental psychology. In developmental neuropsychology, adult brain-behavior relationships can be used only in the context of the potential impact of maturational change in the nervous system. In the context of the behavioral cluster model, such data mean that behavioral cluster membership is likely to vary from age to age, and should do so. The behaviors that contribute to the diagnostic cluster need not be the same at all ages: it is their significance in relation to the relevant neuroanatomic axis/axes, given the developmental stage of the child, that should be consistent across time.

Brain-World Interaction

We have gained our knowledge of brain-behavior relationships largely in terms of "damage" or "experimental breakdown" models, which have emphasized localization and have given pride of place to the brain as the mediator of behavior. The model espoused in this discussion, however, is based on the belief that the brain does not operate independently from the world, and that this interaction plays a significant role in the organ's development and in the utilization of its unfolding skills. We know, for example, from the work of Hubel and Wiesel (1959) that a specific interaction with the world elicits an equally specific response from individual cells in the visual system. Without this brain-world interaction, the individual cells do not "learn" to respond. In the competition for cell connectivity thought to take place in the early differentiation of the nervous system, cells that do not receive the "correct" input may be subverted to entirely different ends. Limitation of the appropriate "world" input affects skill development (and, presumably, neural anatomy) where more complex human functions are concerned: compromised hearing limits oral language use; lack of normal communicative input may limit the acquisition of language itself; inadequate motor skills may impair the development of higher-order organizational capacities with respect to both motor and nonmotor behaviors.

In experiments we can directly influence the nature of the brain-world interaction: subjects can be "set" (by cuing, instructions, or previous experience in the experimental task, for example) to deal with information in one way rather than another. A clinician must be wary of so "setting" a patient. For example, during a professional seminar, Edith Kaplan (personal communication) gave a very elegant demonstration of an erroneous diagnosis of depression based on a clinician's empathic posture in discussion, with a demented patient, of sad and distressing events. In this particular case, changing the topic of discussion to happy and exciting situations elicited a cheerful demeanor. This type of observation makes it very important for the clinician to monitor the demand characteristics of a given clinical situation very precisely. Before hazarding a hypothesis about the possible role that the individual's brain may play in an observed behavior, we must be reasonably certain that the behavior is not, in fact, a product of the clinical testing situation itself.

A good example of this danger comes from use of the *ROCF*. The figure is first copied, then recalled immediately, and then, after a fifteen-to twenty-minute delay, reproduced a third time. While Waber and Holmes (1985, 1986) have developed a scoring system for this test based on overall organization and style, it is important that clinicians do not assume that "organization" and "style" fully characterize the individual's mode of dealing with the material. (Errors, direction of production, placement on the page, associated behaviors, and so forth must all be evaluated clinically.) Especially where children are concerned, the copy may be completed in a slavish, "stimulus-bound" fashion: with the figure directly in view, many children proceed on a line-by-line, matching basis, which eventually leads to an adequate reproduction. Such an approach also can be characterized as "part-oriented." However, many children do not often maintain such a style of production when asked to recall the information from memory, either immediately or after a delay. Whenever they do so, the clinician can put forward the hypothesis, to be tested against other observations, that a part-oriented style of dealing with complex materials is indeed characteristic of the child. However, on recall, many children offer more configurationally oriented products. In spite of their initial slavish approach to the stimulus figure, the elements that they "encoded" for later retrieval had very different characteristics.

A similar demonstration of the demand characteristics of a situation is that of the young man responding to the Vocabulary item *donkey*, described earlier. Here the domain of behavior was language, but the situation also demanded organizational capacities. A third example highlights the constraints on an individual in the testing situation, including both the test materials and the interaction between the examiner and the individual. For example, I had noticed in several youngsters a strong language-implicating behavioral cluster and a striking performance on Block Design, a type of error closely associated with right-frontal brain dysfunction. Good clinical practice argues against interpreting a single behavior as having "brain relevance"; however, the fact that this is a very dramatic error, highly diagnostic in other contexts, plus the fact that I had seen this particular behavior occurring together with the language-implicating profile several times before, prompted me to consider it in more depth. The demand characteristics of this test include not only any single problem, but also all the previously completed items. In evaluating the way a subject reaches a solution, the clinician should not be limited to observing a single test problem but should examine the individual's entire performance.

My observations suggest that on the earlier, four-block items, these children demonstrate difficulty with the analysis of block placement. They frequently struggle with item 5, for example, where the grid indicating block placement is, for the first time, lacking on the stimulus design. Similarly, they may have to use trial and error to establish the structure of items 6 and 8. When the child gets to item 9, his or her insecurity with analysis is compounded by yet another demand characteristic of any task—a marked increase in complexity (in this instance, from four to nine blocks). With this increase in demand, the ability to respond effectively is compromised. Under such constraints, other factors may well come into play.

Under the best circumstances, good clinical rapport will have been established—that is, the child attempts to comply as well as he or she can with the examiner's implied request to produce a design that looks like the one on the card. Note, however, that the child does not have unlimited ways to fulfill the obligation. There are only nine blocks, and these provide the child with only three options—all red, all white, or half red/half white. With insecure analytical skills now overwhelmed by the increased complexity of the task—and yet constrained by the social expectations of offering something as near as possible to the target— the child is forced to give an erroneous response, which nonetheless can be seen as the most reasonable under the circumstances.

In a sense, this suggests that the child's brain has reanalyzed the situation and decided to attempt a goal that is more manageable—the "goal" factor being important for assessing behavior and management strategies. The notion of "demand characteristics" also includes some consideration of what the brain may see as the nature of the task, rather than what the examiner necessarily thinks he or she is actually tapping with a given activity. In the example of the ROCF, on page 121, the examiner's goal in asking for a copy of the complex figure was to elicit information about the individual's thinking/learning style and ability to organize material at this level. However, the goal of the child's brain—at least where the copy production is concerned—may have been to produce as accurate a representation as possible. These two goals may not always be compatible.

Another example of this dissimilarity of goals comes from my observation of a girl I evaluated for benign congenital hypotonia. She was unable to complete the bead-stringing task of the *Stanford-Binet Intelligence Scale* (Thorndike, Hagen, and Sattler 1986), and, as in most confrontational activities, she became extremely frustrated and upset. She could be persuaded to proceed only with sticker rewards. Close observation of a free play period was thus an important part of the evaluative process for this child. In the course of the play period, she knocked a plastic ball off the top of a wire on a toy/mobile that I keep in my office. Now relaxed and happy after an interesting session of play, she set about to "fix Dr. Holmes's toy," replacing with some effort the plastic ball on a wire half the size of a standard pencil lead. Thus, the real-life demand of fixing the toy bypassed the fine-motor coordination problem ("thread the bead with the string") in the formal test. This example highlights the importance for clinicians of building fine-tuned observation skills, especially for evaluating children who are unable to comply with standard task instructions.

Clearly identifying the goal of an action is as important for understanding the brain's role in real-life situations as for defining the relevant behaviors in the diagnostic cluster. Let us draw an example from the music world which highlights the theoretical significance of the demand characteristic construct: a "functional" interpretation of brain-behavior relationships and the goal-oriented approach to brain-world interaction lead to directly opposing neuropsychological explications. If we take the view that the brain primarily mediates function, then generations of string players have been doing it all wrong. The string player's left hand is involved in fast, precise finger movements while the right hand uses the larger movements of the arm musculature. Functionally, however, left-hemisphere systems, directly controlling the right hand, permit precise control of the distal musculature, and the right hemisphere, controlling the left hand, can more easily control larger movements of the arm. Generations of string players have, of course, not been holding their instruments backward. The brain does not appear to be interested in the *how* of output, but the *what*: the string player's fine finger movements change the length of the strings, thereby controlling the pitch of the notes. The long, sweeping movements of the right arm select the notes in the correct order to create the melody. Thus, the right-hemisphere systems have direct responsibility for the sound pattern, and the left-hemisphere systems control the temporal sequence. This accords well with our understanding of hemispheric specialization across a wide range of different clinical and research paradigms (Bryden 1982; Gates and Bradshaw 1977; Gordon 1975; Moscovitch 1979).

Recognizing that the goal of an activity (clinical or real-life) may determine the nature of the strategies used to proceed to a solution and, thus, of the brain systems mobilized to effect the relevant strategies, is crucial if we are to understand the relationships between brain and behavior—and to use this knowledge effectively for clinical intervention and remediation.

Chapter 6

History and Observations

JANE M. HOLMES

The evaluative component of the clinical assessment procedure consists of data derived from the patient's *history,* clinical *observations* and the *testing* process. In this chapter, I will examine the importance of the patient's history and the examiner's observations in the context of a neuropsychological model based on the three brain axes described in chapter 5. I will discuss the contributions of clinical testing to neuropsychological evaluation in chapter 7.

The History

In clinical practice, the clinician typically obtains patients' histories in two ways: (1) by questionnaire and (2) by interview. The relevant informants usually are the child, the parent(s) or guardian(s), one or more teachers, and perhaps a psychotherapist or pediatrician. Historical information provides the first data relative to the anterior/posterior axis. The clinician cannot proceed without some means of knowing just what knowledge is available to this particular child, that is, the general competence of posterior brain systems. For the pediatric population, the necessary first datum must always be "How old?" This single piece of information is critical for evaluating the amount of knowledge to which the child has been exposed. The second crucial piece of information, of which few clinicians take conscious note, is the child's address, which may be a valuable clue to the family's educational history, its vocational success, its social aspirations, and its academic expectations. When working with children from outside one's own geographic area, the clinician must obtain further details of the child's sociocultural experience and the expectations associated with the child's environment. In the case of one child, for example, we learned that learning disabilities are socially unacceptable in her country. Therefore, compensatory strategies for the child were not acceptable—this family wanted a cure. In another case, a socioeconomically advantaged Mandarin Chinese family had sent their sons to school in the United States. In spite of bilingual issues, we diagnosed a language-based learning disorder in the older son: he had been exposed to English at the same time and in the same manner as his brother. The case was further complicated by sociocultural expectations for the oldest son that appeared to get in the way of clear recognition of the learning problem. We finally sought help from a colleague who had been raised in their country.

Simply knowing the range of experiences a child has been exposed to and the expectations of his or her environment, however, is not sufficient; the clinician must also know whether the child has had the opportunity to take advantage of this exposure. Historical variables including the family's medical history, the child's developmental history, and the child's medical history, again, are important. The clinician looks for specific patterns that increase the probability that the child's "failure to cope" has a constitutional, or neuropsychological, basis rather than a purely emotional or socially determined one. Without this knowledge, the clinician cannot evaluate the relative contributions of biological, emotional, and sociocultural factors to the child's overall presentation.

A clear family history of many types of physical disorders increases the likelihood that a patient with similar physical symptoms also has the disorder. The same principle applies for a variety of behavioral disorders: specific learning disabilities sometimes run in families, though the mechanism for transmission is not yet clear (Smith et al. 1983). Specific family members even have been implicated in particular instances: the mother's brother (a maternal uncle) is mentioned as also suffering from similar academic difficulties more frequently than one would expect by chance alone. In the immediate family, symptoms need not match the specific behavior seen in the patient. For example, Geschwind and Behan (1982) and Geschwind and Galaburda (1985) argue that there is an association between dyslexia, handedness, and certain aspects of autoimmune functioning; other disorders of the autoimmune system may be characteristic of families in which one member has a specific reading disorder. A family in which many members are not right-handed may carry a specific, neuropsychologically based difference associated with difficulties in academics. The clinician may have to evaluate the patient's behavioral clusters very carefully in such cases, because they may not conform to those clusters usually seen in the majority of the population. Non–right-handedness in an individual's family members may influence brain-behavior relationships in the individual him- or herself.

Other significant features of the family history include specific medical disorders. For example, where an individual's family has a predisposition to seizure disorder, learning difficulties may be another symptom of the underlying brain difference, paralleling the seizure disorder. Abnormal electrical activity in the brain, marked by lack of concentration, poor attention, daydreaming, and so on, may also lead to attentional difficulties for which the treatment of choice would be anticonvulsant medication, rather than the stimulant medication that might be proposed for a child with a primary attentional disorder.

Further, both maternal and paternal age at conception/birth, and difficulties surrounding the birth process (both low and high maternal age at birth can raise the risk for difficulty in labor and/or delivery), can be associated with later behavioral competence in the child, for example, chromosomal abnormalities. The mother's health during pregnancy is also associated with risk for the child: disordered nutrition, excessive or inadequate weight gain, need for medication, and use or abuse of alcohol, tobacco, or other social drugs during pregnancy can have deleterious effects that may be manifested as behavioral disorders in the growing child.

DEVELOPMENTAL HISTORY

A child's developmental progression is also of critical importance for evaluation. Barring any history of trauma, has the child acquired the usual developmental milestones normally? At the very least, the clinician should review the child's early interaction with the parent(s), gross and fine-motor skills, language skills, separation issues, socialization with peers, feeding behavior, sleeping behavior, block/puzzle/picture play, early school-related series (alphabet, colors, coins, and so on), attentional abilities, and hand preference (right or left, age at which preference was clear). A child for whom early bonding was fraught with difficulty may be at risk for later emotional problems or, possibly, may fail to appreciate the reciprocal nature of communication essential for later language and social interaction. A child who is late in acquiring language skills, either at the first-word level or with respect to more complex language structures, is at significant risk for later insecurity in language skills, especially in the context of more challenging written language, which is not supported by the verbal cues—segmental stress, intonation contours, possibility for repetition, and so on—inherent in oral language.

A history of oromotor apraxia, where the earliest manifestation of a difficulty is seen in early feeding difficulties related to poor sucking, is also implicated in later language disorders. A child with this disorder may need to be taught to suck through a straw and may need help in blowing out the candles on his or her birthday cake. Eventually, an adult realizes that this child still can't whistle and is saying *pisghetti* (for "spaghetti") for far too long. These children frequently have later difficulty with temporal-order concepts (*before, after*), with word order in sentences, and with the arrangement of ideas in paragraphs. This basic problem in serial ordering "replays" at each new level of demand as the child matures.

In the same manner, the child with a history of discontinuities in the development of peer socialization skills may have an underlying neuro-psychologically determined reason for a later-diagnosed "social learning disability," and the child with inefficient fine-motor abilities may have difficulty meeting the production demands that will be an inherent part of academic programming throughout his or her school career. The development of hand preference can also be informative: if the clinician can confirm that hand preference was incontrovertibly established at a very early age (which is not always easy to do), then there may be specific damage to the brain that has limited the child's natural flexibility to work with both hands, at least in the early years, and that may be associated with atypical brain organization.

MEDICAL HISTORY

The child's own medical history may reflect factors associated with his or her birth. Traumatic birth events may be associated with later difficulties in the "thinking" domain accompanied by mild degrees of motor impairment that can be characterized as a "pastel" (or milder) version of cerebral palsy (Denckla 1979a). Intrauterine, perinatal, or early neonatal damage is sometimes associated with change in both the development of hand preference and the basic organization of the brain. The timing, course, and localization of a specific brain injury has different immediate effects as well as different later effects in terms of behavioral outcome (Goldman-Rakic 1981, 1987). Generalized systemic insult to the individual may have specific central nervous system impact, the severity of which depends on the developmental age at which the systemic insult is incurred, for example, lead intoxication (Shaheen 1984) or whole-body irradiation (Waber, personal communication, 1987).

The clinician should also document the child's educational history in detail. How much schooling? How consistent? What are the expectations of the child's school system? What are the parent's expectations for and involvement in the child's education? Has the child ever been held back a grade or required special educational services? The answers to these questions yield information about the child's ability to respond to the various demands imposed by different experiences in the school context, highlighting variables related to the context, as well as the content, of learning. The child's previous school experiences will also play an important role in planning the next interventions—choice of school, classroom type, strategy development, remedial instruction, and so on.

History and Observations

The variables outlined above represent the types of information required from a patient's history. Taken together, these variables form a preliminary picture of the integrity of the child's brain and its ability to take advantage of the knowledge it should have gained thus far. This information is not necessarily limited to the anterior/posterior axis; historical information also reflects the development of the other two brain axes. For example, atypical development of language milestones speaks to a possible disturbance in the "balance" between right- and left-hemisphere systems, impaired motor skills suggest far-reaching consequences for other behaviors mediated primarily by the cortical/subcortical axis, and a history of significant emotional insult can call into question the appropriate development of all behavior (associated with any axis).

Observations

Observational data can be divided into five categories, as follows:

1. Information obtained from questionnaires and interviews completed by people familiar with the child in nonclinical contexts
2. Direct observation of the child-parent interaction during the clinical interview
3. Analysis of the examiner-child dyad
4. Observation of the child under specific performance demands
5. Direct examination of the child's appearance

NONCLINICAL OBSERVATIONS

The importance of eliciting anecdotes, not only from parents but also from other adults in the child's environment, cannot be overestimated. The specific anecdote reveals the actual demand characteristics of a given situation more objectively than parents' or teachers' opinions. It is equally important to get information about a child's peer relationships. Does the child have friends? Does the child have a best friend? Is the best friend of an appropriate age? If not, are there other children of an appropriate age to play with? If the child has trouble with peer relationships, does he or she have trouble making friends? Keeping friends? Do other children tolerate the child or actively shun him or her? A child who has the opportunity to play with other children the same age but who consistently chooses to play with children two years younger is often developmentally young—either in terms of general modulation-of-behavior abilities or in terms of language skills. These children may be very comfortable with adults who can provide a greater degree of support than the peer group. A child who has difficulty making friends and/or is shunned by other children may have fundamental deficits that prevent him or her from appreciating the cues on which normal social interaction is based. A child who has difficulty keeping friends is unlikely to be fundamentally lacking in socially relevant capacities but may have difficulty in modulating behavior appropriately in terms of peer-group expectations. This child's difficulty could indicate a constitutionally based problem in the efficient modulation of behavior or reflect seriously eroded self-esteem or significant emotional distress. This type of problem could be—and, with time, all too often is—a "layer cake" of constitutional and emotional factors (Denckla, personal communication, 1978).

CHILD-PARENT INTERACTION

The clinician obtains details of the child's history from the parent(s) through questionnaires and personal interviews. Difficult-to-discuss and/or psychologically relevant information is discussed with the parent(s) when the child is not present. I frequently obtain further information concerning the child's neuropsychological status and psychological adjustment from the feedback session with the parent(s) and, sometimes, teacher(s) when my knowledge of the child and his or her overall thinking/learning style permits me to ask more precise questions and thereby obtain more focused descriptions. However, I usually do not see the youngster for an extended period of testing prior to a more detailed conversation with the parent(s), preferring to begin with an initial interview of the parent(s) and child together. Indeed, it is my practice to conduct the initial interview with both the parent(s) and the child present. This is reassuring to a child who is usually somewhat anxious about being in a hospital (the setting in which I practice); patients are usually more relaxed and exuberant at the second, now familiar, testing session. It also encourages the child's confidence and trust in the examiner, which is critical for good rapport, and provides the examiner an opportunity for direct observation of the child interacting with the parent.

I have found it very valuable to ask a parent—in the presence of the child—to provide a focus for the evaluation: "What are the specific issues that you would like me to address where the child is concerned right now?" This approach is not intended to elicit elaborate details of the child's history, which has been obtained elsewhere; rather, the brief discussion yields information not only about the child/parent interaction but also about the child's understanding of why he or she is being evaluated. Many children see the type of hospital setting in which I practice as an intimidating one, fearing "shots," "brain tests," and the like. Explaining that the examiner is trying to find out "what sort of a thinker you are—by giving you pictures, puzzles, questions" goes a long way toward reassuring an anxious youngster.

At the beginning of the first session, I indicate to all children that I am going to spend a few minutes talking with Mom and/or Dad about why they are here. I invite older youngsters to take part, and I provide felt-tip markers and clean paper for younger children and invite them to draw and/or listen, as they will. It has been my experience that most younger children (six to eight or nine years old) get quite involved in drawing and listen with only "half an ear"—if at all. An older child's attitude—as well as that of the parent(s)—when the child's deficits are under discussion always provides useful insight. Some parents invite the child to contribute to the conversation and/or reassure the child about the need to go through such potentially negative discussion. In marked contrast, some parents simply talk as though the child were not present, without regard for his or her feelings. Although in my experience most initial interviews of this type are not confrontative (most children appear to be resigned to the fact that adults take them here and there and discuss them in their presence), I always make it a practice to ask a child (when the parent has left the room) whether the parent's account of his or her difficulties was more or less correct. In my experience, most children have a very clear answer to such a question, typically agreeing in a somewhat self-conscious manner that the parent was correct. In those instances where a child clearly disagrees with the parental view of the situation, the child almost always turns out to be the more reliable informant.

THE CLINICAL DYAD

The examiner-child interaction is full of pitfalls for the unwary and, equally, is a source of powerful hypotheses about the child's neuropsychological status—hypotheses that are often firmly in place before any formal psychological instrument is presented. Both the pitfalls and the power of the clinical dyad relate to the examiner's knowledge of self: in the first instance, knowledge of his or her own neuropsychological style and, in the second instance, knowledge of the inherent interpersonal relationships that exist between adults and children in the same culture.

For example, it is important for the examiner to know that he or she works well with the somewhat disorganized, attentionally impaired, and/or hyperactive child. An experienced clinician, comfortable with his or her instruments and able to move through the evaluation in an efficient, fast-paced fashion, is not likely to "see" a hyperactive child, because the highly structured, one-on-one testing situation and the fast pace provide ideal supports for this child and may alleviate hyperactive behavior. Such support is not typical of a standard classroom setting, where the symptoms of the disorder are manifest. If the clinician writes a report without taking into account the contrast between the demand characteristics of these two different settings, he or she may seem incompetent; the description of the child in the ideal testing situation will have almost nothing to do with the classroom teacher's and/or the parent's experiences with the child.

It is equally important for the examiner to recognize his or her own weaknesses in the testing situation, that is, his or her lack of sensitivity to certain aspects of the behavioral domain. This failure to recognize one's own personal and neuropsychological style can lead to poor observation of general context-specific behaviors and to inaccurate scoring of actual tests. For example, many highly verbal individuals choose to pursue careers in psychotherapeutic disciplines because of what they initially perceive as a strong verbal component to such activities. They may be misled by an equally verbal child and may fail to recognize that the child's use of language is actually too adult in nature, that is, out of balance with the child's other competencies. There is a clearly recognizable group of children referred for difficulties in learning whose conversational language with adults is above age expectancy, who do a great deal of talking with adults from whom they get a great deal of support, but who nonetheless have serious *peer* socialization difficulties, as well as major organizational problems in terms of academic materials. Just because a child is a "good talker" in an adult-child conversational interchange does not mean that he or she is behaviorally competent in general. One such ten-year-old girl was described by her mother as being "very good at cocktail parties." Clinical management of this case required a very sensitive touch, given that the mother failed to recognize that it is not normal for a ten-year-old to be taking part in cocktail parties. In another case, a student clinician was totally taken in by the polished verbal abilities of an eight-year-old boy. The student interpreted the entirely appropriate career-advancement strategies of his mother as the cause of the young man's behavioral problems due to a lack of attention and nurturance. The supervising clinician had to intervene in this case, pointing to the extensive evidence for right-hemisphere–mediated dysfunction that indicated a primary, neuropsychologically based reason for the behavioral problems. This particular problem—being misled by an individual's language capacity—is very pervasive in the general population. We all tend to react to other people on the basis of their overt language skills; the verbally facile individual is usually given credit for greater intelligence than the more taciturn person, as noted in chapter 1. However, this everyday perception may turn out to be completely incorrect when two such individuals are asked to complete formal tasks of cognitive ability.

The interplay between the adult examiner and the child in a formal clinical evaluation can also affect the scoring of formal tasks, which is one of the reasons why clinicians use standardized tests in their evaluations. The standardized test keeps the clinician "on the straight and narrow" course with respect to evaluating the child's developmental progress. Even within this context, however, the clinician must pay specific attention to the rigor of scoring, especially in relatively open-ended tasks, such as the Vocabulary or Comprehension subtests from the WISC-R. My neuropsychological style is unlikely to lead me to misinterpret the performance of a child with pseudomature language; however, I regularly consult the WISC-R manual for help with these two subtests. I particularly enjoy the child who can be considered a "good thinker," that is, the child who can mobilize useful strategies in an effort to find information that is not immediately available, who can reason his or her way to correct solutions, and/or who can make optimal use of one more piece of information in solving a problem. Without due care, the strongly positive feelings that I might have about such a child's overall thinking capacity could lead me to give the benefit of the doubt to the child's answers on tests where differential scoring (full-credit or half-credit) is possible. A child's overall score on such a test could be a whole standard deviation better than it would be if responses were scored rigorously. The clinician who explores qualitative, process data thoroughly may be at more risk of being misled by this type of child. Clinical limit-testing of performance (see chapter 7), used as a formal tool for hypothesis testing, may well elicit exactly that type of thinking characterized as the "zone of proximal development": the aspect of a child's competence that reveals his or her readiness to make the next cognitive leap (Vygotsky 1978).

The examiner's interaction with the child is important not only for the influence that their personal styles may have on each other in the ongoing interchange but also for the specific effects the child may have on the examiner's behavior. For example, if a child comes into your office and you feel that your personal space has been invaded, then the child has a "social problem." If a child comes into your office and, after a few phrases or sentences of conversation, you find yourself repeating, rephrasing, simplifying, and/or slowing your utterances, then the child has a problem with processing language. If the child comes into your office and you find yourself talking more loudly and clearly, then the child should probably stop by the Audiology Department on the way out of the building. If the child comes into your office and you find yourself overemphasizing intonation contours and giving grand drama to your utterances, attempting to engage the child more fully in the social and conversational interchange, then the child is probably attentionally dis-ordered or socially dysfunctional and is failing to engage in expected patterns of eye contact. The common element in all of these situations is, of course, the clinician. It is the close monitoring of the change in the *clinician's* behavior that sets up the hypotheses about the *child's* vulnerable areas. It does not appear to matter whether the clinician is particularly socially or linguistically adept. Since the clinician is the com-mon element in all situations, he or she is in a position to evaluate one child against the next; as a competent adult, part of the clinician's social repertoire is supplying to an interaction with the child what he or she perceives (not necessarily at a conscious level) to be missing in the interaction.

The behavior just outlined is not simply that of a trained psychological or neurological clinician; rather, the behavior is a normal part of the armamentarium of the competent adult and appears to be very difficult to resist. It has been discussed at some length in the developmental language literature under the rubric of "motherese" (a somewhat unfortunate label, since it appears to be characteristic of both male and female adults). Adults talking with young children typically modify their language to match that of the child. This match, however, is very sensitive: the adult speaker appears to offer language of a complexity just beyond that degree of complexity used by the child himself or herself, apparently "shaping" the child's use of language. It is, in fact, quite difficult to *resist* offering language in this fashion to a younger person perceived to be less competent in the language domain; similarly, it is difficult to refrain from modifying behavior in response to a perceived need for extra support. The power of this response argues for a considerable force at work in the relationships between adults and children.

In human society, the adults' role toward the young is to inculcate those behaviors and values that will maintain both the society and the species. Adults respond to the biological competence of the developing child at different ages and shape this biological competence to fit the social group to which the child belongs. The adult's response to the child's biological competence is finely tuned: adults appear to have a rather precise internal yardstick of appropriate behavior for individuals of different ages, a yardstick against which they evaluate an individual child's performance. For example, there are very different expectations for three-year-olds, as compared to ten-year-olds, concerning the amount of motor activity that adults will tolerate. A three-year-old who is careening around a room pretending in turn to be a train, a truck, or an airplane, usually elicits—to the extent he is not wrecking the furniture—a tolerant regard for the "energy" of small children; however, a ten-year-old who indulges in precisely the same behavior would be subject to significant disciplinary efforts—and might even be referred to a specialist in an attempt to control this "hyperactive" behavior. Adults have similar internal guidelines for the amount of extra support they provide to a child in a given and specific interaction. Adults expect to put more of their own energies into helping a five-year-old conform appropriately to social standards than into an interaction with a twelve-year-old. To the extent that such extra support is required by the twelve-year-old, the child is likely to be thought of as immature, irresponsible, difficult, and so on.

A primary factor eliciting such behavior in the adult, though not the only variable, appears to be *size*. Where two individuals are of comparable height and weight but one has the smooth skin and light, springing step of an adolescent and the other has the wrinkles, shuffling walk, and stiffness of an eighty-year-old, size is clearly not the salient feature that elicits different expectations from others (although it is worth noting that some of the supportive behaviors that adolescents and eighty-year-olds elicit may be not very different). When the two individuals are children, however, size appears to be a major trigger of expectations in the adult— not surprising, perhaps, given that a major feature of childhood development is increasing size.

One can appreciate the importance of size by considering the experiences of those people who are an unusual size for their developmental competence. Unusually short adults, for example, complain frequently about being "talked down to" by the normal-sized adult population; that is, they are talked to as if they were children (the usual people of less-than-normal height). "Talking down to" short adults reveals the expectation that smaller height indicates less competency. The converse also holds. Exceptionally tall children, who have the height of eighteen-year-olds at the age of eleven, for example, can experience significant psychological distress when the group expects behavior appropriate for an eighteen-year-old from someone who has had only eleven years to develop his or her social and emotional capacities. These children require significant support from professional psychologists to cope with such a discrepancy, especially during adolescence. Likewise, informal observations of both my own behavior and that of my colleagues in dealing with normal-sized but intellectually limited adults reveal that the perceived difference in competence elicits a greater behavioral support from the normally competent adult: slowed and simplified language, very explicit instructions, and carefully tailored expectations for performance.

The child's developmental goal—at least as far as society in general is concerned—is to attain adult competence, that is, to take responsibility for self. When a child is first born, responsibility for his or her well-being rests on adult caretakers. By the time the child is about twenty-five years old, he or she is expected to be able to function independently. However, total responsibility is not expected of the adult in the earliest days of the child's life, nor is total responsibility for self (necessarily) taken by the adult member of society. Work over the two decades has clearly documented the role of the infant in eliciting appropriate interaction from caretaking adults, and few adults, however self-sufficient, are independent of the structure of our societal institutions.

This interaction between child and adult has specific implications for remediation and management. It would appear that the "natural" management strategy of the adult playing/working with the child is to provide what is perceived to be missing "inside the child's head." Many remedial models, however, ignore the reciprocal nature of the child-world interaction and emphasize constant rehearsal of the activity that the child has difficulty performing. This is not what the adult does in normal social interaction with young children. Rather, the adult provides support for the goal of the overall behavioral interchange, not for any one part of it.

The adult's support of the child's behavior is consistent in terms of the underlying brain systems that are presumed to mediate the relevant behaviors; the behaviors themselves can be (and in most cases are likely to be) different. Thus, if the child fails to comprehend, then the adult changes the language delivery style (slowing, simplifying, repeating, rephrasing); if the child makes a serious syntactic error, then the adult models the correct form and continues with the conversational interchange; if the child cannot find an appropriate word, then the adult supplies it and, again, maintains the communication. In all instances, the adult's behavior is complementary to that of the child and maintains the overall social behavior.

Similarly, in the nonlanguage domain, a child with difficulty in modulating behavior, which is thought to reflect relatively immature input from frontal brain systems, elicits from the interacting adult a great degree of organization of his or her environment, an organizational capacity in the adult that is also considered to reflect the integrity of frontal brain systems. Again, the child with atypical social interaction, whose behavioral difficulties are seen in the context of a behavioral cluster implicating right-hemisphere brain systems, will elicit in the interacting adult exaggerated intonational contours and focusing gestures. The mobilization of these behaviors in social interaction has been shown to depend on the integrity of right-hemisphere brain systems in the adult (Ross 1985).

Interestingly enough, this sensitivity of the more competent to the less competent individual is not limited to adults. Children, too, offer extra behavioral support to anyone perceived as less competent than themselves; thus, older children will support younger children, and younger children will actively seek such support. The nature of the critical threshold of differences between competencies, that is, a difference sufficient to elicit interactive support, is not exactly clear. My observations, however, suggest that this is not simply an issue of chronological age; rather, it may require that the two individuals differ by a (possibly brain-based) developmental stage. Thus, a child of a given chronological age appears unable to provide any extra behavioral support for a child of similar age, even when the second child's "developmental age" is clearly discrepant with his or her years. In fact, children with a developmental age/chronological age discrepancy are all too often shunned by children their own age: their "best friends" are younger (matching in terms of developmental age) or older (providing behavioral support in the overall interaction).

OBSERVATION OF SPECIFIC PERFORMANCE

Observing the child under specific task demands reveals two aspects of his or her performance: (1) the *problem-solving strategy* (the *process*) by which he or she proceeds to a solution and (2) the ability to maintain age-appropriate behavioral control when he or she is under the *stress* of performance.

The Problem-Solving Strategy/Process. Almost every complex activity requiring a solution can be tackled in a variety of ways. (To this point, there are few systematic approaches to operationalizing different strategies [Milberg, Hebben, and Kaplan 1986].) Most standardized instruments yield scores that reflect only the level of performance; it is up to the clinician to examine the nature of the problem-solving process. Although there is no reason, in theory, why problem-solving strategies cannot be operationalized, formal measurement of such qualitative aspects of performance does not lend itself to a quantitative approach; rather, the clinician typically proceeds on the basis of binary decisions. For example, in the context of the Block Design subtest, one might ask the following questions:

1. Can the child analyze what is required in terms of individual blocks? (Yes/No)
2. Does the child appreciate the overall configurational parameters of the individual designs? (Yes/No)
3. Can the child maintain the orientational parameters of individual blocks? Of entire designs? (Yes/No)

4. Can the child "resist" stimulus-bound responding to salient but nonrelevant features of the materials? (Yes/No)
5. Can the child maintain problem-solving strategies in the face of increasing complexity (in this case, from four-block to nine-block designs)? (Yes/No)

Note that evidence of problem-solving strategies can be seen in terms of the parameters of performance that are available, as well as the actual errors made. In the context of visually represented materials (block designs, drawings, stick constructions, and so on), where the complementary contributions of different information-processing systems are the focus of examination, intact performance and error are simply different sides of the same coin. On other tasks, however, errors may be of very different types, for example, linguistically based (misnaming on the tasks tapping word retrieval) as opposed to perceptually based.

Careful, verbatim recording of a child's responses, both verbal and nonverbal, is critical to the analysis of problem-solving strategies. The clinician must learn to record exactly what the patient says, not what the clinician knows that the child intended to say, as well as the relative positions of blocks (Block Design) or puzzle pieces (Object Assembly). The clinician can follow a child's production of a complex drawing line-by-line, by noting the direction and sequence of lines (Kirk 1985) or by switching colored pens at specific points (Waber and Holmes 1985). Time-sampling of performance may also be useful, especially if the clinician finds it difficult to follow a particular type of behavior on a moment-by-moment basis. It is particularly important to develop techniques for recording ongoing problem-solving strategies when frank neurological damage is neither known nor necessarily can be assumed. The adult with a documentable brain lesion frequently offers an incorrect response as the solution to a problem; in such cases, the clinician can then examine the nature of the incorrect response (Goodglass and Kaplan 1979). The child, however, often proceeds to the correct solution; the clinician then must examine the nature of the problem-solving strategy employed on a moment-to-moment basis in order to elicit data concerning the diagnostic behavioral cluster.

In evaluating problem-solving strategies, formal clinical limit-testing techniques allow the clinician to test a hypothesis based on some aspect of the individual's performance. We will discuss clinical limit-testing further in chapter 7.

Stress. The concept of *stress* is a very important factor in behavioral assessment, which essentially involves imposing stress in a variety of ways, in an effort to expose vulnerable areas of functioning. Children can be stressed by pushing them beyond age-expected levels of knowledge; by requiring them to perform in their "weak" areas of ability; or by requiring them to maintain general behavioral controls in the face of a demand for performance on abstract activities that require high levels of cognitive/psychological energy. The child's response to such stress also can be used in the diagnostic process, that is, as a contributor to one or another critical behavioral cluster.

We can better understand the clinical uses of stress in the context of the neurological examination of the motor system. The pediatric neurologist determines the child's motor competence in two ways. First, the classical neurological examination determines whether the various parts of the child work correctly or if there are asymmetries, specific pathognomonic signs that highlight dysfunction of one or another important neurological system. Second, the extended neurological examination makes direct use of developmental processes themselves, assessing whether the child can do what is expected of a child his or her age. An examination can find a child at an appropriate level of development—with one striking abnormality. For example, a delightful, poised, and entirely appropriate thirteen-year-old boy was referred for problems in written language at the junior high school level. His concerned and sensitive parents were worried about the amount of effort (and psychological cost) involved in maintaining academic progress at this level of the curriculum, which included a heavy written-language load. The neurological examination documented a right hemi-syndrome with right hemi-atrophy—not remarkable to the untrained eye but nonetheless consistent with the presenting complaint in terms of the associated brain systems. (The patient and his parents, of course, had no reason to associate his written-language problems with the fact that his right foot was a whole shoe size smaller than the left.) In contrast, an examination can reveal that a youngster's motor system could work correctly but at a level more appropriate to a child two or three years younger. This type of profile has been demonstrated repeatedly in children with "hyperactivity," that is, difficulties in the appropriate modulation of motor-activity levels.

Developmental progression, as it concerns the motor system, can be seen as the increasing ability of the brain to send information to specific parts of the body without aspects of that information "overflowing" into other parts. The classic, frequently entertaining, demonstration of this principle, known as *stressed gaits*, is seen daily in neurology departments and offices everywhere. The neurologist stresses a child's system by asking him or her to tackle a nonroutine activity. For example, small children are asked to walk on tiptoe. If the child is only four years old, his or her hands will "walk on tiptoe" also. If the child is asked to walk on his or her heels, the palms of the hands face forward, "heel" down. If the child is asked to walk on the outsides of his or her feet, a small simian strolls down the corridor King Kong style—elbows out, hands curved in and around. If the child is asked to walk on the insides of his or her feet, the arms stiffen and the hands twist back and up. For a four-year-old, all of these associated behaviors are appropriate. The upper extremities pattern their movements in direct response to the gait of the lower extremities. The command to move the lower limbs "overflows" into the upper extremities. These "stressed gaits" are graded in difficulty. As children mature, they gradually become able to carry out each of the gaits—walking on tiptoes, walking on heels, walking on outsides of feet, walking in insides of feet—without overflow of the movement elsewhere in the body. Thus, five-year-olds and six-year-olds can walk on their toes without overflow but not necessarily on their heels or the sides of their feet. Eight-year-olds still have trouble with the insides-of-feet gait but should be able to complete the others cleanly. As the child matures, the nervous system becomes increasingly able to send messages to discrete parts of the body without any overflow. If these associated movements persist beyond the expected age, then the neurologist is alerted to possible developmental problems.

This aspect/correlate of stress can be equally valuable when looking at psychological, rather than motor, behavior. Observation of a small child under the stress of higher-order thinking demands frequently reveals the child's inability to maintain developmentally appropriate inhibitory control of the motor system when he or she is asked to tackle those "nonmotor" tasks that are most stressful. Thus, a child who has to expend an inordinate amount of energy to complete a verbal output task (because he or she has specific difficulty in language output), for example, may well be unable to inhibit an accompanying increase in motor-activity level. The same child, however, may have a perfectly normal level of general motor activity when asked to complete tasks involving, for example, silent reading or drawing. Similarly, increased motor activity may accompany drawing tasks in another child, even though language tasks of any type are not associated with motor-activity levels in other than the normal range. Frequently, such increases in associated motor activity affect the body bilaterally; for example, jiggling, itching, swinging of the legs accompany a verbal output task in one child—or a drawing activity in another.

It is not uncommon to see children demonstrate a specific inability to monitor the side of the body controlled by those brain systems involved in the targeted behavior. One girl, for example, responded, almost like clockwork: whenever a task had an expressive language demand, her right leg would start to swing; as soon as it was her turn to listen, the leg stopped; and so on. This example, in fact, demonstrates the degree of awareness of the child's overall motor-activity level that the examiner must bring to the assessment procedure. Overflow movements need not simply affect the body as a whole but may affect the individual limbs differentially. The clinical examiner should be sufficiently aware of these interactions to sit in a position—and to move appropriately—in which he or she can observe the child's feet, hands, and face—the mouth and tongue, in particular.

The inability to maintain appropriate behavioral control under the stress of other activities is not confined to the motor system. An increase in stress can push a child down a rung on the developmental ladder in terms of specific behaviors, as well as in terms of overall motoric competence. Just as extraneous motor behaviors "go underground" in the older individual, overt verbalization skills also "go underground" in the young child. Early in language development, children typically talk their way through an activity. This overt control of behavior by language, however, should give way to "inner speech" by about the age of seven (Vygotsky 1962). A child who is still overtly talking his or her way through a task at the age of nine or ten, then, raises the hypothesis that there is some specific vulnerability associated with the task at hand.

This vulnerability may not be specific to language, however, and thus imply dysfunction of language. Language skills may be intact—but not yet comfortably "underground." In this case, another task may take so much energy that overt language cannot be effectively inhibited—implicating the brain systems that subserve the nonlanguage task in the diagnosis. A child may not need to talk as he or she works out the answers to verbal questions, but he or she may be completely unable to inhibit such associated conversation while working on a visual-motor task; further, a very specific type of visual-motor task may be needed to elicit the talking-out behavior. Some children cannot inhibit accompanying verbalization when they have a pen in their hand, but they are completely silent and engrossed when tackling block designs, and some children show the reverse pattern. In contrast, the disinhibition of language systems may be seen only when the child is trying to handle verbally presented materials and may be completely absent when the child has a pen or other manipulable materials in hand.

The disinhibition of the language system need not be organized language and/or specifically focused on the task at hand. Some children do talk to themselves and listen to what they are saying, using language to guide their performance directly. Other children simply talk to themselves: they may not be listening to what they are saying, even if the language appears relevant to the task at hand. Sometimes, a good remedial strategy is to ask the child to listen to him- or herself! Accompanying language can also be unconnected nonsense—rhymes, poems, or songs—or vocalization—humming, whistling, clucking—rather than verbalization. (Plosive vocalizations may require further evaluation for the possibility of tics as a factor in a given child's performance.)

In older children, and in very specific task contexts, the presence of (subvocal) verbalization can be cued by silence, which is signaled by a "giveaway" pause in the response pattern. The young child often tells the clinician what he or she is doing in order to solve the problem; this information may help in elucidating patterns of behavior in an older child, for whom the verbal characterization of the problem-solving process has "gone undergound." For example, this specific pattern of behavior emerges in response to backward digits sequences from the Digit Span task. After the examiner presents, say, four digits, the older child often pauses for a measurable period and then presents the last number in the sequence; pauses again and then presents the second-to-last number in the sequence; and pauses a third time before presenting the last two digits as a pair. Thus, 3–4–1–7 is offered by the patient as ".......... 7 . . . 1 . . . 4–3" and recorded on the scoring protocol as 7, 1, 43. The underlying process is immediately recognizable when an obliging seven- or eight-year-old tackles the same task: ". . . . 3–4–1–7 . . . 3–4–1–7 . . . 3–4–1–7 . . . 7! 3–4–1 . . . 3–4–1 . . . 1! 43!" The younger child explicitly signals this forward digit rehearsal strategy, while the older child using the same strategy signals only the pause pattern—the overt recitation of the numbers being carried out at a subvocal level.

The clinician should distinguish this overt verbalization during a problem-solving activity from verbal mediation of behavior. When a behavior that should have "gone underground" (given the child's age) remains overt, the anterior/posterior axis of the brain—specifically, insecure frontal system input—is implicated for this particular child. If the language system is released from inhibitory control, then the clinician may hypothesize that left frontal brain mechanisms are critically involved. Verbal disinhibition is also found in individuals with right-hemisphere dysfunction. In such a case, left-hemisphere systems are "released" from the inhibitory control of their partner (the right hemisphere) on the lateral axis. Such examples only serve to highlight the importance of the diagnostic behavioral cluster in an overall assessment.

Lastly, the extraneous motor activities—jiggling and itching, fidgeting and stretching—that suggest an immature motor system and/or a motor system under stress often are interpreted as reflecting "anxiety." To the extent that the observed "anxious" behavior leads a clinician to explore more thoroughly the source of this anxiety, he or she is proceeding according to the general assessment strategy proposed here. However, "anxiety" is all too often used in clinical practice as an autonomous diagnosis that, at best, leaves the child's specific difficulties undiagnosed and, at worst, may lead to inappropriate, expensive, and time-consuming treatment. An eight-year-old girl, with an IQ score of 140 on the WISC-R, for example, hummed, clucked, wriggled, and fidgeted constantly as she worked. She could not demonstrate age-appropriate motor performance on formal examination, and she responded very positively to stimulant medication prescribed by the pediatric neurologist. An initial diagnosis of "body anxiety," which had led to an insight-oriented psychotherapy, proved far less useful than the pharmacologic support and the behavioral management strategy used both at home and at school.

THE CHILD'S APPEARANCE

In order to get a complete picture, it is important to examine the child directly. If the child's height differs from the norm, for example, then the clinician may be alerted to differences in experience that may be reflected in specific task performance and/or behavioral cluster formation. Anomalies of brain development that may be manifest in later neuro-psychological difficulty can occur as a function of genetic/chromosomal disorder, prematurity, prenatal or postnatal teratogens, treatment for specific disease, and so on, and frequently affect the growth of easily identifiable facial and bodily features. Down's syndrome, Turner's syndrome, fetal hydantoinism, fetal alcohol syndrome, and anomalies of facial growth planes and midline structures—all of these disorders may have specific neuropsychological implications.

The clinician should also take careful note of personal hygiene and dress. Sartorial style, especially in teenagers, often signals psychological and/or social (mal)adjustment, challenging peer-group or parental expectations. The ten-year-old who is "going on thirty" (or six), as manifest in the style of his or her clothing, may be reflecting his or her designated role in the family. The overly neat child may be somewhat obsessive—or may be under excessive parental demands for neat appearance. The disheveled and unkempt child may well be a disorganized individual—to the despair of his or her parent(s) who struggles on a daily basis to send the child off in a reasonably coherent fashion. When both the parent(s) and the child appear disheveled, the clinician will need to take into account the ability of a (possibly disorganized) family to respond to recommendations forthcoming from the evaluation. A child's dress and personal hygiene may also speak to his or her socioeconomic status, knowledge of which may be important not only to intervention strategies but also in terms of specific neuropsychological variables (Waber et al. 1984).

The data gained in review of the child's family and personal history provide a context for the child's performance on standardized test instruments. Specific tests and the process by which they are used as part of the overall assessment are discussed in the following chapter.

Chapter 7

Testing

JANE M. HOLMES

The testing component of neuropsychological assessment is not limited to tests that have been identified as "neuropsychological." The psychological clinicians must choose a range of tests sufficiently wide to allow for converging evidence—from different contexts—to substantiate the presence of a particular deficit or problem. Poor performance on a single measure is not sufficient for diagnosis. The selected tests must evaluate behaviors related to all three brain axes of the neuropsychological model outlined in chapter 5 in order to address issues pertaining to developmental change.

Domains of Behavior

The domains of behavior identified below represent a minimum sampling of behavior necessary for neuropsychological assessment. The depth to which the clinician explores each domain depends on the nature of the referral questions and the initial findings. The clinician now has available a wide range of tests and tasks within each domain that can define quite precisely different aspects of behavior as required for clinical management or research. Before the examiner can address behavioral issues, however, the initial neuropsychological assessment must review the wider, neuroanatomic picture. The domains of behavior relevant for neuropsychological assessment are

- arousal, attention, and modulation of behavior
- motor and sensory capacities
- general cognitive ability
- language and related processing skills
- nonverbal and visually represented materials
- learning new information and manipulating old knowledge
- executive control, planning, and reasoning
- emotional status and personality development
- academic achievement

Not all of these domains are best tapped by means of tests; in fact, they all require data from the patient's developmental history and clinician's observations (see chapter 6) in addition to test results. In this chapter, I will discuss the testing component of assessment, including formal psychological measurement instruments and informal behavioral tasks, which provide evidence for a child's performance in confrontational and spontaneous contexts, respectively. In administering these formal tests and informal tasks, the clinician can identify a diagnostic behavioral cluster by assessing the following types of information:

1. The *level* of performance on a given activity
2. The *quality* of performance on the activity
3. The *relationship* between the level and the quality of performance on different activities
4. The *problem-solving strategy* (process) used to reach a solution

AROUSAL, ATTENTION, AND MODULATION OF BEHAVIOR

The behaviors associated with arousal, attention, and modulation of behavior are derived primarily from observational data, rather than from specific tests. A psychological test is not, after all, needed to demonstrate that a child is asleep, nor that he or she is drowsy because of drug toxicity.

Poor attentional focus and/or concentration difficulty can be elicited by means of continuous performance tasks. However, it is usually direct observation of the child and his or her strategy of performance, rather than formal scores, that identifies the impulsive, distractible, or impersistent behaviors associated with attention disorders.

Observational data include direct observation of the child's behavior (in the assessment as a whole and in the context of specific tasks); observations from interviews with the parent(s) or teacher(s); and observations derived from formal questionnaires, such as the developmental history form completed by the parent(s) prior to the evaluation (see chapter 4).

Behavioral checklists are also valuable starting points for evaluating general competence or well-being. For example, *Conners' Rating Scale for Hyperactivity* (1979) elicits from the parent(s) and/or teachers ratings of ten critical behaviors in a thirty-item questionnaire. Using a four-point scale for each item, a total score of sixteen for the ten critical behaviors raises the possibility of primary attentional difficulty. This instrument repeatedly has been proven valuable in both clinical settings and research. In the clinical setting, the parent's "tolerance" for the target behaviors must also be evaluated. A second behavioral checklist, *Achenbach's Child Behavior Checklist* (1982), contains 118 items for which the parent(s) uses a three-point scale to rate each behavior. The examiner compares the child's behavioral profile with normative standards in order to assess "internalizing" (depressed, somatic complaints, et cetera) and "externalizing" (hyperactive, aggressive, et cetera) characteristics.

The clinician can estimate the child's ability to fulfill age-appropriate behavioral expectations on the basis of information from these or other instruments. He or she can obtain further information from the clinical dyad, task-specific behaviors, and the motor examination. This information—adjusted for developmental competence—forms the basis for assessing the integrity of the cortical/subcortical axis of the brain, that is, the reciprocal relationship between frontal brain systems and the limbic and reticular activating systems.

MOTOR AND SENSORY CAPACITIES

Direct observation of the child is, again, a critical first step in documenting the status of the motor and sensory systems. The experienced clinician treats all behaviors as "tasks" and does not fail to note clumsy play in the waiting room, inability to extend the correct hand in greeting, an asymmetric or uncoordinated gait, anomalous hand use in bimanual activities, or atypical eye movements in face-to-face interaction. All asymmetries should be noted, those involving the sides of the body and the sides of personal space, as well as those involving differential use of test materials, all of which may implicate the left-right axis of the brain. The nature of the asymmetry—motor, spatial awareness—may well point to the anterior/posterior brain axis and also may allow for distinctions within this larger category (motor or premotor cortex versus parietal association areas).

Formal neurological testing should be referred to a neurologist. The neuropsychologist must know when observations warrant referral and when the observed behaviors are "developmental," that is, characteristic of a learning disorder and not indicative of serious, ongoing disease. An ongoing consultative relationship with a pediatric neurologist is clearly valuable in this regard.

The evaluation of the child's motor system includes tests of lateral preference, pegboards, and timed motor skills. Tests of lateral preference use a variety of activities involving fine-motor coordination and whole body use to demonstrate the child's lateral preference (Harris 1958, or Oldfield 1971). Children who are non-right-handed may lack the "standard" brain organization pattern; therefore, behavioral clusters may differ (or may differ in their implications). The clinician should always consider the possibility of pathological left-handedness, especially when there is a history of early trauma or a difference in size between the two sides of the body. In any unconstrained situation, the clinician can identify the child's preference by observing which side he or she leads with. Pegboards tap motor dexterity, coordination, and speed against age-referenced norms (Knights and Moule 1968). The child's ability to manipulate the pegs and/or to judge the peg/hole relationship yields qualitative information as to his or her motor competence. The *Timed Motor Examination* (Denckla 1973) requires the child to perform six different activities using feet, hands, and fingers of both right and left sides of the body. For each task (three are repetitive, three involve patterned movements), twenty contacts are timed, and the times are compared to age-referenced norms, provided separately for males and females, in order to document the child's level of performance. Levels of performance on the two sides are compared to assess asymmetries of both speed and quality (the presence of overflow movements, the rate and rhythmicity of the target movements) in terms of age-expectancy.

Informal neurological observations used routinely in my practice also include the stressed gaits (see chapter 6, pages 160–61); balance; sustentation; strength (eyelids, tongue, fingers, wrist, and so on); winking; whistling; tongue lateralization; repetition of sequenced syllables; eyemovements; axial, buccofacial and limb praxis; and hand postures (sequenced versus alternating). As when examining the motor system generally, the clinician is always on the lookout for (1) the ability to do the task, (2) asymmetries in performance, and (3) the quality of performance. Both the nature of a specific motor deficit and the nature of ongoing motor output provide information concerning subcortical and cortical motor systems. The clinician's careful observations of motor performance (rate, timing, fluency, et cetera), as opposed to accurate programming of individual segments, is especially important.

Tests and tasks tapping sensory capacities include stereognosis (tactile recognition of objects); graphaesthesia (tactile recognition of letters and numbers "written" on the palm of the hand or fingertips); right-left orientation (identification of right and left on self and others); finger gnosis (ability to differentiate individual fingers); and double simultaneous stimulation (ability to discriminate tactile stimulation presented to the hands, the face, or both). Sensory findings implicate parietal brain systems. Children with these findings constitute a small but recognizable percentage of the children referred for learning disorders. We have recently identified a group of children who demonstrate a behavioral cluster consistent with parietal dysfunction, including corticosensory findings, constructional apraxias, and subtle discontinuities in language comprehension, particularly when metaphoric language is involved (Holmes, Urion, and Waber, unpublished manuscript). Complaints about these children typically center on their inability to think independently despite their ability to learn; their failure to "read" the pragmatic underpinnings of social situations; and their difficulty in inferential or deductive reasoning— observations that fit well with our understanding of the role of parietal brain systems, as derived from the study of adults.

Testing

GENERAL COGNITIVE ABILITY

Although the neuropsychological approach focuses on the interaction of different brain systems and their contributions to specific behavioral domains, a preliminary statement about the child's intellectual status is important. A child with, say, a left-hemisphere-implicating profile and an IQ score of 130 (that is, two standard deviations above the mean for his or her age group) is very different from one with a left-hemisphere-implicating profile whose IQ score is 90 (that is, in the average range). At the very least, the difference in scores suggests different compensatory potential in the two children—important for the formulation of management strategies. In terms of the diagnostic process, however, the difference in scores is likely to be associated with different behavioral clusters. A higher level of demand may be required to elicit critical behaviors in the brighter child, who may be able to solve the problems posed by the examiner in terms of the level of performance but who may reveal a discrepancy in the quality thereof. In such instances the behavioral cluster approach becomes critical: where subtle discontinuities in ongoing performance constitute the observable data, the discontinuities in behavior must occur regularly and predictably in relevant contexts throughout the assessment.

There are several standardized intellectual batteries in current use, all of which provide a range of measures of relevant behaviors. Perhaps most widely used of all are the Wechsler scales: *Wechsler Preschool and Primary Scale of Intelligence (WPPSI)*, *Wechsler Intelligence Scale for Children—Revised (WISC-R)*, and *Wechsler Adult Intelligence Scale—Revised (WAIS-R)* (Wechsler 1967, 1974, 1981). The *Stanford-Binet Intelligence Scale*, now in its fourth edition (Thorndike, Hagen, and Sattler 1986), and the *Kaufman Assessment Battery for Children* (Kaufman and Kaufman 1983) also provide up-to-date normative standards for a composite ability score, as well as for age-related performance on individual tasks.

None of these batteries can be considered sufficient for neuropsychological purposes. (In most cases, they were not intended for use in neuropsychological assessment.) Their primary failing is their lack of adequate evaluation of language capacity. Although a serious language impairment is not likely to be missed on verbal subtests, the types of "covert" language problems that occur regularly among learning-disabled children may not inhibit performance on the verbal tasks of comprehensive cognitive batteries. Many children diagnosed as "language-impaired" (relative to their other abilities) on formal tests of language function perform perfectly well on IQ tests. Conversely, the individual with the lower verbal IQ score does not necessarily have a primary language disability; lack of educational exposure (for whatever reason) can markedly limit the acquisition of verbal knowledge.

The Verbal scale of the Wechsler tests is not a gauge of language ability; rather it taps verbal knowledge. A child can have a very high Verbal IQ score and still demonstrate significantly impaired language capabilities. Indeed, this pattern is often seen among children referred for learning disorders (especially as these impact on written-language skills) and is by no means uncommon in children who prove to have documentable brain lesions involving the language systems (usually) of the left hemisphere. Further, the scoring criteria for the Vocabulary subtest allows full credit for very different types of response, even though responses may highlight a significant language (word retrieval?) deficit or even a nonlanguage, right-hemisphere-implicating problem. (See chapter 5, pages 115–16.) As long as the child can somehow demonstrate his or her verbal knowledge, the WISC-R will give credit for it. Similarly, although the questions of the Comprehension subtest seem to require a high degree of linguistic processing, their repeated "if (salient concept), then" format presents the problems in a way that is accessible to many children with minimal recourse to precise linguistic analysis; in this way, the Comprehension subtest is insensitive to subtler degrees of language-processing difficulty.

Careful item analysis of this type is, of course, the very stuff of good psychological assessment practice. It is not simply a strategy applicable at the level of subtest analysis, however. The relationship between the level of performance of the various subscales and their subtests can provide valuable data for an initial hypothesis. For example, if a child's Verbal IQ score is significantly lower than his or her Performance IQ score, then the clinician may hypothesize an underlying insecurity in language capacities—implicating an inadequate left-hemisphere contribution to ongoing behavior. Neither of these may turn out to be the final diagnosis; nonetheless, in the absence of other data, they constitute the best initial hypothesis and mandate formal evaluation of language skills.

In contrast, an equally significant reverse discrepancy (a Verbal IQ score *higher* than the Performance IQ score) does not entail one single hypothesis—and, in particular, does not imply that right-hemisphere systems are "out of balance." Examination of the demand characteristics of Performance subscale items suggests the reason. The Performance tasks all involve visually represented materials; as such, they require dual hemispheric input for their solution. Failure on these tasks can implicate either left-hemisphere or right-hemisphere difficulties. To the extent that the problem is related to the lateral brain axis, the clinician must carefully examine the strategies employed or attempted in solving the task. But the tasks of the Performance subscale are also subject to timing, and the time needed for completion of individual items is part of the data used for establishing the scaled scores. To the extent that speed implies both the ability to solve the problem and the ability to organize the problem-solving approach efficiently, the disorganized child whose problem implicates the anterior/posterior axis (rather than the lateral axis) may have specific difficulty with the timed Performance subtests and thus obtain a lower Performance IQ score. This is particularly likely for children eleven or twelve years old or older: to achieve a sufficiently sensitive measure of the greater "brain power" of the more mature child, speed of problem solution must be used to determine the score.

Similarly, patterns within subtests can provide the data for an initial hypothesis. On the Verbal subscale, for instance, when the Arithmetic and Comprehension scores vary together (against the flow of the other scores), the clinician may conclude that right-hemisphere functioning is important in elucidating the child's thinking/learning style. On the other hand, when Picture Arrangement and Coding scores vary together, left-hemisphere-mediated processing skills may be implicated. In these two instances, the information gained may be both positive and negative; that is, Arithmetic and Comprehension scores that are above the mean for the child suggest effective right-hemisphere-mediated skills, whereas scores that are lower than the mean may imply less competent right-hemisphere input. Positive data of this type are, of course, crucial components of the diagnostic behavioral cluster: in order to identify a specific left-hemisphere-based deficit, the clinician must find that right-hemisphere skills are available. After all, the child may have a problem related to both partners of the lateral axis, the crucial axis for differential diagnosis being the anterior/posterior axis or the cortical/subcortical axis. This can be seen in the case of parietal symptomatology (page 170) or where the clinician finds an ability/achievement discrepancy.

The cluster of tasks is important. A low score on the Arithmetic subtest, standing alone, tells the clinician nothing. In solving the Arithmetic problems, the child needs (at the very least) to be able to attend, to hear, to listen effectively, to process linguistic units at several levels, to retain numeric information in the correct order, to understand the relationships governing numeric symbolism, to handle multiple operations simultaneously, to retain arithmetic facts, and to compute accurately. Without further information, derived from the behavioral cluster, the clinician cannot make an informed decision regarding the relative salience of each of these abilities. The right hemisphere's role in the acquisition of socially relevant knowledge and in the parallel processing of multiple pieces of information in the arithmetic domain is highlighted in the pairing of Arithmetic and Comprehension test results; the left hemisphere's role in serial processing of sequenced information links comparable performance on Picture Arrangement and Coding tests. However, a low Arithmetic score (from the first cluster) and a low Coding score (from the other) in conjunction with a low score on Digit Span may not lead to any conclusions concerning left- or right-hemisphere processing: this triad of subtests is considered to be sensitive to attentional difficulties in many (but certainly not all) children. In all these instances more data are needed to verify the initial hypothesis concerning the critical brain axes involved for a given child; a behavioral cluster of two observations is not sufficient to establish a diagnosis.

Standardized intellectual batteries not only provide a measure of the child's overall ability but also speak to different domains of behavior. Verbal subtests contribute information about language, attention, and verbal learning and memory; performance tasks yield evidence concerning visual-processing skills, nonverbal learning and memory, and planning and organizational ability. The clinician uses the information observed in conjunction with performance on both subscales in evaluating motor and sensory capacities and overall emotional adjustment.

Let us take several examples from WISC-R subtests—to illustrate the neuropsychological approach to these materials. Information and Vocabulary are very powerful subtests with respect to the child's language-processing capabilities. They are, first, usefully contrasted in terms of their demand characteristics: on the Information subtest, the child is required to process a more or less complex utterance and find a precise piece of knowledge; on the Vocabulary subtest, he or she is given a precise piece of language knowledge and asked to provide a self-generated utterance. Children whose underlying neuropsychological deficit can be attributed to a "left-hemisphere down" pattern may differ in the nature of their difficulty in the language domain: one child may benefit from the structure provided by the Information subtest format; another child may do better with the opportunity to wax somewhat lyrical on the relatively unconstrained format of the Vocabulary subtest. The child who scores higher on the Vocabulary subtest may, nonetheless, reveal problems in verbal formulation, giving enough information for credit only by listing associations or by resorting to explanatory gestures, which suggests yet another potential pattern of language-based difficulty. On the other hand, the child may wander completely from the pertinent universe of discourse, raising the hypothesis that the right hemisphere's contribution to effective communication is lacking (see chapter 5, pages 115–16).

The format of the Information subtest is ideal for eliciting word-retrieval problems; indeed, such problems are often seen here first. In order to be quite sure that the child's hesitations ("er! . . . er! . . . er!") and air of searching for a particular word are really indicative of a word-retrieval deficit and not the child's own lack of knowledge, the clinician employs clinical limit-testing, in this case by quickly providing the child with three choices for response and assessing the speed and accuracy with which he or she recognizes the correct answer. At least three choices are necessary in this instance to limit guessing strategies; the examiner must offer the three choices with equivalent intonational emphasis—to avoid cuing the correct answer—and must have three reasonable choices immediately available—to maintain the tempo of the clinical interaction and, again, to avoid cuing the child as to the correct response. For example, I typically say: "Is it Benjamin Franklin, Thomas Edison, or Alexander Graham Bell?" when the child searches for a response to the question, Who invented the electric light bulb? and I vary the order in which I present the choices from one child to the next, to further minimize any tendency to cue the child.

Clinical Limit-Testing. Clinical limit-testing provides for immediate validation of a hypothesis based on some particular observed behavior. The goal is to provide for the child the piece of information that is hypothesized to be lacking in his or her performance. The immediacy and accuracy of the child's subsequent response tells the examiner whether or not the clinical hunch was correct. For example, if the child immediately recognizes the correct answer in a multiple-choice format offered in response to apparent word-finding difficulty, this is support for the hypothesis that a word-finding deficit exists; if the child can quickly arrange the individual blocks of a Block Design problem once the examiner has provided the organizational parameters, then the examiner's hypothesis that the child has a problem with organization is confirmed.

Clinical limit-testing requires considerable rigor on the part of the examiner. It is important that it be systematically undertaken and that its use be noted in the clinical report. Formal instructions for task administration must be observed initially. In some instances, however, it may be very useful to "double score" a test to document, for example, that age-appropriate knowledge is present even when it cannot be demonstrated in a particular task format. On verbal tasks, double scoring can include the knowledge demonstrated according to formal scoring criteria plus that revealed by multiple-choice techniques or by taking the child beyond formal scoring limits because of a repeated error type. On timed tests, double scoring may include the child's timed and untimed performance, especially when the child uses an efficient (albeit time-consuming) strategy that results in accurate completion of the problem on an independent basis within a reasonable time frame. A child's ability to mobilize effective problem-solving strategies (even if it takes time to do so) is a significant piece of information for teachers: after all, the ability to solve a problem, whether in the classroom or in real life, can be more important than the speed with which it is solved.

Formal limit-testing techniques also include strategies to ensure that a child understands the nature of a particular activity. Most standardized tests allow some supportive "over-instruction," where needed, at the beginning of a task. However, some children may need considerable extra assistance in establishing the set of a new task: exemplars, cue phrases, and structuring questions may aid the examiner in dissecting the nature of the child's difficulty when faced with a new problem.

The decision to use a clinical limit-testing technique must be made carefully. It is not appropriate to "test" every response a child makes; indeed, the examiner who needs to test every response does not have a specific hypothesis in mind and, thus, cannot be said to understand the rationale of this assessment strategy. On verbal tasks, individual items can be tested as they arise; after all, there is no inherent relationship between one Information question and the next. On timed tasks involving visually presented materials that require organized problem-solving strategies, however, this is not the case. Since a child can learn from a limit-testing technique, such input on one item could affect later items and thus compromise the information derived from standard scores. On such materials, clinical limit-testing must wait until the child has fulfilled the formal criteria for discontinuing the task.

The issue of learning from clinical limit-testing is also important with respect to future assessments using the same instruments. Is a clinician giving the child information that will invalidate later testing? In my opinion, the information to be gained from careful and systematic limit testing is of crucial importance, not only to effective diagnosis, but also for the development of treatment strategies, and outweighs any potential negative impact on future scoring. Further, the child who can profit by limit testing to the extent that he or she recalls it for later use should, in my opinion, get credit for the learning involved. Efficient use of diagnostic behavioral clusters in any future evaluation would also militate against misdiagnosis because of an anomalous score on one test at that later date.

Clinical limit-testing also helps in establishing rapport between examiner and child, because it communicates the examiner's interest in the child's knowledge, not just in his or her "exam-taking technique." However, the clinician must also remember that some children are only stressed by further "pushing," even when offered supportively; in these instances, the examiner must find critical diagnostic information elsewhere.

Item Analysis. Item analysis of individual WISC-R subtests is often important. On the Information subtest, for example, children with insecure language may well have difficulty with series-based knowledge, especially the date-related series. Right-hemisphere-implicating behavioral clusters often include a discrepancy between discrete (usually formally taught) facts (Who invented X?) and information that is inferred or deduced from knowledge of the relevant variables (How far is it from A to B? How tall is the average Y?). It is typically the latter type of question that elicits "out of the ball park" estimations or guesses from the child with a right-hemisphere-implicating profile, for example. The isolated word format of the Vocabulary subtest also may elicit discontinuities in precise auditory perception that are not easily appreciated where longer utterances provide contextual support. Some children also demonstrate sensitivity to the syntactic class of the target vocabulary words, having greater difficulty in formulating a definition of items other than nouns. The neuropsychologically based vulnerability in this regard may make it easier for emotionally relevant material to intrude in a child with pressing emotional concerns. Questions on the Comprehension subtest are also powerful elicitors of such material: they vary in the degree of structure they provide with regard to the knowledge of social expectations they tap, and they provide opportunity for disinhibited/poorly modulated answers that can cue the clinician not only to emotional concerns and distress but also to the possibility of social imperception or disorganized thinking. The score structure is often revealing on this test: does the child get full credit for few items (with or without disinhibited response) or does the child get half-credit for most of the task?

The Similarities task is all too often overvalued. I am particularly disturbed by the number of children whose "potential" is determined by a high score on this subtest of the WISC-R, even though the rest of their scores on the Verbal scale (or on the test as a whole) are more than a standard deviation below the Similarities score. Such expectations based on the Similarities score alone can put an unfair pressure on a child whose "comfort level" in learning is consistent with that predicted by other test items. Similarities is a limited test of "abstraction" (Edith Kaplan, personal communication, 1975). For the earlier word pairs, at least, the test items can be easily solved by association: one of the highest-frequency associates of any word is, after all, its superordinate; and thus, only one of the words in the Similarities test may be needed to elicit it. Kaplan argues that a better test of the child's ability to deal in abstract concepts would require him or her to provide ways in which the target words are alike and unalike, as in the Likenesses and Differences subtest of the (old) *Detroit Tests of Learning Aptitude* (Baker and Leland 1967). Not surprisingly, perhaps, this test is sensitive to the associative and integrative difficulties with abstract materials observed in children with parietal-implicating behavioral profiles.

The Digit Span subtest can be particularly informative. It provides a measure of auditory span, which is important in evaluating the ability to handle linguistic structures of different lengths and which can be compared with measures of span for visually represented materials, such as the Corsi blocks (Milner 1971) or the Word Order subtest of the *Kaufman Assessment Battery for Children*. Errors on the Digit Span subtest, which include loss of order of elements, loss of information, perseveration of

178

elements within and between trials, stimulus-bound "pull" to the standard number series, and confabulatory response, all have potentially different cluster membership and, thus, different diagnostic significance. The child who encounters difficulty on the backward digits condition (even though he or she can easily accomplish the forward digits trial) may be a disorganized child who is overwhelmed by multiple-operation demands. Such a child often has a low score on the Arithmetic subtest, also, but may demonstrate computational efficiency when given paper and pencil (after fulfilling the formal criteria for discontinuing the task). Discrepancies between forward and backward digit spans can have other implications, as well. A depressed individual, for example, may fail to mobilize adequate resources for a given task until the demand intensifies, which is often displayed in a higher backward score on the Digit Span subtest. Rudel and Denckla (1974) have also demonstrated differential performance on digit spans by two clinical groups with different neurological findings. Children with left hemiparesis (indicating right-frontal brain dysfunction) scored lower in terms of the absolute number of digits expected for age on backward digits, while children with right hemiparesis (left-frontal dysfunction) scored lower on forward digits. Although such findings implicate left- and right-frontal brain systems in forward and backward digits recall, respectively, the performance of an individual (as opposed to a group) must be evaluated very carefully with regard to the identification of a given brain system, especially where actual brain damage cannot be assumed. For example, the child who tackled the backward digits task in terms of forward digits rehearsal (chapter 6, page 163) is very likely to have a significantly lower backward digit span because he or she used a great deal of energy in the rehearsal process. A "right-hemisphere deficit" is not necessarily indicated in the case of this lowered backward digit span, however, since there is no evidence that right-hemisphere-based strategies were mobilized to solve the task.

The Performance subscale often elicits word-retrieval deficits in the search for the missing items in the Picture Completion subtest. Poor performance on both Picture Completion and Coding implicates insecurity in linear processing. A child may be able to solve the Picture Arrangement and Object Assembly subtests by referring to real-world knowledge that is not so useful or available for other tasks. One child may find Block Design especially difficult because of its abstract organizational demands; however, another child may have no problem with

A   B

FIGURE 7.1

the subtest because a target model is always present; thus, he or she does not have to generate or maintain the goal of the activity, as seems to be the case for both Picture Arrangement and Object Assembly subtests.

Children can, of course, make different types of errors on Performance items. The child's inability to appreciate details carries a different implication in terms of behavioral cluster membership than failure to appreciate the point of the social situations in the Picture Arrangement subtest. Block Design elicits information relevant to organizational capacity, including the child's problem-solving strategy and the time/solution relationship (the anterior/posterior axis), and to information-processing style, as measured by the child's specific manipulation of blocks (the lateral axis). In figure 7.1, example A is frequently seen in response to example B in the presence of a right-hemisphere or right-frontal behavioral cluster (see also chapter 5, page 141). Figure 7.2 is the production of another nine-block design by a sixteen-year-old boy with a longstanding language-based learning disorder (left-hemisphere-implicating behavioral cluster). This design represents a routine verbatim record of the young man's performance: the sequence of blocks is numbered; and a dot indicates red color on the blocks (which have all-red, all-white, and half-red/half-white sides). Note the consistent maintenance of the configurational parameters (three-by-three matrix) of the design with the constant readjustment of individual blocks, the extent of the trial-and-error strategy needed for the right side as opposed to the left side of the figure and the amount of time (lower right) needed for this problem-solving approach to be completed (two minutes is the limit for this item). This young man

180

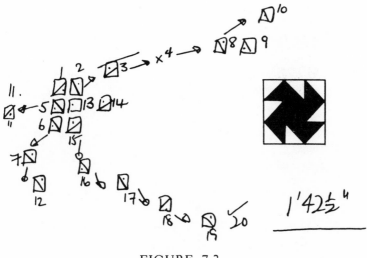

FIGURE 7.2

did not get a particularly good formal score for his Block Design performance, because he is near the age limit of the task and is heavily penalized
for lack of speed; the quality of his performance continues to cluster,
however, with other left-hemisphere-implicating behaviors (developmental history, spontaneous and formally elicited language, motor and
academic skills development) that he has repeatedly demonstrated over
several years. The precise composition of the diagnostic cluster has
changed over time in response to different environmental demands, in
accordance with Rudel's (1981a) "time-referenced symptoms" and the
"natural history" of learning and learning issues (Holmes 1987); however,
the implication of the diagnostic cluster has remained the same. At this
relatively late age, the cluster is largely, but not entirely, qualitative; a
careful delineation of problem-solving strategies, as on Block Design, is
thus of critical importance in the diagnostic process (Goodglass and Kaplan
1979).

LANGUAGE AND RELATED PROCESSING SKILLS

In evaluating the efficacy of language-processing abilities within the
neuropsychological model, the clinician first needs to know whether language skills in general are available. He or she first obtains insight through
conversational interaction with the child and careful monitoring of his
or her own language and related behavior. The clinician tries to distinguish

between the processing (registration, encoding, comprehension) of incoming language at different levels and the ability to produce organized, intelligible utterances that are relevant to a conversation (the anterior/ posterior axis). Basic skills typically tapped by the neuropsychologist include:

- word retrieval in response to pictured objects and under rapid naming demands
- word generation
- digit repetition
- sentence repetition
- recall of orally presented text
- ability to handle utterances of increasing length and syntactic complexity
- auditory discrimination
- vocabulary knowledge
- written language formulation (relevant to the lateral axis)

Not all of these abilities may require the administration of a formal test, however. Few clinicians would use a test of sound discrimination, such as the *Auditory Discrimination Test* (Wepman 1958) in a child whose speech was clear, language fluent, comprehension smooth, and reading phonically accurate; nor would the clinician mobilize the relatively lengthy *Peabody Picture Vocabulary Test—Revised* (Dunn and Dunn 1981) to assess single-word vocabulary knowledge in a child with good oral-language abilities and above-average ability on the Information and Vocabulary subtests of the *WISC-R*. Rather, the direct observation of the child's language use on these tasks and in ongoing, spontaneous conversation provides the relevant data concerning intact vocabulary or auditory processing skill for the behavioral cluster.

Word-retrieval skill has been repeatedly demonstrated to be an important component of both oral language-processing abilities and (in children) the secondary—written—language skills predicated upon them (Wolf 1982). The clinician taps these skills directly with naming tasks of various types: *The Boston Naming Test* (Kaplan, Goodglass, and Weintraub 1983); *Expressive One-Word Picture Vocabulary Test* (Gardner 1979); and *Rapid Automatized Naming* (Denckla and Rudel 1976). These tasks typically require the child to name line drawings of objects or other symbols, the names being graded in accordance with their frequency of usage in the language. When a task involves items of equivalent difficulty, speed of naming a complete set of items is the basis of the score. Beyond establishing the age-related level of performance, a child's responses frequently differ in quality: dysphonemic errors have different import (in neuroanatomic terms) from semantic paraphasias, over-inclusive category labels, or perceptually based misnamings. For example, dysphonemic errors are often part of a behavioral cluster that includes insecure rapid-naming skills, oromotor apraxia, poor control of fine finger and/or oculomotor movements, asymmetric (right-sided) motor findings, syntactic production errors, deficits in the ordering of higher-order concepts, and a relative lack of attention to detail in complex, visually represented materials. Where such discontinuities in performance are present, however, language comprehension, organizational skills, configurationally based processing strategies, and general motor and sensory capacities can all be available in an individual with age-appropriate exposure to relevant materials and no specific emotional stressors or concerns. From a neuropsychological point of view, this cluster highlights the relative inefficiency in overall behavioral function that is referable to left-frontal brain systems. A behavioral cluster including perceptually based misnamings could include poorly modulated intonation, discontinuities in social interaction, loss of gestalt parameters in complex visual materials, figure-ground distortions in constructional activities, and poor planning or reasoning abilities—seen in the context of age-appropriate verbal knowledge, intact rote memorization, efficient control of linguistic structures, and so on. The neuropsychological diagnosis here would involve right-hemisphere mechanisms.

The child's level of vocabulary knowledge, ability to manipulate syntactic structures, and comprehension skills are first evaluated in the clinical interview with the child and in ongoing conversation as testing proceeds. Thus, it is important to record the child's language forms accurately. Vocabulary knowledge can be further assessed by means of the *Peabody Picture Vocabulary Test—Revised* and the Vocabulary subtest from the WISC-R. The *Token Test* (DiSimoni 1978) assesses the child's ability to handle syntactic structures of increasing length and syntactic complexity in a reduced semantic context. Sentence repetition tasks, such as the *Sentence Repetition Test* (Spreen and Benton 1969) and *The Stanford-Binet Intelligence Scale,* and narrative recall tasks, including *Logical Memory for Children* (Taylor, date unknown) and *Logical Memory Passages* (Wechsler 1945), highlight insecure mastery of syntactic structures and/or linguistic comprehension as well as uncertain recall for different types of verbal materials. The child's ability to recall the paragraphs in *Logical Memory Passages* and *Logical Memory for Children* yields information pertaining to a potentially discrepant child's abilities in dealing with order of elements, with specific details, with more general ideas, or with the overall gist of the material. Narrative composition, either self-generated or in response to a pictured scene, such as the "Cookie Theft" picture from the *Boston Diagnostic Aphasia Examination* (Goodglass and Kaplan 1972) or the *Test of Written Language* (Hammill and Larsen 1983), provides information concerning not only linguistic units but also verbal formulation, organization of discourse, spelling, and graphomotor control. Such narrative skills in written language often shed light on comparable skills in oral language and complement observations of discontinuities in language processing in both spontaneous conversation and formal test procedures.

NONVERBAL AND VISUALLY REPRESENTED MATERIALS

This category of behavior includes but is not limited to tests of drawing, construction, visual matching, closure, topographic space appreciation, mazes, face recognition, and musical appreciation. As in the case of language skills, the primary questions speak to the anterior/posterior and lateral axes:

1. Does the child have the relevant knowledge?
2. Can the child demonstrate it in an appropriately organized fashion?
3. What is the quality/style of his or her approach to the materials (part-oriented or configurational)?

In most instances, the child's ability to produce reasonably well organized responses attests to a basic perceptual competence with visually represented materials; therefore, elaborate tests of basic perceptual abilities are not routinely required. The *Rey-Osterrieth Complex Figure* (*ROCF*) is a powerful clinical instrument that offers a great deal of information about organizational strategies/competence and the style in which a particular child approaches complex visual materials (see chapter 5, pages 120–22). By comparing the child's copy of the figure with the immediate and delayed recalls, the clinician can distinguish deficits in organization from problems in appreciation of the material. For example, many disorganized (developmentally immature) children copy the figure in a stimulus-bound fashion, slavishly moving from one line to another without any particular strategy in evidence; yet they produce coherent, configurationally intact representations of the figure under recall conditions—attesting to the intactness of their knowledge/appreciation of the materials, in contrast to their production/organizational problems. The *Developmental Test of Visual Motor Integration* (Beery 1982) provides good normative data—as well as valuable developmental examples—of less complex figures. When children are encouraged to tackle all twenty-four items on the test (unless clinical concerns preclude this), then the clinician can not only generate the developmental-age score (based on the number of correct items up to three consecutive failures) but also determine the highest level at which the child can accurately produce the design. For many learning-disordered children with underlying insecurity in language, a significant discrepancy between their formal developmental-age score and the most complex figure that they can produce adequately not only highlights the intra-individual differences in skills that are characteristic of this population but also underscores the importance of examining the demand characteristics of a given task's scoring system. In this test, the scoring criteria place a high value on precision, which "catches" the child who is less facile with detail-oriented processing (left hemisphere) than with configurationally based appreciation (right hemisphere). On the more complex figures toward the end of the task, the critical scoring features emphasize the organizational aspects of the items, rather than the details, which may allow the child to "solve the problem." The clinician can use both the *ROCF* and the *Developmental Test of Visual Motor Integration* to evaluate left-right differences—in use of space and in the accuracy of the figures themselves—as well as of graphomotor control. These tasks both can be usefully compared with constructional tasks like Block Design, where the contrast between unimanual and bimanual manipulation of materials may be important. All of these tasks, in turn, may reveal difficulty in integrating elements across the vertical axis of the materials, behaviors that occur with some regularity in children with dysgenetic facies (particularly involving the midline) and with problems in reciprocal movements involving the two sides of the body where even relatively complex single-side movements are performed bilaterally (Christensen 1975).

Mazes (Porteus 1965; Wechsler 1974, 1981) can offer further information concerning organizational abilities, especially when the clinician is investigating impulsive versus deliberate response styles. Even in the deliberate processor, strategies can vary between a "move the pen, make a decision, move the pen, make a decision" iteration and a "stop—evaluate the situation—complete the maze in one move" approach. The *Locomotor Maze* is useful when questions of extrapersonal organization and orientation arise (Denckla, Rudel, and Broman 1980). *Embedded Figures* (Witkin et al. 1971), *Gestalt Closure* (Kaufman and Kaufman 1983), *Mooney Faces* (Mooney 1957), and *Face Recognition* (Benton et al. 1983) all may be important, in particular instances, for elucidating perceptual functions specifically referable to right-posterior brain systems.

LEARNING NEW INFORMATION AND MANIPULATING OLD KNOWLEDGE

In evaluating a child's recall of materials, the clinician should recognize the various components of the process loosely called "memory": registration of the stimulus, encoding, organization, storage, and retrieval. To the extent that specific brain systems are known to be involved in these different processes, the neuropsychologist can make the case that the developmentally learning-disabled child cannot have "real" memory problems in the sense that they have specific damage to temporal, hippocampal, and related subcortical systems, as experienced by adults. Early disruption of such core brain structures is likely to be incompatible with life itself or to severely limit learning potential to the point of severe retardation. Without core memory systems, the child cannot learn; without the ability to learn, he or she will not be labeled as learning-disabled.

Learning-disabled children, however, are constantly described in the psychological and educational literature as having memory deficits of various types, usually "visual" or "auditory" (short-term or otherwise). In almost all cases, the impairment involves either the initial encoding or the effective retrieval of information. (All of the children who demonstrated adult-like memory problems that I have evaluated on formal testing turned out to have midline brain tumors or temporal lobe dysfunction [typically, seizure disorder].) Therefore, "memory" testing in learning-disabled children usually focuses on the encoding and retrieval processes for different types of information.

From the neuropsychological perspective, one of the most striking aspects of human memory capacity is the difference in the brain's handling of verbal versus nonverbal or visual materials. The relationships between left-sided brain systems and verbal memory, and right-sided brain systems and visual memory, are perhaps the best-documented relationships in brain-behavior literature. This is the primary distinction that the clinician tries to make in evaluation: the availability of encoding, organization, and/or retrieval abilities in terms of verbal and visual materials.

While word-retrieval skills are particularly important in language assessment, the clinician can use naming tasks of various kinds to explore different aspects of the naming/retrieval skill. The ability to retrieve stored knowledge is also crucial to successful completion of the Information subtest of the Wechsler scales, to any task of narrative composition, and to the demonstration of formal academic skills. On the Information subtest, for example, the clinician may need to demonstrate the availability of knowledge, perhaps through clinical limit-testing techniques, before he or she can comment on retrieval deficiencies (see pages 175–77). Different types of information may be differently available to a child on such a task—without this reflecting memory deficits. Although missing factual data that are usually taught in the classroom may implicate memory issues, an inability to respond to questions that require independent linking of ideas (estimation, inference, and so on), may reflect a lack of "thinking" that is referable to parietal brain systems or right-hemisphere mechanisms, rather than lack of remembering. Similarly, reported "memory problems" are frequently based on rote series (alphabet, dates, numbers) or closed sets (directions, coins) where the child may confuse the knowledge even in the absence of a recall demand—and where the diagnostic behavioral cluster as a whole points to problems in organization, rather than in memory.

In evaluating a child's inability to perform at an age-appropriate level on tasks tapping verbal memory, the clinician must distinguish between recall for, and processing of, the relevant language structures. Retrieval of accurate fragments from orally presented text, as in *Logical Memory Passages* and *Logical Memory for Children*, may well implicate problems in memory; however, the recall of details in distorted syntax, with failure to grasp the import of grammatical constructions and with poor comprehension and (possibly) confabulation, suggests primary language-processing deficits, rather than an inability to remember. Presenting a passage for recall a second time (or a second, equivalent paragraph) may be helpful to the child with attentional difficulties or organizational problems, as it allows him or her to estimate the parameters of the task—thus eliminating an apparent "memory" deficit.

Tests that require both immediate and delayed recall of verbal materials also allow the clinician to distinguish memory from processing or retrieval deficits. Where a delayed recall condition elicits essentially what was initially retrieved (even if initial recall was limited), information storage problems are unlikely to be primary. On the other hand, deficits in immediate recall, followed by better performance under delayed recall conditions, raise questions about short-term encoding skills; the clinician may need to distinguish the child's use of "primary memory" as opposed to "working memory" strategies for short-term verbal recall (Craik and Rabinowitz 1984).

Recall of verbal materials can speak to different brain systems, depending on the type of information to be retrieved. Although errors involving structural components of language almost always reflect inefficient left-hemisphere input, errors of order of elements may cluster with either left-hemisphere or frontal-implicating profiles, or both. Retrieval of detail information without appreciation of the overall gist of the material is frequently a component of the right-hemisphere-implicating behavioral cluster; conversely, retrieval of a few details in an effective paraphrase may be seen in the context of other discontinuities of language, highlighting a less-than-optimal contribution from left-hemisphere systems.

Retrieval of different aspects of the material is also characteristic of performance on complex tasks of visual processing. Where the task involves copying, recall for the material is critical to reveal what the child has efficiently encoded. Figure 7.3 demonstrates a delayed recall condition on the ROCF: example A illustrates the loss and distortion of inner detail and of right-side elements seen in the context of left-hemisphere dysfunction; example B reveals the loss of gestalt and the poorly related fragments that highlight right-hemisphere dysfunction. (The two examples are reproduced on the same scale.)

By comparing immediate and delayed recall of simpler forms in the *Visual Reproductions* subtest (Wechsler 1945) to that of the more complex ROCF (Waber and Holmes 1986), the clinician can assess the nature of the encoding strategies, for example, motor versus figural codes (Waber and Bernstein, submitted for publication) available to a child for recall of complex materials. Recognition and matching tasks serve the

FIGURE 7.3

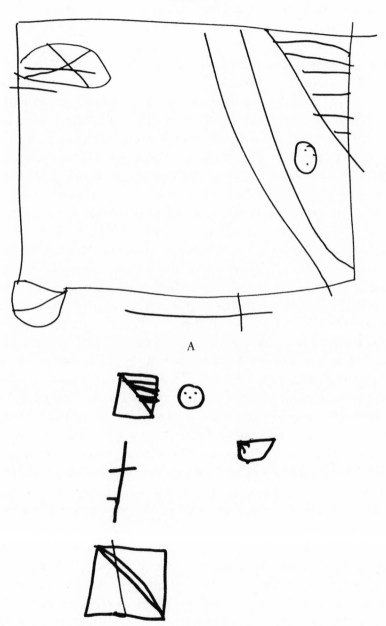

A

B

nonverbal domain in much the same way as the multiple choice-plus-recognition techniques used in clinical-limit testing of language. Where recall for visual materials is absent or incorrect, the examiner must demonstrate that the child has the ability to perceive the material accurately before diagnosing a specific retrieval deficit.

The clinician also systematically evaluates the role of complexity in the recall of both verbal and visual information. Some children are unable to retain much information beyond their basic auditory or visual spans in the Digit Span and Corsi blocks tests. Many children, especially those who can demonstrate good thinking skills in spite of subtle language difficulties, achieve better scores on more complex materials, where meaningfulness supports encoding and organization in memory. These children demonstrate good recall of configurational parameters of complex visual materials of all types; therefore, they are likely to do better on *Logical Memory Passage* recall, where ideas are the basis of the score, than on Sentence Repetition, which assesses verbatim recall, or Digit Span, which is not linguistically organized. Given that many remedial strategies in education are based on the belief that the student must proceed from simple to more complex exemplars in a given domain, the neuropsychologist's clear description of a child's ability to work with more complex materials, despite an inability to handle the apparently simpler subcomponents, is crucial to effective management.

The examiner can obtain an initial examination of a child's learning strategies on such tasks as the *Rey Auditory Verbal Learning* (RAVL) test (Rey 1964) or the *California Verbal Learning* (CAVL) test (Kramer et al. 1984), which involve learning lists of words—unrelated words in the Rey version and semantically related groups of words in the California version. The examiner administers five learning trials, then gives a second word list as a potential interfering activity. After the appropriate interval, he or she assesses the child's recall—immediate, short-delay, or delayed. The RAVL test also taps immediate and delayed recognition with a written narrative containing the target words (immediate recognition) and a longer list containing a mix of words, some of which have been learned previously (delayed recognition). The CAVL test uses semantic categories to probe the child's knowledge of the target words. The clinician not only evaluates the child's level of performance in terms of words learned but also assesses the child's learning strategies. The learning curve documented over the five trials highlights different learning strategies that may belong to different diagnostic clusters and that may have specific implications for treatment planning. For example, many children with difficulties in actual retrieval of the list are able to demonstrate learning through their recognition of the target items or with the help of a structured probe.

Another valuable distinction in the general domain of memory comes from the careful examination of adults with known neurological disorders—memory for skill versus memory for knowledge (Butters 1984). To the extent that the brain can be demonstrated to mediate these different aspects of a skill differentially, this distinction is likely to be important in the formulation of a remedial plan. The pediatric clinician needs to be alert to the possibility that the child may have difficulty learning or recalling the production demands of a task, rather than simply failing to learn or to remember the actual knowledge involved.

When the clinician suspects specific deficits in information storage that can be related to temporal system dysfunction, clear discrepancies in recall of verbal (as opposed to nonverbal or visual) materials are likely to be the primary data for diagnosis. The clinician also needs to be aware that the verbal/nonverbal distinction can often herald frontal-system dysfunction where the recall problem involves temporal ordering of the material to be recalled (Milner 1973). Major subcortical lesions (tumors, for example) may be attended by persistent complaints of memory deficit from the child, parent(s), or teacher(s), even though the child's performance on specific tasks is not particularly poor. In such cases, the clinician needs to be alert to the possibility that the task format and/or structure of the testing situation are supporting the child's performance. At home and at school, he or she may be unable independently to attend and focus on a moment-to-moment basis to register and encode information for adequate storage in those situations. Where there is reason to suspect a head injury, the clinician can expect memory disturbance in various areas. Therefore, careful documentation of the extent of retrograde and anterograde amnesia and delineation of the pattern of memory dysfunction—beyond the initial neuropsychological assessment—are required.

EXECUTIVE CONTROL, PLANNING, AND REASONING

Executive control, planning, and reasoning skills depend heavily on the integrity of frontal brain systems, although any activity at this level of complexity must also involve attention, memory, and language and visual processing skills that engage systems throughout the brain. Tests for this behavioral domain tap Denckla's (1976) ISIS (initiate—sustain—inhibit—shift) functions; sorting and classification abilities; planning and sequencing skills.

The examiner can formally assess inhibitory capacities that involve the motor system in terms of the quality of performance: can the child inhibit extraneous (synkinetic/mirrored) motor movements in performing the target activity? The examiner monitors the child's ability to modulate his or her motor activity level constantly throughout the evaluation as part of the data gathered under the rubric of Observations. Consistent, age-appropriate inhibitory control of the motor system is a well-documented problem for hyperactive and attentionally disordered children (Conners 1970).

The examiner can further assess the child's ability to inhibit potentially interfering stimuli by means of the *Stroop Color and Word Test*, which also yields information relative to the automaticity of reading, to rapid naming skills, and to maintaining continuous performance (Golden 1978). *Go/No Go* paradigms (Weintraub and Mesulam 1985) and the alternating sequences of *Trail Making* (Reitan and Davison 1974) tap the ability to shift set on a continuing basis. The *Wisconsin Card Sorting Test* (Chelune and Baer 1986; Heaton 1981) taps both sustaining and shifting abilities in the context of a hypothesis-testing activity. The Digit Span and Corsi blocks assess the ability to sustain performance in terms of attention (auditory and visual, respectively). The examiner can also employ cancellation tasks to evaluate sustained performance with respect to different categories of stimuli (consonant trigrams, digit trigrams, visual figures, et cetera) (Denckla, Rudel, and Broman 1978).

The *Wisconsin Card Sorting Test*, the *Booklet Category Test* (De-Filippis and McCampbell 1979) and *Raven's Standard/Coloured Progressive Matrices* (Raven 1960, 1965) examine different aspects of reasoning skills. All three tasks require the identification of a specific principle (or principles) for problem solution. Maze activities lend insight into planning and reasoning skills (Porteus 1965; Denckla, Rudel, and Broman 1980). Tests tapping complex visual organization (Block Designs, the *ROCF*, et cetera) yield further information in this regard.

Items from elsewhere in the assessment, for example, informal conversation, the Comprehension and Information subtests of the *WISC-R* and the Word Comprehension subtest from the *Woodcock Reading Mastery Tests* (Woodcock 1973) reflecting social judgment, manipulation of knowledge (drawing inferences, appreciating cause-and-effect relationships), and abstract relationships all speak to reasoning skills. The child's general comportment in the testing situation attests to the integrity (adjusted for age) of his or her interpersonal and situational judgment and organizational capacities.

EMOTIONAL STATUS AND PERSONALITY DEVELOPMENT

The child's overall emotional status, at least with respect to mood, affect, motivation, and self-esteem, will not await formal exploration with projective instruments. These aspects of a child's functioning necessarily are revealed by his or her ability to take part effectively in the assessment procedure at all. Although typically considered as potentially moderating variables with respect to performance on cognitive tasks, behaviors that suggest emotional factors are an important part of the diagnostic behavioral clusters within the neuropsychological model. For example, Pribram (1981) has made a case for the role of specific limbic circuitry in maintaining and modulating motivational capacities. In the clinical context, depression may not always be easy to distinguish from the apathy and hypoactivity of the frontally involved individual. While these types of behaviors have been described more extensively for adults than for children, they can be seen in children with neoplastic brain lesions. Hypoactivity, rather than hyperactivity, is also occasionally seen in the presence of the behavioral cluster that typically accompanies primary attentional disorders in children (consistent with disturbance of fronto-limbic circuitry). Another patient presented with apparently flattened affect that turned out to reflect an underlying deficit in programming the motor musculature of the face. Children with right-hemisphere dysfunction are often misdiagnosed as having primary psychiatric disorder because their anomalous social interaction is interpreted psychologically, rather than neuropsychologically.

The language-impaired individual who avoids linguistic interaction is all too quickly diagnosed as "hostile," "oppositional," "denying," or "constricted": in such cases, the diagnostician has interpreted a behavior that signals the language difficulty in psychological terms. A developmentally immature child who is constitutionally unable to modulate his or her behavioral output may reveal psychologically interesting material that is, however, not inappropriate for the age group but which is usually accessed (if at all) only in the privacy of an ongoing psychotherapeutic relationship. In such a case, it may be easy availability of the emotional material that is "pathologic," rather than the nature of the material itself.

Such behaviors can, of course, signal both neuropsychological and psychological issues: one does not preclude the other. Indeed, by the time a child who has struggled with the impact of neuropsychologically based difficulties for most of his or her life is referred for evaluation, he or she is likely to present the examiner with a neuropsychological/psychological "layer cake"; determining the various ingredients may well require all of the examining clinician's experience and acumen. Specific responses also may yield both psychological and neuropsychological data; for example, a child may consistently have difficulty in defining verbs, rather than nouns, and under the neuropsychological stress of trying to define verbs, he or she may be unable to contain emotionally relevant material. A constitutionally disinhibited child may reveal his or her vulnerability in poorly modulated responses on, say, Vocabulary items. For example, in response to the task of defining *brave*, the child who answers "Jumping off a building" when he or she is sitting near the window in an eleventh floor office displays behavior that is rather different in its psychological implications from that of the child who answers "Beating up on (a named person)" with evident relish.

The use of projective instruments is extensively discussed in the psychological literature (French, Graves, and Levitt 1983; Krahn 1985). Where children with specific neuropsychologically determined thinking differences are concerned, specific attention must be paid to the interpretation of projective materials. Differences in performance between the *Rorschach* test, the *Roberts Apperception Test for Children* (McArthur and Roberts 1982), and the *Tasks of Emotional Development* (Cohen and Weil 1975), for example, should be evaluated for both psychological and neuropsychological relevance. The inherent structure of these tasks varies in terms of real-world meaning, a difference that may be relevant for neuropsychological diagnosis. For example, with the *Rorschach* test, a child who is unable to find words easily in ordinary conversation is not likely to give much in the way of imaginative responses to unformed inkblots; nor is the child who lacks appreciation for configurational aspects of complex materials (on a cognitive/neuropsychological basis) likely to see beyond single-feature percepts. The clinician's psychological interpretations of *Rorschach* responses from either of these children must be undertaken with extreme circumspection.

Other, more structured tasks elicit projective material by offering (age-related) meaningful situations (*Roberts Apperception Test for Children* and *Tasks of Emotional Development*), initial cues (Sentence Completion), and specific drawing activities (Draw a Person, Family Kinetic Drawing, squiggle games, et cetera). These tasks typically reveal the erosion of self-esteem common in most children with learning disorders. In addition to insecurity about self-worth and general competence, children with learning problems frequently experience difficulty in the mastery of developmental tasks, particularly as these involve separation, autonomy and individuation, management of aggressive feelings, and socialization skills within the peer-group. The clinician must distinguish such discontinuities in personality development from primary, neuropsychologically determined disorders of social cognition, impulse control, or attentional deficits. Further, in the context of neuropsychological assessment, the clinician needs to evaluate the extent and severity of any identified emotional concerns, not only for their impact on the child's actual test performance and, thus, on diagnostic behavioral clusters, but also for their effect on the child's ability to take advantage of recommendations. Energy that is diverted to maintain emotional equilibrium—putting on a good face to the world—is not usually available for academic work. In such cases, the most elegant of intervention strategies based on the child's neuropsychological profile may be useless in the absence of ongoing psychotherapeutic support.

ACADEMIC ACHIEVEMENT

Although most children referred for evaluation arrive with detailed academic test results, frequently documenting their progress over several grades, it is frequently necessary to administer academic tests within the neuropsychological assessment. In fact, the neuropsychologist often acts as a referee when the parent(s) and teacher(s) disagree about the child's level of skills. Using a different type of test may well clarify the nature of the disagreement: this may demonstrate the child's sensitivity to different kinds of testing formats, thus documenting a potential difference between the child's knowledge of the material and his or her ability to produce it in specific contexts. Academic tasks that document age-related changes in skill profiles are familiar to the clinician working within a developmental neuropsychological model, but they are frequently incomprehensible to the parent(s) and teacher(s) viewing the child at one point in time. By administering academic tests directly, the clinician can also examine qualitative aspects of performance that typically cluster in a consistent fashion with other features of the child's cognitive profile. The information so gained is important not only for formulating intervention strategies but also for working with the individuals who will implement these strategies (Holmes and Waber, in press). Parents and teachers will constitute a more effective treatment team to the extent they see the same child—manifesting different aspects of his or her overall skills under different demands.

Relevant domains of academic skills include reading, writing (narrative composition and penmanship), spelling, and mathematics; and documenting these skills typically requires more than one test. Not all tests need be administered by the neuropsychologist, however: direct observation of the child's performance on one task may be sufficient for comparison with performance documented by school personnel on other instruments whose format is well known. Where reading skills are concerned, the *Gray Oral Reading Test—Revised* (Wiederholt and Bryant 1986), the *Gilmore Oral Reading Test* (Gilmore and Gilmore 1968), the *Woodcock Reading Mastery Test*, and the *Analytic Reading Inventory* (Woods and Moe 1985) are all useful for documenting level of performance in terms of decoding skills, oral reading, and comprehension. It is important to know whether single-word decoding skills hold up under the demands of more complex text or whether inefficient decoding skills are supported by the meaningfulness of more complex material. Comprehension of facts and comprehension of text that requires inferential reasoning constitute very different problems at different ages. Children whose formally measured comprehension skills are age-appropriate at the third grade level, for instance, when recall of facts is the critical scoring variable, may not do well at higher grade levels, when it is important to derive information from more complex text by means of inferences about what has been read. This type of child's learning disorder thus may remain hidden until he or she is halfway through his or her school career.

The clinician evaluates writing skills in the context of both reading and oral language abilities. Errors in speaking are often equally prevalent in written text. Narrative formulation deficits in oral language are typically replayed in composition. A child's lack of appreciation of discourse relationships is frequently highlighted when he or she creates a story from a sequence of pictured scenes, as in *The Test of Written Language* (Hammill and Larsen 1983). The request for "a paragraph, that is, three or four sentences, about what is happening on this picture" when administering the "Cookie Theft" picture from the *Boston Diagnostic Aphasia Examination,* can reveal a discourse problem that is independent of overall ability, as with the child with an above-average IQ who offered the following response:

1. The mother is washing the dishes, and the boy is stealing cookies.
2. The mother is washing the dishes, and the boy is stealing cookies.
3. The mother is washing the dishes, and the boy is stealing cookies.
4. The mother is washing the dishes, and the boy is stealing cookies.

Content, vocabulary choice, syntactic structures, spelling, and punctuation are all accurate: the failure to understand "paragraph" and the literal interpretation of the "three or four" sentences reveal, nonetheless, a significant problem in language use.

Written narrative also elicits information relative to spelling and handwriting. Again, spelling errors are evaluated in light of oral-language-processing skills; for example, a child with auditory-processing and/or phonological production deficits may spell accurately what he or she "hears" or (mis-)produces. The clinician compares the child's spelling in context with spelling of unconnected word lists, as in the *Wide-Range Achievement Test—Revised* (WRAT-R) (Jastak and Jastak 1984): does the child lose control of spelling rules and patterns under the excitement and stress of formulating the narrative? Spelling errors also highlight phonically regular misspellings, visually based misspellings, and irregular spelling attempts (Boder 1973; Rourke 1985). Handwriting may also deteriorate under the stress of producing a continuous narrative. Given the age of the child, a choice of printing or using cursive script may signal motor-programming deficits that belong in a behavioral cluster with early evidence of oromotor apraxia, sequence errors in spelling, and insecurity with ordered elements in abstract materials. The nature of the hand/arm use may reflect problems in rate, fluency, and so on that can be referenced to discontinuities in subcortical control of motor systems.

Tics, tremors, and choreiform movements have characteristic effects on written output. The clinician can compare the child's performance on the Repeated Patterns task (Roach and Kephart 1966), which taps continuous graphomotor control of single/alternating and angular cursive forms, with spontaneous handwriting.

The clinician documents arithmetic skills by means of the Arithmetic subtest of the WRAT-R. It is also useful to make some assessment of a child's ability to successfully complete items beyond the time limit for the task. Especially in the case of the older child, who may require a waiver of time constraints in formal examinations, it is important to know whether extra time does indeed facilitate the level of performance. Careful evaluation of historic information pertaining to actual classroom performance will be necessary in such cases. The clinician's item analysis should focus on potential deficits associated with computation, as opposed to conceptual understanding or lack of familiarity with age-expected procedures. For younger children, the clinician may compare the level of performance on the WRAT-R with that on the *KeyMath Diagnostic Arithmetic Test* (Connolly, Nachtman, and Pritchett 1976), for example. A child may be able to demonstrate familiarity with even complex computational procedures if they are presented one conceptual domain at a time, as in the *KeyMath* test; in contrast, the Arithmetic subtest of the WRAT-R requires careful examination of which arithmetic procedure is needed, item by item. The clinician may need to document foundation skills in mathematics, rather than formal arithmetic achievement: basic counting (forward; backward; counting on; skip counting by tens, fives, and twos; and the like), cardinality, conservation of number, one-to-one correspondence, appreciation of place value, appreciation of fractions, and so on, are prerequisite for mathematic skill development at different ages (Davidson and Marolda 1978). The clinician can use dictated problems to tap knowledge of numeric symbolism, as well as computational algorithms. He or she draws a neuropsychological diagnosis and recommendations for management from the following questions:

1. Can the child write (as well as read) numbers of different lengths?
2. Can he or she maintain the correct orientation of symbols?
3. Can he or she maintain multidigit numbers in the correct order?
4. Are similar reversals or misorderings seen in the writing of letters?
5. Can he or she lay out a multidigit problem that is accurate in space as well as in time?

While these factors may be irrelevant to the development of conceptual understanding in mathematics, they are critical to production skills and, thus, will affect the child's classroom achievement.

Management Strategies

The goal of evaluation and diagnosis is not to diagnose a deficiency in the child but to construct the Child-World System, which forms the basis for intervention (Holmes and Waber, in press). The neuropsychologist seeks to optimize the match between child and world, using management strategies that effectively address both sides of the equation. In this final section, I will address issues of managing this intervention as part of the neuropsychological assessment process. Chapter 8 will conclude with a discussion of what can be done "beyond the diagnosis."

In all three evaluative domains (history, observation, testing), the clinician looks for behavioral clusters that speak to the three neuroanatomic axes: the domains of behavior observed in the evaluation must be sufficiently various to yield the necessary observations. The brain-world interaction—in the guise of the specific demand characteristics of each situation—is carefully examined as the clinician outlines the diagnostic behavioral clusters. The clinician bases the evaluation of the child's performance on his or her performance on other tasks and the expectations derived from his or her previous experience, asking, How does the person *solve* the problem? The goal of the evaluation is to identify the nature of the solving system, that is, the brain. Figure 7.4 illustrates the various parameters involved.

In beginning to formulate intervention strategies or treatment plans, the clinician reiterates this question but with a new emphasis: *how* does the person solve the problem? Once the clinician knows something about the child's "solving system" (figure 7.4), he or she can reexamine the child's problems and goals in the real world (figure 7.5).

The clinician must explore the demands of the child's real-world goals with respect to the formulation of treatment goals even more carefully than with respect to evaluation. The specific demands faced by school-age children include specific content goals, specific context demands,

FIGURE 7.4

Subject variables

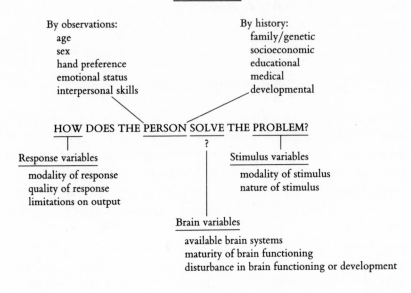

By observations:
  age
  sex
  hand preference
  emotional status
  interpersonal skills

By history:
  family/genetic
  socioeconomic
  educational
  medical
  developmental

HOW DOES THE PERSON SOLVE THE PROBLEM?
?

Response variables
  modality of response
  quality of response
  limitations on output

Stimulus variables
  modality of stimulus
  nature of stimulus

Brain variables
  available brain systems
  maturity of brain functioning
  disturbance in brain functioning or development

FIGURE 7.5

Subject variables

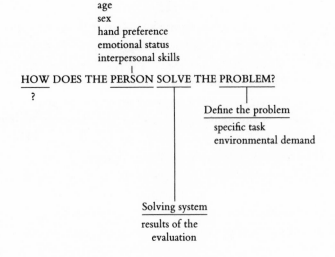

age
sex
hand preference
emotional status
interpersonal skills

HOW DOES THE PERSON SOLVE THE PROBLEM?
?

Define the problem
  specific task
  environmental demand

Solving system
  results of the
  evaluation

and longer-term challenges (Holmes 1987). Thus, the school-age child's goals encompass not only the acquisition of reading or math skills but also the acquisition of such skills in the usual classroom context, the application of the skills to get information, and the requirement to complete the standard number of years of schooling with a basic set of competencies. Children can fail because of different aspects of the various demands made upon them: one child can fail to learn to read; another child can have difficulty in applying reading skills; yet another can read adequately in a structured setting but cannot "hold it all together" when faced with the reading expectations at an upper grade level. While all these children present problems in written language, the clinician's definition of the specific demand, drawn from the diagnosis generated by the evaluation, will provide the critical focus of the treatment plan.

Optimizing the match between child and world requires precise definition of the contribution of both to a particular skill/task/situation, not only in immediate, grade-referenced terms, but also in the context of the longer-term goal of overall adult competence. Approaches to neuropsychological assessment in children that do not place the child in a developmental context thus are inadequate to address the varied, and changing, patterns of learning profiles that are so strikingly limned in individuals with learning disorders. More comprehensive—and with wide-ranging implications for both evaluation and management—is the systemic approach that emphasizes the interrelationship of the child and his or her environment, placing both in the context of neurobehavioral development (Holmes and Waber, in press).

PART THREE

EDUCATIONAL

IMPLICATIONS

Chapter 8

Beyond the Diagnosis

JOAN RUDEL PARDES

A diagnosis is only as good as the degree to which it provides methods and means for effective learning. The clinician draws plans for remediation from the diagnosis and should include both short- and long-term goals: while the short-term goals may suggest specific remedial programs, the long-term goals should support the view that an effective educational program for the child facilitates the development of a competent adult. Ideally, the child will grow to be an independent and productive member of our highly complex society—with its many educational, social, and vocational requirements. Short-term goals should reflect a thorough consideration of the more global expectations the child will face in society. In fact, one useful long-range goal may well be to help the child navigate the educational system with as many life-effective skills as his or her learning capacity will permit and with as few psychological and emotional stresses as the school and family can prevent.

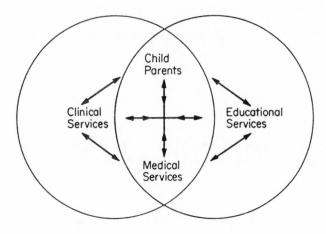

FIGURE 8.1

Treatment Team

Without question, the total effectiveness of any remedial plan depends upon the availability and quality of its support systems (Johnson 1978), including those family members, educators, psychologists, and medical personnel who work together to evaluate and manage the child's learning program. Figure 8.1 illustrates one view of the treatment team and how they can best interact to maximize their efforts on behalf of the child.

In order for the learning plan to be most effective, the child should be engaged in the planning and evaluation, as well as the act of learning (Wittrock 1978). In this way, the child is a pivotal member of the treatment team and, as such, is encouraged to adopt a "responsibility for self" model of learning (see chapter 5). Motivating the child through active involvement in all aspects of the learning process is the key to success for any educational program (Pardes 1979).

The parent(s) also commands an important position on the treatment team—attending the interview, planning, and evaluation sessions, prepared to participate productively (see chapter 4). The clinician can ensure goal-directed participation at each session by supplying a "focus sheet," on which the parent(s) can include a list of questions they would like answered. The focus sheet should also contain the parent's written personal assessment of the child's educational and interpersonal skills—the child's strengths and weaknesses in learning as well as in social and emotional behavior. The focus sheet serves two major functions: (1) it helps direct the discussion to the specific abilities and disabilities that shape the child's behavior and learning, and (2) it helps keep the team meetings on track and productive. Since each member of the treatment team comes to the task with different types and levels of expertise, the focus sheet is an important means of enlisting everyone's cooperation.

The parent(s) is the "home team": any techniques adopted to modify the child's at-home behavior, from changes in homework rules to adjustments in diet, are enforced by the parent(s) with little or no direct professional supervision. Therefore, good rapport between the parent(s) and the educational and psychological professionals is critical. Lack of cooperation could very well sabotage a large part of a treatment program. Thus, one primary objective for the psychologists and educators on the treatment team is to help the parent(s) and child feel as comfortable as possible with all of the diagnostic procedures. This objective involves much more than just professional courtesy: it encourages cooperation, total effort, and optimal performance by all those concerned with the success of the child. In this regard, the parent(s) and child must never be made to feel that the diagnosis is the end of the line, just a label for what is wrong with the child. Many parents arrive at the testing and interview sessions already aware of the child's problems. It is up to the professional team members to communicate an open-minded approach and to handle the test results as a point of departure for a complete and well-considered understanding of what, when, and how the child will learn most effectively.

Since the child is the focus of the testing and will be expected to participate fully in the remedial program, it seems only natural to discuss with him or her, at least in part, the diagnosis itself. The depth of this discussion, however, depends on several factors: (1) most importantly, the age of the child; (2) the child's level of interest in the information; and (3) the child's ability to understand and accept the information. The clinician might ask a very young child, "Do you have any questions that you would like to ask about the games we played and the things we have done here together?" In the case of an older child, the clinician might ask, "Would you be interested in reading or speaking about a report on your learning abilities and problems?" If the child indicates interest, the clinician could prepare a condensed and understandable explanation of the test results, avoiding technical jargon and editing input from the educational and psychological team members with care. The report should stress the child's learning abilities as well as his or her limitations (see chapter 2). The professional team members should jointly decide what diagnostic information should be shared with both the child and parent(s). However, the manner in which the information is shared must reflect the view that the diagnosis is the beginning of an understanding and a clear direction for the education of the child.

Diagnosis and the Role of Change Over Time

A diagnosis is a formative description of a child's learning capacity at a given point in time; therefore, it should serve as a beginning, a starting point for the child's continued development. As the child grows and matures, his or her learning strengths and weaknesses will change as well. In view of the changes in the developing child over time, it will be necessary to reevaluate the learning program several times during the course of the child's schooling. Even though this reevaluation does not necessitate formal retesting, it should be carefully timed to maximize its usefulness in maintaining a successful learning program for the child.

The clinician can set the most productive times for program updating and diagnostic reevaluation only after considering two critical elements of change and charting the relationship between them. The first change-element is developmental change in the cognitive, psychological, and physical domains of the child's behavior over time. For example, the cognitive style and capacity—linguistic ability, complexity, and thought-processes—of any six-year-old, whether learning disabled or not, is dramatically different from that of a twelve-year-old, as are differences in behavior patterns and physical stature.

The second change-element is the learning environment, which has two component parts. First, the child faces new demands created by changes in what has to be learned. For example, a major demand of the first-grade curriculum is learning to read. In junior high school, however, the focus shifts to tasks that require the child to organize what he or she reads in order to learn. The junior high school student needs to know much more than the words in the social studies text, and reading through the chapter will likely be only the beginning of the task. He or she may need to read the material, then outline it, compare or contrast it with a previous unit or chapter, organize the material in historical sequence, and draw conclusions and inferences: a far cry from the reading tasks demanded of a primary school student. Although this shift takes place gradually over time, keeping pace with the cognitive development of the learning-disabled child, a good treatment plan is periodically revised to realign the child's abilities and limitations with changes in the curriculum. The second component of the learning environment is the learning context—the setting in which learning takes place. The learning context includes the school and classroom structure and organization, as well as the effects of changes in the teacher-pupil ratio and the resources (texts, computers, and other media) available to support the learning effort. For example, the typical first grade is characterized by a highly structured and supportive teacher-pupil context that provides a learning context that is organized and directed for the students. In contrast, the junior high school learning context usually involves departmentalized classes with different teachers for different subjects, less supportive teacher-pupil interactions, and greater student-directed learning. In fact, most average students find the adjustment to the myriad of contextual changes of junior high school challenging. Thus, even if a learning-disabled child is mainstreamed for only a few classes a day, the contextual demands of junior high school can be the source of many problems.

These changes in the learning content and context create critical stress-points at specific times in the child's school years (Holmes 1987). Unless the clinician accurately predicts these stress-points when establishing and reevaluating a learning program, they can eventually break down a child's learning progress.

In preparing the learning program, the clinician must consider not only these two change-elements—changes in the developing child and the changing demands of the learning environment over time—but also the critical interaction *between* the two. It is important to be able to predict whether the child, when confronted by increases in content demand and decreases in contextual support, will be equipped to respond with a repertoire of learning skills that can counterbalance the changes in the learning environment. For example, outlining skills aid in handling increased content-load and in coping with the decreasing amount of teacher-directed support. Therefore, the child should learn outlining skills before he or she reaches junior high school; otherwise, the child is left without training to find a strategy appropriate for content and context. Only when the strategies for learning become part of the child's repertoire of skills will the child be able, when the learning environment demands, to provide his or her own context for learning.

It is within this framework that both Rudel and Holmes argue the concept of change in the child's learning parameters across time. For Rudel, there are "time-referenced symptoms": symptoms of a learning disability that appear at one point in time and then change in relation "to new educational and vocational requirements" (Rudel 1981a). When the demands of the environment create a critical interface with the learning parameters of the child, there is a need to reassess at least some components of the treatment program. Holmes, on the other hand, describes the "natural history of the child" as that "interaction between a child's given style of thinking and the regular patterns of changing demands in the education process" (Holmes 1987). A clear understanding of this critical interaction between child and environment allows the clinician to predict probable stress-points in a child's educational program and to suggest appropriate strategies for teaching and learning that may forestall frustration and failure for the child. Being able to predict how and when a child's abilities and limitations will critically interact with the learning environment is the hallmark of a good clinician. If this clinical skill can be matched with an equally astute educational plan for teaching critical learning techniques and strategies at the most appropriate time, then the child's education will progress with less stress and greater success.

Critical Educational Landmarks

Holmes's (1987) content/context construct is most helpful in evaluating the "right" times to reevaluate the child in relation to the demands of the learning content and context. Figure 8.2 illustrates the relationships

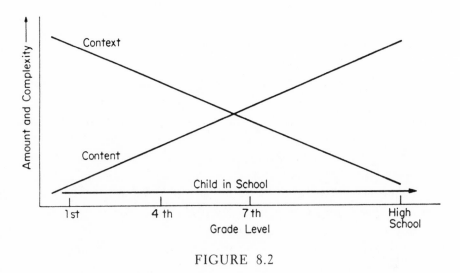

FIGURE 8.2

between the learning content, the learning context, and the child over time.

The learning content and context are inversely related: as the curriculum content increases in quantity, depth, and complexity, the amount of contextual support decreases. This loss of contextual support in the educational structure, coupled with increases in content demand, causes critical stress-points, especially at the fourth grade, junior high school, and high school levels. For example, the first-grade curriculum demand, "learning to read," is a source of difficulty for many children whose language-processing skills are not adequate for the task. Thus, stress-points occur when a critical time in the development of the child or a major shift in the content demand interfaces with a decrease in the amount of contextual support available. These stress-points are likely to cause learning problems when the child's abilities cannot stretch to meet the demands of content, context, or both. These changes are likely to create stress and learning problems for most children. Children with learning disabilities, however, are at higher risk and have a lower threshold for change in general: they are more sensitive to imbalances in contextual support and less able to respond to increases in content demand.

FIRST GRADE

For the first grader whose learning disability (language and language-related processing difficulty) makes learning to read difficult, if not seemingly impossible, a high level of contextual support is mandatory. This child needs small-group and/or individual tutoring to maximize his or her chances of success. In addition to individualized instruction, which may or may not take place in the mainstreamed classroom, this child will need more time and more practice in order to learn. Thus, the reading content materials require supplements that provide more time and more practice. The traditional contextual and content constraints created by a graded primary school may not be in the best interests of this child, and the treatment team should consider placing the child in an ungraded primary school environment and/or allowing the child four or five years to cover the curriculum content usually covered in three to four years.

The child who demonstrates poor modulation of behavior from the very earliest school experiences needs early educational planning with high levels of contextual support (Rudel 1984). His or her behavior management program should include a consistent reinforcement schedule. Learning in small groups with simple but clearly enforced rules for behavior will provide this child with the best chance for learning success. He or she needs structured activities and task features selected for ease of focus and attention. While a child who has difficulty learning to read demands more time and more practice for success with a learning objective, a child with poor attentional focus is hard pressed to sit for even the minimum number of learning exercises (see chapter 3). This child requires carefully spaced learning activities that provide the same number of activities—but not as many at one time.

FOURTH GRADE

Fourth grade is a critical time of content/context interface, when the content demand shifts from learning to read to reading to learn and there is a subtle decrease in contextual support (Holmes 1987). Learning to read is a highly skills-oriented activity in the primary grades, involving letter-sound relationships, phonics rules, and reading stories for sight vocabulary development. Reading activities are teacher-directed or

212

workbook-directed, and the content is limited in the amount of information that the reader must bring to it. For example, the reader does not need to expend much cognitive power to understand "See Dick run." In fact, the child who is referred for clinical diagnosis in the fourth grade may not have a problem with classroom learning *until* learning to organize and process information for comprehension replaces phonics drills as the primary curriculum goal. In other words, as long as the demands of the curriculum are limited to rather simple decoding and repetition tasks, the child who is often diagnosed as learning disabled in the upper elementary grades may be equipped to meet the skill demands of the primary school content.

The content of the fourth-grade curriculum, however, demands more from the learner's cognitive reservoir. In order to comprehend social studies and science texts, the child must be able to draw on knowledge accumulated from language read and heard. His or her reading tasks are no longer limited to decoding and phonics skills; the content demand has increased as the teacher-input context has decreased. This shift comes at an age-appropriate time in intellectual development: fourth graders usually develop "learning to learn" skills in tandem with reading skills. However, for many learning-disabled children, especially those with organization and comprehension difficulties, fourth grade provides a learning environment laden with difficulty. These children need direction and specific guidance in developing learning strategies, and they must receive contextual support to help them mobilize whatever skills they have. They need skills training directed toward learning to recognize inference, cause and effect, and sequence in what is read. Their lack of organizational strategies and their poor language-processing skills wreak havoc with writing-skills development as well; therefore, tutorials in composition are a necessary part of a good remedial program.

When the language-impaired child, who struggled during the first three years of school in order to learn to read, reaches fourth grade, a new battle begins. He or she must now work even harder to learn all that has to be learned from written materials. Because content load may be overwhelming, the learning program may need to be adjusted. Time is a critical factor. Since the language-impaired child's decoding of printed text is often too slow for successful comprehension, he or she is not able to extract the required information in the allotted amount of time. Therefore, this child needs more time for each task; shortening each task and reducing the number of similar examples that must be completed could allow the extra time required. In addition, more scheduled "work" sessions could allow for ample practice time for each skill. Further, alternate visual or auditory media may aid the child in acquiring the necessary information. In language-impaired and organizationally and conceptually impaired children, the goal of the treatment program is to match the skills of the child to the demands of the learning environment.

For the child diagnosed with attentional deficit disorder (ADD), the intensity of the problems revealed in the fourth grade depend in part on the success of an early intervention program (see chapter 3 for a detailed discussion of ADD). If the child has benefited from early intervention, his or her behavior may be improved. However, a reevaluation of the program may be necessary at this juncture, because many of the new cognitive tasks differ significantly from the previous ones. The fourth-grade curriculum replaces the basic skills taught in the primary grades with more student-initiated activities—reports and projects that the disorganized, skill-poor, language-impaired, and ADD students will find difficult, if not impossible, to accomplish without clear and consistent direction from a teacher or tutor. Without adequate planning and management, the child's work will be disorganized, messy, and often incomplete.

Classroom behavior, in anything but the most structured situations, will still need monitoring. Because the child's work habits are poor, behavior often mitigates against successful task completion. The child with poor behavior modulation will be a reluctant choice of classmates for work in committees, much like the child who is chosen last for the baseball team. As it is customary for upper elementary school curricula to require group projects, it is necessary to build structure and control into these projects in order to promote a successful learning outcome. The rationale for these group assignments is sound: in order to learn about working with others, children need to practice these skills. However, these tasks not only put the cognitive skills of the child to the test but also put social and interpersonal skills under stress as well. In such situations, many learning-disabled children are at risk for failure. Armed with this information, the clinician should recommend highly structured work assignments, perhaps allowing the child to work within a group but with responsibility for only one small segment of the total project—first in the resource center and then in the mainstreamed classroom. In this way, the learning-disabled child has the opportunity to work as fully as possible in the regular learning environment.

Homework. Homework is another part of the curriculum that is ripe for problems, particularly by the fourth grade. While there isn't a home in the United States that hasn't been subjected to the stress and crisis of homework, the learning-disabled child requires specific consideration. Homework in the primary grades is usually limited in amount and complexity, but fourth-grade homework assignments can be fraught with difficulties—social studies reports may require the use of outside sources, and a science project may introduce the child to the lab report. Homework requires a more complex set of skills, frequently involving the student in reading and writing assignments that call for student-initiated learning.

The treatment team needs to clarify how much and what kind of assistance the parent(s) should give. Regardless of the child's learning difficulty, the parent(s) should provide contextual support only; in other words, it is the parent's responsibility to provide the child with a well-lighted and quiet (but not necessarily silent) place to study and to establish a daily routine that allows ample study time (see chapter 3). The parent(s) should plan the number of after-school activities to maximize time-value; if the child is too tired to do an adequate job on his or her homework, then after-school programs must be limited. On the other hand, the child should never be expected to spend all of his or her after-school time doing homework. The parent(s) must establish a balance that permits the child enough study time and an appropriate number of extra-curricular activities. This balance will change as the child grows; thus, decisions about the appropriate amount of study time and play time will be periodically reevaluated.

The parent(s) should not provide tutorial support with homework. This is important for two reasons. First, a major thrust of the learning context beyond the primary grades is the development of independent learning skills. Parents who are too actively involved in the content of the child's homework undercut not only the learning goal but also the child's self-esteem. Second, parents of children with learning disabilities run a greater risk of confusing the child or confounding the remedial strategy that is part of the treatment plan. Good management of a remedial program demands that the parent(s) understand the goal of the child's homework assignment. If the goal of the homework assignment is to practice or rehearse a specific skill learned in class, then practice time should be spaced for maximum retention. For example, three 15-minute practice sessions are far more learning-effective than one 45-minute session. If extra help is needed, perhaps the resource room teacher can assist the child with sample homework problems before the end of the school day. If the major goal of the homework is simply to train the child to work independently, then the parent(s) must encourage such a context. Thus, the place where homework is done and the way in which it is explained must be consistent with the child's learning goals.

Copying from the Blackboard. By the end of primary school, another area of concern for learning-disabled children is copying from the blackboard. Although the blackboard is used in earlier grades, more complicated tasks, such as receiving, understanding, and duplicating instructions, notes, and even assignments, are introduced by the fourth grade. In chapter 3, Rudel describes copying from the blackboard as a "tracking operation" that causes particular difficulty for children with attentional problems. It may also present problems for children whose reading skills are impaired by slow visual processing: the information on the blackboard is not processed in "meaningful" chunks but is seen as individual figures (letters or words) that must be looked at, remembered, and then copied onto the paper next to the previous figure. This process is often slow, painful, and woefully inaccurate. The slowness of processing causes the child to look up at the blackboard so many times that he or she frequently loses the place on the paper and on the board; further, the inaccuracy of the final result reflects the inevitably poor quality of learning attained from such a transcription.

The child with organizational problems may also have difficulty extracting information from the blackboard, due to poor written-language skills. Because this child frequently has difficulty producing coherent discourse, the notes copied from the blackboard often contain disconnected thoughts instead of concept-bearing information.

With such a dismal list of problems caused by requiring some children to copy from the blackboard, it would seem wise to simply recommend that all copying from the blackboard be stopped. Such a recommendation is certainly one way to eliminate the problem, but in most schools it is not a practical solution. Without question, copying from the blackboard is so difficult for learning-disabled children that it should be used sparingly. However, there are alternative solutions. For example, educators can use small, individual, desk-size chalk slates for practice in copying information.

One slate is placed on each child's desk, thereby eliminating one critical aspect of the blackboard-copying problem: continually looking up and looking down (vertical to horizontal axis). With this method, tracking is limited to following less information on a smaller, closer surface. Further, this information is framed in two ways for ease of focus: (1) the individual slate provides its own literal frame and (2) the child can place a simple straightedge under the line to be copied or a cutout around the individual item that is to be transferred from slate to paper.

Alternatively, the teacher can give each child a typed facsimile of the work as it will appear on the blackboard. In this way, the child's learning is not dependent upon his or her copying ability. The key to this approach is training: as the child progresses in the ability to process printed material, the teacher deletes from the handout larger and larger sections of the board notes and expects the child to fill in the missing notes by careful copying from the blackboard. If one of the curriculum goals is to learn outlining skills, then the teacher can hand out board notes written in outline form. As the child achieves greater copying skill, the handouts should include less subtopic detail. Eventually, the outline is only a skeleton, containing only the major headings. The child should be able to fill in the details by copying the notes from the blackboard. With this approach, two important skills are acquired simultaneously: (1) blackboard-transcription skills and (2) note taking in an organized and clearly structured format.

JUNIOR HIGH SCHOOL

The stress-points encountered by the child at the fourth-grade level are frequently attributed to changes in curriculum content. However, the problems the child encounters at the junior high school level, another critical stress-point, are more likely caused by shifts in the context of the learning environment as well as by major developmental changes in the child.

Junior high school has been described by Holmes (1986) as the time when the child must learn to organize his or her own learning. In order to do this, the child must call into play learning-effective and efficient organizational strategies. These strategies are important tools of learning: although the teacher may direct their use, the student surveys the available methods and means of organizing the material for effective processing, and then selects the ones that will best serve the demands of the task and his or her own learning strengths and weaknesses. In the junior high school context, then, the teacher relinquishes the firm grasp on the reins of the organizational strategies of learning, and the student takes up the responsibility for selecting, with guidance when necessary, the most learning-effective means of organizing the concepts covered in the curriculum.

The structural organization of the typical junior high school reflects this major contextual change, replacing the self-contained classrooms of the elementary school with a departmentalized organization. The child must move from one classroom to another in different parts of the school within a limited period of time. The doors are shut when the late bell rings, and there is little sympathy for the child who can't get from the cafeteria on the main floor to the gym on the fourth floor in four minutes. The security of having one teacher who knows each child well, simply because they spend the entire school day together, is gone in a departmentalized system. In junior high school, the child must not only meet the content demands of many diverse subjects but also adapt to the contextual demands of different teaching styles. Even something as simple as the way the math notebook is organized or the method of completing the social studies homework can cause confusion and, ultimately, task-failure for the child. Because the contextual demands of junior high school place all but the most adaptable learners at risk, many learning-disabled children are not mainstreamed at this juncture in the educational system.

There are several alternative solutions for these problems in the junior high school context. For example, a buddy system may help children with organizational and directional problems get from the cafeteria to the gym on time, or the child's schedule could be adjusted to eliminate long and complicated between-class changes. In order to cut down on the stress related to organizing and completing work for different teachers with different rules and styles of teaching, the school administrator can arrange for teachers to coordinate their teaching plans and requirements. Simplifying the contextual and organizational demands made on the students is a matter of effective communication and professional skill, one that should not be overlooked as a way of reducing stress-points for the student.

In addition to these major contextual changes encountered in junior high school, the child also faces formidable developmental changes at this time. Hormones wreak havoc, not just with facial complexions, but also with physical, psychological, emotional, and cognitive changes within the child (Manning 1977; Rogers 1978). During this time, the child frequently turns his or her attention inward and away from academics, worrying about his or her appearance, how many friends he or she has, and how others see him or her. In addition, the junior high school student is often focused on an overriding concern with peer-group acceptance. It is not surprising, then, that this child seems less than enthusiastically involved with schoolwork. While learning cannot be abandoned at this time, it can instead be structured to meet the changing interface of child and environment.

In planning an appropriate learning program, the clinician must evaluate the critical shifts in context and the major changes in the developing child. For the child who experienced difficulty with basic language and reading skills in the primary grades, each new wrinkle in the educational system provides another opportunity to fall further behind. Even if decoding skills remain poor at this time, however, it would be wise to deemphasize phonics and to devote time and practice to extracting meaning from the printed text. Because the child must meet the requirements of many different subjects and is often frustrated by the sheer volume of what must be read, learned, and written, it is important to plan remedial time efficiently: tutoring sessions must help the child find those organizational strategies that will enable him or her to successfully complete as many tasks as possible; alternate media effectively supplement reading as the major mode of learning; class time can be divided between short presentations of material to be learned and short small-group practice sessions; and notes, outlines, and organizational techniques for classwork can be customized to fit the child's needs and to maximize learning.

Task-analysis techniques are of great value at this level of learning because they allow the teacher an opportunity to evaluate the child's reservoir of available skills in relation to the demands of the task (Gagné 1975). The child with language and language-related processing difficulty will likely be struggling to read a seventh-grade science text with third-grade skills. Even if the teacher's manual boasts a seventh-grade readability, the concepts that must be grasped from a reading of the book are simply beyond the scope of readability formulas and beyond the conceptual skills of children with a language-impairment or organizational difficulties (McLaughlin 1969; Klare 1963). The teacher or clinician must be able to assess the concepts and skills to be learned and decide how best to guide this child to the most effective use of his or her skills. If, for example, the social studies text contains a reading on immigration to the United States that is too lengthy for the student, the resource room teacher might supplement the reading material with photographs of immigrants entering Ellis Island. (These photographs are available in many media centers and school libraries.) With careful planning, the teacher can easily guide the learning-disabled child to the concepts and facts to be mastered through the use of photographs. Photographs and other visual media, carefully selected and used with preplanned, concept-directed questions and discussion, can be a highly successful enrichment, as well as remedial, technique.

Filmstrips that show and tell the story of the framing of the Constitution, puzzle maps of the United States, historical photographs, and magazine articles that reinforce the material found in the text all provide the child with alternative avenues for learning the required content. Whereas the computer might offer the most sophisticated forms of learning assistance, including spelling and grammar checks for written work, less formidable audiovisual aids can provide the child with the opportunity to learn more independently and with greater ease and success.

Most learning-disabled children need remedial help with writing tasks in junior high school. Dictating the answers to comprehension questions into a tape recorder often eases the pain and frustration caused by poor language and handwriting skills. This technique frequently allows the child, who just can't get started with a task, an effective means of getting his or her ideas down. With guidance, dictation may prove to be a productive alternative to the blank or scribbled page. The tutor or teacher can then train the child to transcribe the dictated assignment from the tape using a typewriter or word processor. When the child is able to use these mechanical aids without assistance, he or she will benefit, not just in the types of information learned, but also in the level of self-initiated learning.

Limiting the extent and length of reading and writing assignments should not be viewed as a weakening of standards but as a practical means to an end—successful task completion. Simple logic suggests that four questions and answers carefully completed are more learning-effective

220

than ten items done poorly because of limited attention and feelings of overwhelming task demand. If additional practice on a skill is necessary, then it is done more effectively at spaced intervals than at one sitting. Similarly, a child who is diagnosed as having problems with conceptualization should learn math concepts by focusing on one formula or algorithm for each problem type. Again, when the goal is to help the student meet the content demands, the methods and means chosen should ensure the achievement of that goal without sacrificing the child's goodwill.

In order to effectively plan a remedial program for the junior high school child, the clinician must consider the critical developmental changes in the child, the major shifts in the context, the complexities of the multisubject content, and the stress-points inherent in the interaction of these factors. Finally, the remedial plan must also anticipate the next set of stress-points that the child will face in high school.

HIGH SCHOOL

High school is viewed as a time for reevaluation, not because of any dramatic changes in the student or in the learning environment, but because of several specific curriculum decisions necessary for guiding the child through to the end of the educational system. Holmes (1986) describes high school as the time when the student controls the reading and the organization of learning. The shift here is not dramatic, but it places the student further from contextual support. High school students are expected to find primary source materials in the library and use the information to understand and perhaps solve the problems presented in class or in the text. The high school student with organizational and conceptual difficulties, however, will still suffer from an inability to organize work, write an integrated paragraph, follow through and complete an assignment, or understand a complex concept. The student who began school with a language-processing deficit and difficulty in learning to read still has difficulty with the longer and more complex reading and writing assignments in the high school curriculum. The student who was diagnosed as having an attentional deficit disorder early in his or her schooling has, by high school, lost many of the outward negative behavioral symptoms; the processes of maturation have worked to modulate his or her behavior. However, this student will still have problems with organization, focus, independent work, and even poor or inappropriate responses to the contextual demands of the high school environment. At higher levels of academic training, when the complexities of the concepts are implicit and not explicit in the text, many learning-disabled children experience added cognitive stress (see chapter 3).

Even if language-impaired students have been able to avoid foreign language in junior high school, high school graduation requirements may include a two- or three-year foreign language component. This content demand is often a source of difficulty for learning-disabled students (Rudel 1985). Given the parameters of the child's abilities and disabilities, the clinician must help the child and the parent(s) answer several questions. First, does the school offer Latin as a foreign language choice? If so, Latin might answer the requirement with less stress on the learning abilities of the child, because Latin has a static grammar, does not need to be pronounced, and is not a conversational language. If Latin is not a possible choice, then Spanish may be the next-best alternative: its grammar, spelling, and pronunciation are more regular than French, for example. Second, is any foreign language either spoken or known by family members living at home? If so, that language would be a more learning-efficient choice than one that the child has never heard or spoken before. Finally, given the diagnostic profile of the child, do the long-range educational goals include the possibility of college? Whether or not the colleges under consideration have language requirements is an important factor. The team must evaluate whether the student has the ability to meet that requirement with additional time, with tutorial help, or (possibly) by substituting a computer language for the required foreign language.

If college is indeed a viable option, then the student must prepare to take the Scholastic Aptitude Tests (SATs) which are required of most college applicants. Some learning-disabled students obtain special permission to take an untimed SAT, which may be helpful for some students. Alternatively, some colleges do not require SAT scores, and others have special programs for the learning-disabled student. The student can check out all these possibilities with the high school's guidance department. The team must keep long-range vocational and educational goals in sight when making decisions regarding the student's remedial program. Problems can be solved by finding acceptable curriculum alternatives, providing more time and help for learning activities, or deciding that a specific learning activity should be abandoned. If, for example, no foreign language alternative turns out to be possible, and tutorial help proves to be insufficient, then the team needs to find an alternative curriculum plan that best meets the student's short- and long-range goals.

Educational planning, especially at the high school level, involves more than just determining which tutorial programs are best for the student. The team must also come to grips with how, when, and if future educational experiences will enhance the student's vocational goals. As was stated earlier, one of the treatment team's major goals is to assist the child's growth into a productive and competent adult.

General Principles for Effective Remedial Learning

In addition to predicting stress-points in the learning environment, the clinician must be able to evaluate the effectiveness of the learning program and the manner with which it is administered. The clinician can not only track stress-points across time and within different learning contexts but also apply effective learning principles to many levels of learning ability. Research on both normal and learning-disabled children, which sought to better understand their differences and to find ways in which to direct the educational planning of the disabled learner, provided the basis for these learning principles. Although these principles apply to all learning programs, they may mean a more dramatic difference between success and failure for the learning-disabled child. If these principles are not judiciously practiced in the standard educational context, the normal learner may simply utilize a self-generated compensatory cognitive strategy in order to complete the task. A child with limited resources is unlikely to be able to draw on self-generated learning strategies. Although some researchers have argued that all children should be trained in the generation and utilization of cognitive strategies (Kreutzer and Flavell 1975; Flavell 1971), children with clear learning limitations *must* be so trained in order to increase their chances for successful learning (Brown and Barclay 1976; Brown 1975; Denckla 1979b; Torgensen and Goldman 1977).

THE "MORE" PRINCIPLE

In a review of remedial reading programs, Guthrie (1978) concludes that although the quality of instruction is critical, the quantity of instructional time is a key factor in measuring learning results. This "more" principle emphasizes the importance of more task repetitions, more teacher supervision, more practice activities, more opportunities to practice the learning skill, more time for oral instructions, more senses involved in task practice and learning, and more time to organize and complete the task.

Tallal, Stark, and Mellits (1981) demonstrated that tasks requiring rapid processing of information could easily (98 percent of the time) distinguish language-impaired children from normal children. In a classroom setting, instructions and information given at the normal processing rate clearly would result in poor comprehension for language-impaired children. The teacher should be aware that slowing down oral instructions and allowing more time for each instruction to be processed will likely result in better comprehension for these children. In a similar study, Tallal and Piercy (1973) demonstrated that speech sounds had to be presented at a much slower rate for language-impaired children than for normal children. Denckla (1978) also described this phenomenon, explaining that since many dyslexic children process incoming language slowly, receiving too much information too fast will overload the process and may lead to a total lack of comprehension. In addition, Denckla notes that comprehension is affected by complexity of syntax: when syntax is simple, comprehension is better. Thus, Denckla recommends repeating questions with smaller bits of information at a time, using simple and direct syntax, and giving information and instructions more slowly.

The "more" principle also advocates a more individualized learning environment and more adult supervision. In recommending more supportive supervision for the learning-disabled student, Denckla adds that an educational plan must not neglect the child's need for a "time-consuming adult presence." Indeed, this may well be one of the greatest needs of many children with attentional and organizational deficits (Denckla 1979b, 266). Zigmond (1978) stresses the need for more individualized instruction and declares that such instruction may be the most promising aspect of many remedial techniques. Rudel (1978) commented that whatever learning deficit is diagnosed, the teacher is often forced to teach to the deficit by helping the child overlearn the task. Overlearning implies more time, more practice, more feedback, and more effort.

When discussing the remediation of children with language-processing problems, Menyuk and Flood (1981) also emphasized the importance of "more." The child needs more opportunities to play with language; he or she should be encouraged to recognize and create rhymes, riddles, puns, and stories, and to enjoy language experiences that include the many meanings, sounds, and ambiguities of words. The language-experience approach is not merely a technique of language remediation; it is also a call for the incorporation of the "more" principle into the treatment plan of learning-disabled children in order to stimulate their understanding and use of language.

Similarly, many remedial programs use a multisensory approach to learning. In brief, a multisensory approach calls for an increase in the number of sensory pathways through which a child experiences a task. This approach recognizes the visual-processing and/or auditory-processing limitations of many learning-disabled children and concludes that if one or more sensory pathways is deficient, then tapping alternative sensory pathways can aid in the learning process. Researchers have studied the effectiveness of this approach, and in spite of some inconclusive results, it is fair to say that the proponents advocate a remedial plan that utilizes more of the learner's senses. They argue that by inputting and processing information through *more* than just two sensory channels, the child will have a greater chance for learning success (Rupley and Blair 1983).

THE TRADE-OFF PRINCIPLE

The "more" principle often is not the most time-effective remedial route to follow. The clinician must frequently ask: does this child need more work in this skill area, or is the quality of the progress being made simply not worth the amount of time that is being expended to achieve a result? If the time being expended outweighs the learning gains, then it is time for a *trade-off*. The clinician is called upon to evaluate the return-on-investment for the child's learning efforts many times for many tasks and must be prepared to recommend a shift in content and/or remedial learning approach that will improve the child's chances of success. In discussing the diagnosis of motor deficits in learning-disabled children, Denckla (1978) states that a child with inadequate fine-motor skills simply cannot produce neat handwriting and fast handwriting at the same time. This child has to make a trade-off—time for legibility, the pen for a word processor.

Trade-offs can be viewed from at least two perspectives. First, the clinician recommends one type of remedial approach over another. For example, when exercises in "summarizing the main idea" continually stymie the child who is unable to organize printed text, more practice using the same program will be futile. The teacher may need to switch to structured rules and easy-to-follow learning recipes that can cue reading to the summarizing task. When one remedial program does not pay off for a child (not enough learning accomplished for the amount of time and effort being expended), the clinician must be ready to trade the program in for a more learning-efficient approach. If the goal of the reading task is to extract information from the printed text, and there is no inviolate sequence of remedial activities that must be completed by every child in order for comprehension of the text to be achieved, then fifty poorly completed phonics exercises might well be traded for activities that enhance the ultimate goal. For example, a series of short paragraphs with controlled vocabulary and sentence complexity could be used in a "treasure hunt" activity where the text is read first with, and then without, teacher assistance. The object of the game is to find "clues" (details from the text) that lead to the ultimate "treasures" (inference, cause/effect, summary, and/or conclusion).

The second perspective in which trade-offs can be viewed is one of compensation. The clinician should know the comparative benefits of each approach, and know whether or not trading one remedial program for another will provide the child with the needed help toward the learning goal. The treatment team must look for ways around the learning problem and toward the goal. For example, foreign language study, discussed earlier, supports this view of trade-offs. Similarly, a child who fails for years to master the rules of arithmetic computation, whose columns of numbers are never straight enough for accurate figuring and whose multiplication tables are forever new, would probably profit more from concentrating on mathematical concepts and using a calculator for computation. Since we have the luxury of using calculators and computers for simple computations (and more), we can abandon the program that relies on memorization, at least for a time, and plan a program that helps the child understand math concepts. It does not make sense, given time limitations, to compel a child to continue, with little or no success, with exercises in computation at the expense of understanding important mathematical concepts.

THE STRESS-ABILITIES PRINCIPLE

In addition to knowing when to apply the principles of remedial and compensatory trade-offs, and when to plan for "more" time and practice at the learning task, the clinician also must be able to assess whether the quality of the child's learning progress is sufficient to counterbalance any temporary negative effects on his or her self-concept. The most highly acclaimed remedial program will be a certain failure if the child believes that he or she cannot learn, no matter what. Thus, the clinician must ensure that the learning program includes elements that bolster the child's self-esteem and emphasize his or her abilities while also working to re-mediate and/or compensate for the disability. For example, when a young child is relatively better at temporal processing tasks than spatial processing tasks, the clinician might well recommend a phonics reading program that includes the blending of sounds. By stressing this relative learning strength, the clinician may provide a key to some reading success for this child. On the other hand, the learning-disabled child who does well on a spatial-spatial task might have greater success associating a whole-word configuration with its pictorial equivalent. An emphasis on this learning strength may well provide the child with the opportunity to develop an initial sight-word vocabulary. In either case, the clinician needs to know which process available to the child is stronger and to stress this ability when recommending a learning approach (Rudel and Denckla 1976).

When a dyslexic child is having great difficulty processing sequential information, the program must shift away from activities that emphasize this weakness. If those learning activities cannot be avoided, however, the treatment team can arrange additional contextual support: individ-ualized tutoring, extra time, and supplemental learning materials. For example, the teacher may use story cards to help the child put a story in sequence. In order to strengthen the child's ability to sequence a story accurately, the teacher may help the child to tell the story out loud as the child puts the pictures in proper sequence. The number of activities that press on a child's disability must be strictly limited, and the teacher can deemphasize the problem tasks by interspersing them with tasks that stress the child's learning abilities. For example, if the child has difficulty with drawing conclusions or predicting a probable outcome for a story, perhaps he or she can try an activity that shows how selecting an appropriate title or detecting cause and effect in the action of the story can aid in the overall comprehension of the material. With a clear focus on the learning goal and the child's learning strengths, the clinician is able to set up a learning plan that emphasizes the individual child, not the remedial program.

Rudel (1980) recommended that "learning disability" not be viewed as a global diagnosis and noted the importance of finding strengths and weaknesses of ability, even within a single diagnostic classification. For example, there are some dyslexic children with language-processing difficulties, whose capacity to utilize spatial-configurational information is not only adequate but often superior to the capacity of normal controls. Thus, it is important to stress the child's abilities while recognizing his or her disabilities. A child's relative strength in the use of spatial-configurational information might be incorporated into a total plan for developing sight vocabulary by having the child draw or outline the shapes of new words in order to better commit the words to memory. Additionally, a child's relatively strong spatial-configurational ability may well provide a key to learning mathematics through lessons that emphasize geometric shapes and relationships. The use of geometry also lends itself to manipulatives and activities with tangible objects. When the treatment team commits itself to stressing the abilities of the child, it is declaring its faith in the child and acknowledging his or her individuality as well.

The importance of stressing abilities does relate to the establishment of a strong program but, even more, impacts significantly on the health of the child. Continually hammering away at a skill that demands abilities that the child simply does not have is a sign of poor learning management and, also, a warning that a healthy self-concept may be at risk. When a child continues to fail at the learning process, he or she loses not only the content material but also self-confidence. With the child's confidence goes not only a positive self-concept but also motivation to learn.

Motivation to Learn

Motivation to learn is one of the most complex components of behavior. Theories of motivation range from explanations of the mechanisms of stimulus-response to involved psychological interpretations of behavior (Weiner 1972). Research on cognitive performance has attempted to ascertain those task variables that could determine the level of motivation for learning (Pardes 1979; Ballif 1974; Weiner 1972). In trying to make a practical assessment of whether or not a child will engage in, persist at, and complete a learning task, the clinician should evaluate the child. The child's motivational disposition and attitude toward the task and himself or herself determines not only the level of task involvement but also the degree of learning success.

Rotter, Seeman, and Liverant (1962) have asserted that when a child believes that success or failure at a task is determined only by luck and/or task difficulty, he or she demonstrates an external locus of control. The child sees learning as controlled by the teacher, the school, the program, or any number of external content and contextual variables— but not by the learner. It is easy to see how such an outlook on learning would not bode well for successful task involvement. Unfortunately, this motivational disposition is not only counterproductive for the learning-disabled child but also quite predictable. Diagnostic testing, medical and psychological evaluations, special classes, and tutoring focus so much attention and concern on a child that the child may well come to believe that, without all the help and special treatment, he or she simply *couldn't* learn. The treatment team may also unwittingly fall victim to this same conclusion. When the child's learning skills and limitations are the subject of countless meetings and discussions, the sheer volume of clinical and educational effort may undermine and overwhelm the very goal toward which the team is working: the development of an independent and competent adult. If the mature learner feels that he or she is not in control of the learning process, then his or her level of motivation will not be adequate for active participation in a remedial program, no matter how skillfully the program is constructed. Without the active involvement of the learner, the treatment plan may not be worth the paper upon which it is written.

229

The questions then must be: How can we enlist the involvement of the learner in his or her learning? How can we foster the belief that control of the learning process can ultimately rest in the hands of the learner? How can we test, interview, diagnose, plan, and manage learning problems without causing the learner to lose self-confidence? These questions are of critical importance and probably can be answered by describing several different theoretical constructs. However, the answers discussed here involve techniques for creating within the learner a positive motivational disposition. The learner must come to believe that remedial help will ultimately lead to control of his or her own learning. In fact, all learners should be in control of their own learning; however, the learning-disabled child probably will need more convincing, and more active involvement from adults, in order to achieve this goal.

Just as an external locus of control mitigates against learner motivation, the child who attributes success and failure at learning tasks to his or her own effort and ability displays an internal locus of control. This ascription of control to internal forces more frequently produces adequate levels of motivation (Rotter, Seeman, and Liverant 1962; Weiner 1972). When the learner feels that success at learning results from his or her own efforts and capabilities, then the learner is more likely to ascribe success to his or her own ability and effort. Thus, how a learner develops a feeling of competence is a critical component in motivational disposition.

One cognitive model of motivation contends that motivation to learn is determined by several learner-controlled variables (Ballif 1974), including (1) the learner's evaluation of the learning task in terms of his or her own expectations of positive affect and (2) the learner's assessment of probable success at the task. The learner decides whether participation in the task will bring positive or negative feelings, and the learner knows whether or not he or she has a good chance of doing well at the task. This evaluation is based on an assessment of previous performance at similar tasks and a *general* appraisal of self as a good or poor learner. It is highly probable that the strength and accuracy of the learner's self-image as a learner is directly related to the number and kind of previous learning experiences. If his or her learning history contains a high percentage of learning failures, particularly at similar tasks, then the learner will decide that the chances for success and positive affect are poor, and this evaluation will mitigate against participation in the learning task. For example, when a learner has repeatedly failed to master the multiplication tables, a fresh attempt at teaching this task, no matter how well packaged or well intentioned, will be met with less-than-enthusiastic participation. Conversely, if the learner is able to evaluate past learning experiences favorably, because of frequent success and generally positive affect, the odds are greater that the learner will participate and successfully complete the task (Parsons and Ruble 1977; Ames, Ames, and Felker 1976).

A child's learning history seeks a pattern, and if failure and frustration are the focus of that pattern, then he or she will require a great deal of time, effort, and success at subsequent learning tasks in order to avoid developing a negative motivational disposition. Planning and managing a learning program is most efficient when the child's disability is diagnosed and treated early, so that a negative motivational attitude is not allowed to take a stranglehold on the learning process. Rudel comments that in a longitudinal study by Satz and Fletcher (1978), children who were thought to have only a mild reading disorder in second grade were seen in fifth grade as being severely reading-impaired. Even a mild disability, if not effectively treated, may expand into a learning problem of much greater magnitude with time. Without early detection and treatment, the child stands a greater chance of falling further behind academically, losing confidence as a learner, and developing a more complex set of learning problems over time.

The rationale for prompt diagnosis and treatment speaks not only to the importance of efficient remediation but also to the need for the early establishment of a positive motivational disposition in the learner. Once the learner considers himself or herself as a poor learning risk, he or she becomes less likely to engage in the very learning tasks necessary to remediate his or her specific learning problems. Thus, the problem is clear: unless a child can be made to view himself or herself as an able learner, even though limited by a disability, these problems, academic and motivational, will multiply over time.

On the other hand, learning professionals often assume that their expertise affords them the opportunity to control, through the use of well-chosen materials and techniques, the child's participation, success, and even attitude toward the task. Research and day-to-day classroom evidence, however, testify otherwise (Greiner and Karoly 1976; Master, Furman, and Barden 1977). The learner's decision whether or not to participate is based on an evaluation of past success and past experience with similar and general learning tasks, not on a teacher's pleasant demeanor or a colorful new learning packet. This is not to say that the teacher and the materials do not play an important role in the involvement of the learner in the task; rather, the learner's own motivational disposition is the more likely source of the decision of whether or not to participate in learning.

The learner's evaluation of past performance and assessment of probable results can be strengthened considerably if the learner has an effective and efficient repertoire of strategies that can improve chances for task success. What Ballif (1974) describes as the "knowledge of instrumental steps" is another critical variable in the cognitive model of motivation. Instrumental steps are those cognitive strategies that the learner must be able to select and utilize in order to solve a learning problem successfully. It is unlikely that a child will view his or her chances of success at a task in a favorable light if he or she has little, if any, idea of how to begin or how to mediate the processing of the task. It is also improbable that a child will look forward to positive affect from a task similar or identical to one that he or she has never been able to solve before. For example, the child who still cannot read after two years of school is unlikely to be enthusiastic about an opportunity to engage in yet another reading activity.

Learning-disabled children are likely to have inadequate search and organizational strategies. As the content of the learning shifts from memorization of facts to retrieval of self-generated information, these children experience problems that prevent their effective task participation. Thus, it is critically important to train these children with effective cognitive strategies over time—as the learner matures, as the content increases in complexity, and as the educational context decreases its support.

A considerable body of research and literature is concerned with the description and analysis of those cognitive strategies that can affect accurate processing and retrieval of information (Hilgard and Bower 1975). Researchers have found that training children to attend to task-relevant information when processing new material increases their learning capacity (Lehman 1972; Kobasigawa 1974). Children trained in specific strategies of rehearsal, chunking, sorting, and organization of incoming information are better able to control their learning processes (Neimark, Slotnick, and Ulrich 1971; Ornstein, Naus, and Liberty 1975; Worden 1975). Researchers have also studied strategies that could help normal and slow readers learn how to organize text for efficient and effective processing (Brown and Smiley 1978; Brown 1975; Paris, Lindauer, and Cox 1977). In addition to finding that training in these strategies positively affects recall and comprehension of text, Brown (1975) found developmental differences suggesting that, while older children may have a larger and more effectively utilized repertoire of strategies, age differences on many learning tasks can be reduced significantly if young children receive instruction and support in the use of task-processing strategies.

Some researchers attribute the learning-disabled child's failure to perform adequately in a variety of task settings to an inability to adapt to the cognitive requirements of a task and to use active and efficient task strategies (Torgensen and Goldman 1977). Poor readers may fail to comprehend partly because they fail to approach reading tasks in a planned, organized, and active way (Gibson and Levin 1975). Holmes (1986) describes many learning-disabled children as plagued by a "jumping the gun" syndrome: instead of attending to salient task features and then selecting the most productive task strategy, these children begin to work at the task without benefit of a plan or organized processing strategies. Rudel (1981a) explains that many learning-disabled children lack the capacity to mobilize self-monitoring, self-initiated organizational and information-processing strategies. Without this capacity, the learner continues to be dependent upon those who can help solve the learning problem. These support services, however, should be teaching the *child* to select and apply the appropriate strategies for solving an ever-increasing number of tasks.

Knowledge of and facility in the use of specific information-processing strategies (ideally) places the learner in a position of "executive control"; in this position of control, the learner is better able to participate in his or her own learning. Cognitive strategies must be taught, learning must be organized for efficient processing and retrieval, and curricula must develop from the belief that learning to learn is a critical factor in establishing a positive motivational disposition in the learner. Holmes (1986) calls for the teaching of strategies that prepare the learner to anticipate and adapt to the content and contextual changes in the learning environment. Zigmond (1978) suggests teaching response patterns that are appropriate to changes in the learning tasks. Mahoney (1974) proposes a systematic training program for problem-solving skills with modeling of learning strategies that can deliver extensive improvements in task performance. Training the learner in the effective and efficient use of cognitive-processing strategies can improve task performance, place more responsibility for learning in the hands of the learner, and positively influence the learner's motivation to learn.

Conclusions

Once the treatment team has referred, tested, interviewed, and evaluated the child, it must focus on the child's long-term goals of independence and competence. With full knowledge of the child's limitations and abilities, the treatment team must be prepared to periodically reevaluate the child's interactions with the learning environment over the course of his or her schooling. The learning program must be tailored to fit the child's needs: needs that will change as the content increases in complexity, as the context decreases its support, and as the child grows and matures. With proper planning and management, this child will come to have a positive self-image as a learner because he or she will be trained to anticipate and adapt to changes in the learning environment and he or she will know how to utilize effective and efficient cognitive strategies that place him or her in control of learning. If the treatment team succeeds at these tasks, then they clearly have moved beyond the diagnosis.

List of Tests

Achenbach, T. M. and Edelbrock, C. S. 1982. *Manual for the child behavior checklist and child behavior profile*. Burlington: University of Vermont, Child Psychiatry.

Baker, H. and Leland, B. 1967. *Detroit tests of learning aptitude*. Rev. ed. Indianapolis: Bobbs-Merrill.

Beery, K. E. 1982. *Revised manual for the development test of visual motor integration*. Cleveland, OH: Modern Curriculum Press.

Bellak, L. 1949. *The children's apperception test*. New York: C. P. S. Co.

Bryant, N. D. 1975. *Diagnostic test of basic reading decoding skills*. New York: Columbia University, Teachers College.

Cohen, H. and Weil, G. R. 1975. *Tasks of emotional development*. Brookline, MA: TED Associates.

Connolly, A. J., Nachtman, W., and Pritchett, E. M. 1976. *KeyMath diagnostic arithmetic test*. Circle Pines, MN: American Guidance Service.

Davidson, P. S. and Marolda, M. R. 1978. *Mathematics diagnostic/prescriptive inventory*. New Rochelle, NY: Cusinaire Company of America.

DeFilippis, N. A. and McCampbell, E. 1979. *The booklet category test*. Vol. 2. Odessa, FL: Psychological Assessment Resources.

Denckla, M. B. and Rudel, R. G. 1976. Rapid automatized naming (R.A.N.): Diplexia differentiated from other learning disabilities. *Neuropsychologia* 14 (4):41–79.

Di Simoni, F. 1978. *The token test for children*. Allen, TX: DLM Teaching Resources.

Dunn, L. M. and Dunn, L. M. 1981. *Peabody picture vocabulary test*. Rev. ed. Circle Pines, MI: American Guidance Service.

Forer, B. R. 1967. *The Forer structured sentence completion test*. Los Angeles: Western Psychological Services.

Gardner, M. F. 1979. *Expressive one-word picture vocabulary test*. Novato, CA: Academic Therapy Publications.

Gilmore, J. V. and Gilmore, E. C. 1968. *Gilmore oral reading test*. New York: Harcourt Brace Jovanovich.

Golden, C. J. 1978. *Manual for the Stroop color and word test*. Chicago: Stoelting.

Gray oral reading test. 1963. Indianapolis: Bobbs-Merrill.

Hammill, D. D. and Larsen, S. C. 1983. *The test of written language*. Austin, TX: Pro-Ed.

Harris, A. J. 1958. Harris test of lateral dominance. In *Manual of directions for administration and interpretation*. New York: Psychological Corporation.

Heaton, R. K. 1981. *Manual for the Wisconsin card sorting test*. Odessa, FL: Psychological Assessment Resources.

Iowa test of basic skills. 1965. New York: Houghton-Mifflin.

Jastak, J. F. and Jastak, S. R. 1978. *The wide-range achievement test*. Wilmington, DE: Jastak Associates.

———. 1984. *The wide-range achievement test manual*. Rev. ed. Wilmington, DE: Jastak Associates.

Kaplan, E. F., Goodglass, H., and Weintraub, S. 1983. *The Boston naming test*. Philadelphia: Lea and Febiger.

Kaufman, A. S. and Kaufman, N. L. 1983. *Kaufman assessment battery for children*. Circle Pines, MI: American Guidance Service.

Kramer, J. H., Delis, D. C., Kaplan, E., and Ober, B. A. 1984. *California verbal learning test—children*. N.p.

McArthur, D. S. and Roberts, G. E. 1982. *Roberts apperception test for children*. Los Angeles: Western Psychological Services.

Osterrieth, P. A. 1944. Le test de copie d'une figure complex. *Archives de psychologie* 30:206–356.

Porteus, S. D. 1965. *Porteus maze·test: 50 years' application*. Palo Alto, CA: Pacific Books.

Raven, J. C. 1960. *Guide to the standard progressive matrices*. London: H. K. Lewis; Psychological Corporation.

———. 1965. *Guide to using the coloured matrices*. London: H. K. Lewis; Psychological Corporation.

Reitan, R. M. and Davison, L. A. 1974. *Clinical neuropsychology: Clinical status and applications*. New York: Hemisphere.

Rey, A. 1941. L'examen psychologique dans le cas d'encephalopathie traumatique. *Archives de psychologie* 28:286–340.

Roach, E. and Kephart, N. C. 1966. *Purdue perceptual and motor skills survey*. Columbus, OH: Charles Merrill.

Rorschach, H. 1942. *Psychodiagnostics: A diagnostic test based on perception*. New York: Grune & Stratton.

Spreen, O. and Benton, A. L. 1969. *Sentence repetition test*. Victoria, B.C.: University of Victoria, Neuropsychology Laboratory.

Taylor, L. B. n.d. *Children's stories*. Montreal: Montreal Neurological Institute.

Thorndike, R. L., Hagen, E. P., and Sattler, J. M. 1986. *The Stanford-Binet intelligence scale*. 4th ed. Chicago: Riverside.

Wechsler, D. 1967. *Wechsler preschool and primary scale of intelligence*. New York: Psychological Corporation.

———. 1974. *Wechsler intelligence scale for children*. Rev. ed. New York: Psychological Corporation.

———. 1981. *Wechsler adult intelligence scale*. Rev. ed. New York: Psychological Corporation.

Wepman, J. M. 1958. *Auditory discrimination test*. Chicago: University of Chicago Press.

Wiederholt, J. L. and Bryant, B. R. 1986. *The Gray oral reading tests*. Rev. ed. Los Angeles: Western Psychological Services.

Witkin, H. A., Oltman, P. K., Raskin, E., and Karp, S. A. 1971. *Children's embedded figures test—manual*. Palo Alto, CA: Consulting Psychologists Press.

Woodcock, R. W. 1973. *Woodcock reading mastery tests*. Circle Pines, MI: American Guidance Service.

Woods, M. L. and Moe, A. J. 1985. *Analytical reading inventory*. 3d ed. Columbus, OH: Charles Merrill.

References

Ackerman, P. T., Dykman, R. A., Holcomb, P. J., and McCray, D. S. 1982. Methyl-phenidate effects on cognitive style and reaction time in four groups of children. *Psychiatry Research* 7:199–213.

American Psychiatric Association. 1980. *Diagnostic and statistical manual of mental disorders*. 3d ed. Washington, D.C.: American Psychiatric Association.

Ames, C., Ames, R., and Felker, D. W. 1976. Informational and dispositional determinants of children's achievement attributions. *Journal of Educational Psychology* 68:63–69.

Ballif, B. L. 1974. Components of motivation for learning and procedures for increasing them. *New York State Personnel and Guidance Journal* 9:3–17.

Barkley, R. A. 1981. *Hyperactive children: A handbook for diagnosis and treatment*. New York: Guilford.

Basso, A., Berti, A., Capitani, E., and Fenu, E. 1981. Aphasia and acalculia: Relationship and recovery. Paper presented at the Fourth International Neuropsychological Society European Conference, Bergen, Norway.

Benbow, C. P. and Stanley, J. C. 1983. Sex differences in mathematical reasoning ability: More facts. *Science* 222:1029–31.

Benson, D. F. and Denckla, M. B. 1969. Verbal paraphasia as a source of calculation disturbance. *Archives of Neurology* 21:19–46.

Benson, D. F. and Geschwind, N. 1969. The alexias. In *Disorders of speed, perception, and symbolic behavior*, ed. P. J. Vinken and G. W. Bruyn. Vol. 4, *Handbook of clinical neurology*. Amsterdam: North Holland.

Benton, A. L. 1975. Neurological aspects. In *Advances in neurology*, ed. W. J. Friedlander. New York: Raven.

Benton, A. L., Hamsher, K. deS., Varney, N. R., and Spreen, O. 1983. *Facial recognition*. New York: Oxford University Press.

Best, C. T., ed. 1985. *Hemispheric function and collaboration in the child*. New York: Academic Press.

Blank, M., Berezweig, S. S., and Bridges, W. H. 1975. The effects of stimulus complexity and sensory modality on reaction time in normal and retarded readers. *Child Development* 46:133–40.

Boder, E. 1970. Developmental dyslexia. *Journal of School Health* 40:289–90.

———. 1973. Developmental dyslexia: A diagnostic approach based on three atypical reading-spelling patterns. *Developmental Medicine and Child Neurology* 15:663–87.

Broman, M. and Rudel, R. 1982. Inter and intrahemispheric visual reaction time of dyslexic and normal children. Paper presented at the Twenty-seventh Annual Convention, International Reading Association, Chicago, Illinois.

237

Brown, A. L. 1975. The development of memory: Knowing, knowing about knowing, and knowing how to know. In *Advances in child development and behavior,* ed. H. W. Reese. Vol. 10. New York: Academic Press.

Brown, A. L. and Barclay, C. 1976. The effects of training specific mnemonics on the metamnemonic efficiency of retarded children. *Child Development* 47:71–81.

Brown, A. L. and Smiley, S. S. 1978. The development of strategies for studying text. *Child Development* 44:1076–88.

Bryden, M. P. 1982. *Laterality: Functional asymmetry in the intact brain.* New York: Academic Press.

Butters, N. 1984. The clinical aspects of memory disorders: Contributions from experimental studies of amnesia and dementia. *Journal of Clinical Neuropsychology* 6:17–36.

Cameron, M. I. and Robinson, M. J. 1980. Effects of cognitive training on academic and on-task behavior of hyperactive children. *Journal of Abnormal Child Psychology* 8:405–19.

Cantwell, D. P. and Satterfield, J. H. 1978. The prevalence of academic underachievement in hyperactive children. *Journal of Pediatric Psychology* 3:161–71.

Caplan, D., ed. 1980. *Biologic studies of mental processes.* Cambridge, MA: The MIT Press.

Caplan, P. and Kinsbourne, M. 1979. *Children's learning and attention problems.* Boston: Little, Brown.

Carey, S. and Diamond, R. 1980. Maturational determination of the developmental course of face encoding. In *Biological studies of mental processes,* ed. D. Caplan. Cambridge, MA: The MIT Press.

Ceci, S. J. 1986. *Handbook of cognitive, social and neuropsychological aspects of learning disabilities.* Hillsdale, NJ: Erlbaum Associates.

Chall, J. and Mirsky, A. 1979. *Education and the brain.* Chicago: University of Chicago Press.

Chelune, G. J. and Baer, R. Z. 1986. Developmental norms for the Wisconsin card sorting test. *Journal of Clinical and Experimental Neuropsychology* 8:219–28.

Christensen, A. 1975. *Luria's neuropsychological investigation: Manual.* New York: Spectrum.

Cohen, J. 1976. Learning disabilities and conditional brain activity. In *Developmental psychophysiology of mental retardation,* ed. R. Karrer. Springfield, IL: Charles C. Thomas.

Cohen, N. J. and Douglas, V. I. 1972. Characteristics of the orienting response in hyperactive and normal children. *Psychophysiology* 9:238–45.

Coltheart, M. 1979. Lexical access in simple reading tasks. In *Strategies of information processing,* ed. G. Underwood. New York: Academic Press.

Cone, T. E. and Wilson, L. R. 1981. Quantifying a severe discrepancy: A critical analysis. *Learning Disability Quarterly* 4:359–71.

Conners, C. K. 1970. Symptom patterns in hyperkinetic, neurotic and normal children. *Child Development* 41:667–82.

———. 1973. Rating scales for use in drug studies with children. *Psychopharmacology Bulletin,* Special Issue, 24–29.

———. 1979. A teacher rating scale for use in drug studies with children. *American Journal of Psychiatry* 126:884–88.

Corkin, S. 1974. Serial-ordering deficits in inferior readers. *Neuropsychologia* 12:347–54.

References

Critchley, M. 1964. *Developmental dyslexia*. Springfield, IL: Charles C. Thomas.

———. 1970. *The dyslexic child*. Springfield, IL: Charles C. Thomas.

Curtiss, S. 1977. *Genie: A psycholinguistic study of a modern-day "wild child."* New York: Academic Press.

Decker, S. N. and DeFries, J. C. 1980. Cognitive abilities in families with reading-disabled children. *Journal of Learning Disabilities* 13:53–58.

Denckla, M. B. 1973. Development of speed in repetitive and successive finger-movements in normal children. *Developmental Medicine and Child Neurology* 15: 635–45.

———. 1979a. Childhood learning disabilities. In *Clinical neuropsychology*, ed. K. M. Heilman and E. Valenstein, 535–76. New York: Oxford University Press.

———. 1979b. Minimal brain dysfunction. In *Education and the brain*, ed. J. Chall and A. Mirsky. Chicago: University of Chicago Press.

Denckla, M. B. and Rudel, R. G. 1976. Rapid automatized naming (R.A.N.): Dyslexia differentiated from other learning disabilities. *Neuropsychologia* 14:471–79.

———. 1978. Anomalies of motor development in hyperactive boys. *Annals of Neurology* 3:231–33.

Denckla, M. B., Rudel, R. G., and Broman, M. 1980. Development of a spatial orientation skill in normal, learning disabled and neurologically impaired children. In *Biological studies of mental processes*, ed. D. Caplan, 44–59. Cambridge, MA: The MIT Press.

Dennis, M. 1980. Capacity and strategy for syntactic comprehension after left or right hemidecortication. *Brain and Language* 10:287–317.

Dennis, M. and Kohn, B. 1975. Comprehension of syntax in infantile hemiplegics after cerebral hemidecortication: Left-hemisphere superiority. *Brain and Language* 2:472–82.

Dennis, M. and Whitaker, H. A. 1976. Language acquisition following hemidecortication: Linguistic superiority of the left over the right hemisphere. *Brain and Language* 3: 404–33.

Diamond, M. C., Rosenzweig, M. R., Bennett, E. L., Lindner, B., and Lyon, L. 1972. Effects of environmental enrichment and impoverishment on rat cerebral cortex. *Journal of Neurobiology* 3:47–64.

Doehring, D. G. 1968. *Patterns of impairment in specific reading disability*. Bloomington: Indiana University Press.

Dykman, R. A., Ackerman, P. T., Clements, S. D., and Peters, J. E. 1971. Specific learning disabilities: Attentional deficit syndrome. In *Progress in learning disabilities*, ed. H. R. Myklebust, Vol. 2. New York: Grune & Stratton.

Dykman, R. A., Ackerman, P. T., and Oglesby, D. M. 1979. Selective and sustained attention in hyperactive, learning-disabled, and normal boys. *Journal of Nervous and Mental Disease* 167:288–97.

Edelman, G. M. 1978. Group selection and phasic reentrant signalling: A theory of higher brain function. In *The mindful brain*, ed. G. M. Edelman and V. B. Mountcastle. Cambridge, MA: The MIT Press.

Edelman, G. M. and Mountcastle, V. B., eds. 1978. *The mindful brain*. Cambridge, MA: The MIT Press.

Fantz, R. L. 1965. Visual perception from birth as shown by pattern selectivity. In *New issues in infant development*, ed. H. E. Whipple, 793–814. *Annals of New York Academy of Science*, no. 118.

Filskov, S. B. and Boll, T. J. 1981. *Handbook of clinical neuropsychology*. New York: Wiley.

Finucci, J. M. 1978. Genetic considerations in dyslexia. *Progress in Learning Disabilities* 4:41–63.

Finucci, J. M., Isaacs, S. D., Whitehouse, C. C., and Childs, B. 1982. A quantitative index of reading disability for use in family studies. *Developmental Medicine and Child Neurology* 24:733–44.

Firestone, P. and Douglas, V. I. 1975. The effects of reward and punishment on reaction times and autonomic activity in hyperactive and normal children. *Journal of Abnormal Child Psychology* 3:201–15.

Flavell, J. H. 1971. What is memory development the development of? *Human Development* 14:272–78.

French, J., Graves, P. D., and Levitt, E. E. 1983. Objective and projective testing of children. In *Handbook of clinical child psychology*, ed. C. E. Walker and M. C. Roberts. New York: Wiley and Sons.

Gagné, R. M. 1975. *Essentials of learning for instruction.* Hinsdale, NJ: Dryden Press.

Gardner, R. A. 1986. *The psychotherapeutic techniques of Richard A. Gardner.* Cresskill, NJ: Creative Therapeutics.

Gates, A. and Bradshaw, J. L. 1977. Music perception and cerebral hemispheres. *Cortex* 13:390–401.

Gazzaniga, M. S., ed. 1979. *Handbook of behavioral neurobiology*, Vol. 2, *Neuropsychology.* New York: Plenum Press.

Geschwind, N. 1962. The anatomy of acquired disorders of reading. In *Reading disability*, ed. J. Money, 115–29. Baltimore: Johns Hopkins University Press.

Geschwind, N. and Behan, P. 1982. Left-handedness: Association with immune disease, migraine, and developmental learning disorder. In *Proceedings of the National Academy of Sciences*, no. 79, 5097–5100.

Geschwind, N. and Galaburda, A. M. 1985. Cerebral lateralization. In *Biological mechanisms, associations and pathology: A hypothesis and a program for research*, 428–59. *Archives of Neurology*, no. 42.

Geschwind, N. and Galaburda, A. M., eds. 1984. *Cerebral dominance: The biological foundations.* Cambridge, MA: Harvard University Press.

Gibson, E. J. and Levin, H. 1975. *The psychology of reading.* Cambridge, MA: The MIT Press.

Goldman, P. S. 1974. An alternative to developmental plasticity: Heterology of CNS structures in infants and adults. In *CNS plasticity and recovery of functions*, ed. D. G. Stein, J. Rosen, and N. Butters. New York: Academic Press.

Goldman-Rakic, P. S. 1981. Development and plasticity of primate frontal association cortex. In *The organization of cerebral cortex*, ed. F. O. Schmitt, F. G. Worden, S. G. Dennis, and G. Adelman. Cambridge, MA: The MIT Press.

———. 1987. Development of cortical circuitry and cognitive function. *Child Development* 58:601–22.

Goodglass, H. and Kaplan, E. 1972. *Assessment of aphasia and related disorders.* Philadelphia: Lea and Febiger.

———. 1979. Assessment of cognitive deficit in the brain-injured patient. In *Handbook of behavioral neurobiology*, ed. M. S. Gazzaniga. Vol. 2, *Neuropsychology.* New York: Plenum Press.

Gordon, H. W. 1975. Hemispheric asymmetry and musical performance. *Science* 189: 68–69.

———. 1980. Cognitive asymmetry in dyslexic families. *Neuropsychologia* 18:645–56.

References

Grant, I. and Adams, K. M., eds. 1986. *Neuropsychological assessment of neuropsychiatric disorders*. New York: Oxford University Press.

Greiner, J. M. and Karoly, P. 1976. Effects of self-control training on study activity and academic performance: An analysis of self-monitoring, self-reward, and systematic planning components. *Journal of Counseling Psychology* 23:495–502.

Gross, K., Rothenberg, S., Schottenfeld, S., and Drake, C. 1978. Duration thresholds for letter identification in left and right visual fields for normal and reading disabled children. *Neuropsychologia* 16:709–15.

Guthrie, J. T. 1978. Principles of instruction: A critique of Johnson's "Remedial approaches to dyslexia." In *Dyslexia: An appraisal of current knowledge*, ed. A. L. Benton and D. Pearl. New York: Oxford University Press.

Halperin, J. M., Gittleman, R., Klein, D. F., and Rudel, R. G. 1984. Reading disabled hyperactive children: A distinct subgroup of attention deficit disorder with hyperactivity? *Journal of Abnormal Child Psychology* 12:1–14.

Held, R. and Hein, A. 1963. Movement-produced stimulation in the development of visually guided behavior. *Journal of Comparative and Physiological Psychology* 56:607–13.

Helfgott, E., Rudel, R. G., and Kairam, R. 1986. The effect of Piraretam on short and long term verbal retrieval in dyslexic boys. *International Journal of Psychophysiology* 4:53–61.

Hilgard, E. R. and Bower, G. H. 1975. *Theories of learning*. Englewood Cliffs, NJ: Prentice-Hall.

Holmes, J. M. 1987. Natural histories in learning disabilities: Neuropsychological difference/environmental demand. In *Handbook of cognitive, social and neuropsychological aspects of learning disabilities*, ed. S. J. Ceci. Hillsdale, NJ: Erlbaum Associates.

Holmes, J. M., Urion, D. K., and Waber, D. P. Developmental learning disorders associated with parental dysfunction. Unpublished manuscript.

Holmes, J. M. and Waber, D. P. In press. Developmental neuropsychological assessment: The systemic approach. In *Neuromethods 15: Neuropsychology*, ed. A. A. Boulton, G. B. Baker, and M. Hiscock. Clifton, NJ: Humana Press.

Hoy, E., Weiss, G., Minde, K., and Cohen, N. 1978. The hyperactive child adolescence: Emotional, social, and cognitive functioning. *Journal of Abnormal Child Psychology* 6:311–24.

Hubel, D. H. and Wiesel, T. N. 1962. Receptive fields, binocular interaction and functional architecture in the cat's visual cortex. *Journal of Physiology* 160:106–54.

Ivinskis, A., Allen, S., and Shaw, E. 1971. An extension of Wechsler Memory Scale norms to lower age groups. *Journal of Clinical Psychology* 27:354–57.

Jansky, J. and DeHirsch, K. 1972. *Preventing reading failure: Prediction, diagnosis, intervention*. New York: Harper & Row.

Johnson, D. J. 1978. Remedial approaches to dyslexia. In *Dyslexia: An appraisal of current knowledge*, ed. A. L. Benton and D. Pearl. New York: Oxford University Press.

Johnson, D. J., Blalock, J. W., and Nesbitt, J. A. 1978. Adolescents with learning disabilities: Perspectives from an educational clinic. *Learning Disabilities Quarterly* 1:24–36.

Kagan, J. and Lewis, M. 1965. Studies of attention in the human infant. *Journal of Behavior and Development* 11:95–127.

Kaplan, E. F. 1976. The role of the non-compromised hemisphere in patients with local brain disease. In *Alterations in brain functioning and changes in cognition*, ed. H.-L. Teuber. Symposium presented at the meeting of the American Psychological Association, Washington, D.C., August 1976.

Keogh, B. K. 1971. Hyperactivity and learning disorders: Review and speculation. *Exceptional Children* 38:101–10.

Kinsbourne, M. and Caplan, P. J. 1979. *Children's learning and attentional problems*. Boston: Little, Brown.

Kirk, U. 1985. Hemispheric contributions to the development of graphic skill. In *Hemispheric function and collaboration in the child*, ed. C. T. Best. New York: Academic Press.

Klare, G. R. 1963. *The measurement of readability*. Ames: Iowa State University Press.

Knights, R. M. and Moule, A. D. 1968. Normative data on the Motor Steadiness Battery for children. *Perceptual and Motor Skills* 26:643–50.

Kobasigawa, A. 1974. Utilization of retrieval cues in recall. *Child Development* 45:127–34.

Kohn, B. and Dennis, M. 1974. Selective impairments of visuo-spatial abilities in infantile hemiplegics after right hemidecortication. *Neuropsychologia* 12:505–12.

Krahn, G. L. 1985. The use of projective assessment techniques in pediatric settings. *Journal of Pediatric Psychology* 10:179–93.

Kreutzer, M. A. and Flavell, J. H. 1975. An interview study of children's knowledge about memory. *Monograph of the Society for Research in Child Development*, Vol. 40, no. 1. Chicago: University of Chicago Press.

Lassen, N. A., Ingnar, D. H., and Skinhj, E. 1978. Brain function and blood flow. *Scientific American* 239:62–71.

Lehman, E. B. 1972. Selective strategies in children's attention to task-relevant information. *Child Development* 43:197–210.

Levine, M. D. 1980. *The ANSER system: Aggregate neurobehavioral student health and educational review*. Cambridge, MA: Educators Publishing Service.

Lezak, M. D. 1983. *Neuropsychological assessment*. 2d ed. New York: Oxford University Press.

Liberman, I. Y. and Shankweiler, D. 1979. Speech, the alphabet, and teaching to read. In *Theory and practice of early reading*, ed. L. Resnick and P. Weaver. Hillsdale, NJ: Erlbaum Associates.

McFie, J. and Zangwill, O. L. 1960. Visual-constructive disabilities associated with lesions of the left cerebral hemisphere. *Brain* 83:243–60.

McLaughlin, H. G. 1969. SMOG grading—A new readability formula. *Journal of Reading* 12 (no. 8):639–46.

MacLean, P. D. 1973. A triune concept of brain and behavior. In *The Hincks memorial lectures*, ed. T. J. Boag and D. Campbell. Toronto: University of Toronto Press.

Mahoney, M. J. 1974. *Cognitive and behavior modification*. Cambridge, MA: Ballinger.

Manning, S. A. 1977. *Child and adolescent development*. New York: McGraw-Hill.

Marcel, T., Katz, K., and Smith, M. 1974. Laterality and reading proficiency. *Neuropsychologia* 12:131–39.

Marcel, T. and Rajan, P. 1975. Lateral specialization for recognition of words and faces in good and poor readers. *Neuropsychologia* 13:489–97.

Master, J. C., Furman, W., and Barden, R. C. 1977. Effects of achievement standards, tangible rewards, and self-dispensed achievement evaluations on children's task mastery. *Child Development* 48:217–24.

References

Mattis, S., French, J. A., and Rapin, I. 1975. Dyslexia in children and young adults. *Developmental Medicine and Child Neurology* 17:150–63.

Mazziotta, J. C. and Phelps, M. E. 1986. Positron emission tomography: Studies of the brain. In *Positron emission tomography and autoradiography: Principles and applications for the brain and heart*, ed. M. E. Phelps, J. C. Mazziotta, and H. R. Schelbert. New York: Raven Press.

Menyuk, P. and Flood, J. 1981. Linguistic competence, reading, writing problems and remediation. *Bulletin of the Orton Society* 31:13–28.

Mesulam, M. M., ed. 1985. *Principles of behavioral neurology*. Philadelphia: F. A. Davis.

Milberg, W. P., Hebben, N., and Kaplan, E. 1986. The Boston process approach to neuropsychological assessment. In *Neuropsychological assessment of neuropsychiatric disorders*, ed. I. Grant and K. M. Adams. New York: Oxford University Press.

Miller, G. A. 1956. The magical number seven plus or minus two: Some limits on our capacity for processing information. *Psychological Review* 63:81–97.

Milner, B. 1971. Interhemispheric differences in the localization of psychological processes in man. *British Medical Bulletin* 27:272–77.

———. 1973. Hemispheric specialization: Scope and limits. In *The Neurosciences: Third study program*, ed. F. O. Schmitt and F. G. Worden. Cambridge, MA: The MIT Press.

Mooney, C. M. 1957. Age in the development of closure ability in children. *Canadian Journal of Psychology* 2:219–26.

Mooney, C. M. and Furguson, G. A. 1951. A new closure test. *Canadian Journal of Psychology* 5:129–33.

Mosher, F. S. and Hornsby, J. R. 1966. On asking questions. In *Studies in cognitive growth*, ed. J. S. Bruner, P. Olver, and P. Greenfield. New York: Wiley.

Moscovitch, M. 1979. Information processing and the cerebral hemispheres. In *Handbook of behavioral neurobiology*, ed. M. S. Gazzaniga. Vol. 2, *Neuropsychology*. New York: Plenum Press.

Muehl, S. and Forell, E. 1974. A follow-up study of disabled readers: Variables related to high school reading performance. *Reading Research Quarterly* 9:110–23.

Murray, H. A. 1938. *Explorations in personality*. New York: Oxford University Press.

Neimark, E., Slotnick, N. S., and Ulrich, T. 1971. Development of memorization strategies. *Developmental Psychology* 5:427–32.

Neimark, F. D. and Lewis, N. 1967. The development of logical problem-solving strategies. *Child Development* 38:107–17.

Nelson, H. E. and Warrington, E. K. 1974. Developmental spelling retardation and its relation to other cognitive abilities. *British Journal of Psychology* 65:265–74.

Ojemann, G. A. 1975. Language and the thalamus: Object naming and recall during and after thalamic stimulation. *Brain and Language* 2:101–20.

Ojemann, G. A. and Mateer, C. 1979. Human language cortex: Localization of memory, syntax and sequential motor-phoneme identification systems. *Science* 250:1401–3.

Oldfield, R. C. 1971. The assessment and analysis of handedness: The Edinburgh inventory. *Neuropsychologia* 9:19–113.

Ornstein, P. A., Naus, M. J., and Liberty, C. 1975. Rehearsal organization processes in children's memory. *Child Development* 46:818–30.

Osterrieth, P. A. 1944. Le test de copie d'une figure complex. *Archives de psychologie* 30:206–356.

Owen, F. W., Adams, P. A., Forrest, T., Stolz, L. M., and Fisher, S. 1971. Learning disorders in children: Sibling studies. In *Monograph of the Society for Research in Child Development*, no. 36, 1–77. Chicago: University of Chicago Press.

Pardes, J. R. 1979. Effects of a strategy training program on motivation for learning. Ph.D. diss., Fordham University, New York.

Paris, S. G., Lindauer, B. K., and Cox, G. L. 1977. The development of inferential comprehension. *Child Development* 48:1728–33.

Parry, P. 1973. The effect of reward on the performance of hyperactive children. Ph.D. diss., McGill University, Montreal.

Parson, J. E. and Ruble, D. N. 1977. The development of achievement-related expectancies. *Child Development* 48:1075–79.

Pennington, B. F. and Smith, S. D. 1983. Genetic influences on learning disabilities and speech and language disorders. *Child Development* 54:369–87.

Phelps, M. E., Mazziotta, J. C., and Schelbert, H. E., eds. 1986. *Positron emission tomography and autoradiography: Principles and applications for the brain and heart.* New York: Raven Press.

Poppel, E. and Shattuck, S. R. 1974. Reading in patients with brain wounds involving the central visual pathways. *Cortex* 10:84–88.

Prechtl, H. and Stemmer, C. 1935. The choreiform syndrome in children. *Developmental Medicine and Child Neurology* 4:119–27.

Pribram, K. H. 1981. Emotions. In *Handbook of clinical neuropsychology*, ed. S. B. Filskov and T. J. Boll. New York: Wiley.

Rakic, P. and Goldman-Rakic, P. S., eds. 1982. Development and plasticity of the cerebral cortex. *Neurosciences Research Program Bulletin*, Vol. 20, no. 4. Cambridge, MA: The MIT Press.

Raven, J. C. 1960. *Guide to the standard progressive matrices.* London: H. K. Lewis; Psychological Corporation.

———. 1965. *Guide to using the coloured matrices.* London: H. K. Lewis; Psychological Corporation.

Reitan, R. M. and Davison, L. A. 1974. *Clinical neuropsychology: Clinical status and applications.* New York: Hemisphere.

Rey, A. 1941. L'examen psychologique dans le cas d'encephalopathie traumatique. *Archives de psychologie* 28:286–340.

———. 1964. *L'examen clinique en psychologie.* Paris: Presses Universitaires de France.

Reynolds, C. R. 1981. The fallacy of two years below grade level for age as a diagnostic criterion for reading disorders. *Journal of School Psychology* 19:350–58.

Rogers, D. 1978. *Adolescence: A psychological perspective.* Belmont, CA: Wadsworth Publishing.

Ross, E. D. 1985. Modulation of affect and non-verbal communication by the right hemisphere. In *Principles of Behavioral Neurology*, ed. M. M. Mesulam. Philadelphia: F. A. Davis.

Rotter, J. B., Seeman, M., and Liverant, S. 1962. *Internal vs. external control of reinforcement*, Vol. 2, *Decisions, values and groups.* London: Pergamon Press.

Rourke, B. P. 1985. *Neuropsychology of learning disabilities: Essentials of subtype analysis.* New York: Guilford Press.

Rudel, R. G. 1978. Neuroplasticity: Implications for development and education. In *Education and the brain*, ed. J. Chall and A. Mirsky. Chicago: University of Chicago Press.

References

————. 1980. Learning disability diagnosis by exclusion and discrepancy. *Journal of the American Academy of Child Psychiatry* 19:547–69.

————. 1981a. Residual effects of childhood reading disabilities. *Bulletin of the Orton Society* 31:89–102.

————. 1981b. Definition of dyslexia: Expressive language and motor deficits in children with reading impairment. Paper presented at the Institute for Child Development Research Symposium, Current Status and Future Directions, Philadelphia, Pennsylvania.

————. 1984. Reading-disabled hyperactive children: A distinct subgroup of attention deficit disorder with hyperactivity. *Journal of Abnormal Child Psychology* 12 (no. 1).

————. 1985. Hemispheric asymmetry and learning disabilities: Left, right, or in-between? In *Hemispheric function and collaboration in the child*, ed. Catherine T. Best. New York: Academic Press.

Rudel, R. G. and Denckla, M. B. 1974. Relationship of forward and backward digit repetition to neurological impairment in children with learning disabilities. *Neuropsychologia* 12:109–18.

————. 1976. Relationship of IQ and reading score to visual, spatial, and temporal matching tasks. *Journal of Learning Disabilities* 9:42–51.

Rudel, R. G., Denckla, M. B., Broman, M., and Hirsch, S. 1980. Word finding as a function of stimulus context: Children compared with aphasic adults. *Brain and Language* 10:111–19.

Rupley, W. H. and Blair, T. R. 1983. *Reading diagnosis and remediation: Classroom and clinic.* Boston: Houghton-Mifflin.

Rutter, M. 1970. Children of sick parents: An environmental and psychiatric study. In *Institute of Psychiatry Monographs*, no. 16, 615–21. New York: Oxford University Press.

Rutter, M. and Yule, W. 1975. Concept of specific reading retardation. *Journal of Child Psychology and Psychiatry* 16:181–97.

Safer, D. and Allen, R. 1976. *Hyperactive children: Diagnosis and management.* Baltimore: University Park Press.

Santostefano, S. 1978. *A biodevelopmental approach to clinical child psychology: Cognitive controls and cognitive control therapy.* New York: Wiley.

Satz, P. and Fletcher, J. M. 1978. Predictive validity of an abbreviated screening battery. *Journal of Learning Disabilities* 11:347–51.

Satz, P., Taylor, H. G., Friel, J., and Fletcher, J. 1978. Some developmental and predictive precursors of reading disabilities: A six-year follow-up. In *Dyslexia—An appraisal of current knowledge*, ed. A. L. Benton and D. Pearl, 313–47. New York: Oxford University Press.

Schmitt, F. O., Worden, F. G., Dennis, S. G., and Adelman, G., eds. 1981. *The organization of cerebral cortex.* Cambridge, MA: The MIT Press.

Shaffer, D., Bijur, P., Chadwick, O., and Rutter, M. 1980. Head injury and later reading disability. *Journal of the American Academy of Child Psychiatry* 19:592–610.

Shaheen, S. J. 1984. Neuromaturation and behavior development: The case of childhood lead poisoning. *Developmental Psychology* 20:542–50.

Smith, M. D., Coleman, J. M., Dokecki, P. R., and Davis, E. E. 1977. Recategorized WISC-R scores of learning disabled children. *Journal of Learning Disabilities* 10: 437–43.

Smith, S. D., Kimberling, W. J., Pennington, B. F., and Lubs, M. A. 1983. Specific reading disability: Identification of an inherited form through linkage analysis. *Science* 219:1345–47.

Smith, S. D., Pennington, B. F., Kimberling, W. J., and Lubs, M. A. 1979. Investigation of subgroups within specific reading disability utilizing neuropsychological and linkage analysis. *American Journal of Human Genetics* 31:83–91.

Sprague, R. L. and Sleator, E. K. 1976. Drugs and dosages: Implications for learning disabilities. In *The neuropsychology of learning disorders: Theoretical approaches*, ed. R. M. Knights and D. J. Bakker. Baltimore: University Park Press.

Squire, L. S. 1981. Two forms of human amnesia: An analysis of forgetting. *The Journal of Neuroscience* 1:635–40.

Stanley, G. and Hall, R. 1973. Short-term visual information processing in dyslexics. *Child Development* 44:841–44.

Stein, D. G., Rosen, J., and Butters, N., eds. 1974. *CNS plasticity and recovery of function*. New York: Academic Press.

Strag, G. A. 1972. Comparative behavioral ratings of parents with severe mentally retarded, severe learning disability and normal children. *Journal of Learning Disabilities* 5:52–56.

Strag, G. A. and Richard, B. O. 1973. Auditory discrimination techniques for young children. *Elementary School Journal* 73:447–54.

Stuss, D. T. and Benson, D. F. 1986. *The frontal lobes*. New York: Raven Press.

Sweeney, J. and Rourke, B. 1978. Neuropsychological significance of phonetically accurate and phonetically inaccurate spelling errors in younger and older retarded spellers. *Brain and Language* 6:212–25.

Symmes, S. and Rapoport, J. 1972. Unexpected reading failure. *American Journal of Orthopsychiatry* 42:82–91.

Tallal, P. and Piercy, M. 1973. Developmental aphasia: Impaired rate of non-verbal processing as a function of sensory modality. *Neuropsychologia* 11:389–95.

Tallal, P., Stark, R., and Mellits, D. 1981. Classification of language impaired and normally developing children on the basis of rapid perception and production skills. Paper presented at the Fourth International Neuropsychological Society European Conference, Bergen, Norway.

Taylor, J., ed. 1931. *The selected writings of John Hughlings Jackson*, Vol. 2. London: Hodder and Stoughton.

Taylor, L. B. n.d. *Children's stories*. Montreal: Montreal Neurological Institute.

Thomas, C. J. 1905. Congenital "word-blindness" and its treatment. *Opthalmoscope* 3: 380–85.

Torgensen, J. and Goldman, T. 1977. Verbal rehearsal and short-term memory in reading-disabled children. *Child Development* 48:56–60.

Varlaam, A. 1974. Educational attainment and behavior at school. *Greater London Council Intelligence Quarterly* 29:29–37.

Vogel, S. A. 1974. Syntactic abilities in normal and dyslexic children. *Journal of Learning Disabilities* 7:103–9.

———. 1977. Morphological ability in normal and dyslexic children. *Journal of Learning Disabilities* 10:35–43.

Vygotsky, L. S. 1962. *Thought and language*. Cambridge, MA: The MIT Press.

———. 1978. *Mind in society*. Cambridge, MA: Harvard University Press.

Waber, D. P., Carlson, D., Mann, M., Merola, J., and Moylan, P. 1984. SES-related aspects of neuropsychological performance. *Child Development* 55:1878–86.

References

Waber, D. P. and Holmes, J. M. Remembering the Rey-Osterrieth complex figure: A dual code model. Manuscript submitted for publication.

————. 1985. Assessing children's copy productions of the Rey-Osterrieth Complex Figure. *Journal of Clinical and Experimental Neuropsychology* 7:264–80.

————. 1986. Assessing children's memory productions of the Rey-Osterrieth Complex Figure. *Journal of Clinical and Experimental Neuropsychology* 8:563–80.

Walker, C. E. and Roberts, M. C., eds. 1983. *Handbook of clinical child psychology.* New York: Wiley.

Warrington, E. K., James, M., and Kinsbourne, M. 1960. Drawing disability in relation to laterality of lesion. *Brain* 89:53–82.

Wechsler, D. 1945. A standardized memory scale for clinical use. *Journal of Psychology* 19:87–95.

Weiner, B. 1972. *Theories of motivation: From mechanism to cognition.* Chicago: Rand McNally.

Weiner, B. J., ed. 1974. *Cognitive views of human motivation.* New York: Academic Press.

Weintraub, S. and Mesulam, M. M. 1985. Mental state assessment of young and elderly adults in behavioral neurology. In *Principles of behavioral neurology*, ed. M. M. Mesulam. Philadelphia: F. A. Davis.

Wender, P. 1971. *Minimal brain dysfunction in children.* New York: Wiley.

Wittrock, M. C. 1978. Education and the cognitive processes of the brain. In *Education and the brain*, ed. J. Chall and A. Mirsky. Chicago: University of Chicago Press.

Wolf, M. 1982. The word retrieval process and reading in children and aphasics. In *Children's language*, Vol. 3, ed. K. Nelson. New York: Gardner.

Worden, P. E. 1975. Effects of sorting on subsequent recall of unrelated items: A developmental study. *Child Development* 46:687–95.

Yule, W., Rutter, M., Berger, M., and Thompson, J. 1974. Over and underachievement in reading: Distribution in the general population. *British Journal of Educational Psychiatry* 44:1–12.

Zigmond, N. 1978. Remediation of dyslexia: A discussion. In *Dyslexia: An appraisal of current knowledge*, ed. A. L. Benton and D. Pearl. New York: Oxford University Press.

Index

Index

Index

"More" principle, 224–25
Moscovitch, M., 143
Mosher, F. S., 59
Motivation for learning, 15, 229–33
Motor: activity levels, 126, 160; bilaterality and, 162; capacities, 167, 169–71; codes, 188; control, 71, 119, 192; coordination, 85; cortical/subcortical axis and, 126, 197; dexterity, 169; findings, left-sided, 115; immaturity in preschool children, 61; movements, extraneous, 164, 192; responses, excessive, 126; restlessness, 51; skills, 126, 139, 149; system asymmetries, 120, 169
Muehl, S., 6

Nachtman, W., 198
Naming: of conditions, 3; of problems, 102
Neimark, E., 232
Neimark, F. D., 59
Nelson, H. E., 33
Nesbitt, J. A., 24
Neuroanatomic axes, 113–15, 117–23, 125–29, 132, 139, 144, 149, 164, 168–69, 173, 180, 184
Neuropsychological: approach to diagnosis, 10–16, 20; theory, developmental, 112–13
Neurosurgical intervention, for learning disorders, 11

Ober, B. A., 190
Object naming, 26–27
Observations: clinical, 144–65; erroneous, 140; five categories of, 149; direct, importance of in assessment, 169; initial, 77, 78; nonclinical, 149–50; of specific performance, 158–64
Obsessive behavior, 66, 69–70
Oculomotor movements, 183
Oglesby, D. M., 17
Ojemann, G. A., 29
Oldfield, R. C., 169
Oltman, P. K., 186
Ordering, serial, 4
Organizational skills, 174, 183, 186, 220, 233
Orientation-habituation responses, 53
Ornstein, P. A., 232
Osterrieth, P. A., 120, 127
Overindulgence, as compensatory mechanism, 70
Over-instruction, 176
Overlearning, 225
Owen, F. W., 12, 49, 78

Paraphasia, 4, 28, 183
Pardes, J. R., 206, 229
Parent(s): age of at conception/birth of child, 146; -child interaction, 147, 150–51; collusion of with child in inappropriate behavior, 98; conflicts between, 91; denial of child's problems by, 80; educational level of, 102; excuses of for child's learning disorders, 8; focus sheet and, 206–7; helping child with homework and, 215–16; interviewing, 89–99; language skills of, 102; love of child by, 96; objectivity of regarding child and, 96; paranoia of, 95; recall of child's developmental milestones by, 90–91; referral by of child for clinical diagnosis of learning disorders, 7–8; tolerance of for target behaviors, 168; withholding of child's past test results by, 75–76
Parietal symptomology, 173
Paris, S. G., 232
Parry, P., 56
Parson, J. E., 231
Passivity index, 88
Pathology, and brain-behavior relationships, 118
Peabody Picture Vocabulary Test, 12, 182–83
Peers, 147, 149–50, 219
Pennington, B. F., 78
Perceptual: deficit hypothesis of reading disability, 12–13; error, 28; impairment, 3, 7
Performance: cognitive, 229; continuous, 192; level of on given activity, 167
Personality development, 167, 193–95
Personal space, asymmetries of, 169
Peters, J. E., 58
Phelps, M. E., 123
Phoneme-grapheme correspondence, 34, 36
Phonemic-sequencing error, 28
Piaget, J., 58
Piercy, M., 42, 224
Planning, 167, 174, 191–93
Play, *see* Games
Poppel, E., 42
Porteus, S. D., 185
Praxis, 170
Prechtl, H., 128
Pregnancy, health of mother during, 146–47
Pribram, K. K., 193
Pritchett, E. M., 198
Problem(s): serial order, 28–30; -solving strategy/process, 158–59, 167
Processing, slow visual, 15, 42
Procrastination, 68
Projective instruments, 194
Psychiatric: disorders, 14, 100; evaluation of for learning disabilities, 15; referral for literacy problems in college, 9
Psychometric: model, 120; obstacles to using grade levels or school years as discrepancy measures, 20–21

Index